SCHOOLING FOR A GLOBAL AGE

SCHOOLING FOR A GLOBAL AGE

JAMES M. BECKER, *EDITOR*

CHARLOTTE ANDERSON

LEE ANDERSON

LILLIAN K. DRAG

BRUCE R. JOYCE

DAVID C. KING

M. FRANCES KLEIN

ROBERT LEESTMA

DONALD N. MORRIS

ALEXANDER M. NICHOLSON

STEPHEN H. RHINESMITH

JUDITH V. TORNEY

KENNETH A. TYE

Foreword by John I. Goodlad

McGraw-Hill Book Company

New York St. Louis San Francisco
Auckland Bogotá Düsseldorf Johannesburg London Madrid Mexico
Montreal New Delhi Panama Paris São Paulo Singapore
Sydney Tokyo Toronto

The editors of this book were Thomas Quinn and Michael Hennelly for
McGraw-Hill Book Company and Judith S. Golub for |I|D|E|A|. Elaine
Gongora was the designer. Thomas Kowalczyk and Sally Fliess supervised
the production. This book was set in Century Schoolbook by University
Graphics, Inc. It was printed and bound by R. R. Donnelley and Sons, Co.

Library of Congress Cataloging in Publication Data

Main entry under title:

Schooling for a global age.

  (A Study of schooling in the United States)
  "Conducted under the auspices of the Institute for
Development of Educational Activities."
  Bibliography: p.
  Includes index.
  1. Education, Elementary—United States—Curricula.
2. Education, Secondary—United States—Curricula.
I. Anderson, Charlotte C. II. Becker, James.
III. Institute for Development of Educational
Activities. IV. Series.
LB1570.S3468   373.1′9   78-9335
ISBN 0-07-004190-3

1 2 3 4 5 6 7 8 9   RRDRRD 7 9 8 7 6 5 4 0 9

Acknowledgments for permission to use exerpts from copyrighted material include:

John A. Carpenter and Judith V. Torney, "Beyond the Melting Pot to Cultural Plurism," from *Children and Intercultural Education: Overview and Research,* p. 20. Reprinted by permission of the Association for Childhood Education International, 3615 Wisconsin Avenue, N.W., Washington, D.C., 20016. Copyright © 1974 by the Association.

Robert J. Goldstein, "Elementary School Curriculum and Political Socialization," in *Political Youth, Traditional Schools: National and International Perspectives,* edited by Byron G. Massialas, © 1972. Reprinted by permission of Prentice-Hall, Inc., Englewood Cliffs, N.J.

John I. Goodlad, "A Perspective on Accountability," *Phi Delta Kappan,* vol. 57, no. 2, October 1975.

E. Hicks and Barry K. Beyer, "Images of Africa," *Journal of Negro Education,* vol. 39, 1970.

"It's a Small World," © 1963 Wonderland Music Company, Inc. Words and Music by Richard M. and Robert B. Sherman.

David C. King and Charlotte C. Anderson, *Windows on Our World: United States,* copyright © 1976. Reprinted by permission of Houghton Mifflin Company.

Wallace E. Lambert and Otto Klineberg, *Children's Views of Foreign People,* copyright © 1967. Used by permission of Irvington Publishers, Inc.

Skip Redwine, "Big Blue Marble," 1973. The song is printed courtesy of Alphaventure Music, Inc.

Edwin Reischauer, *Toward the 21st Century: Education for a Changing World.* Copyright © 1973, reprinted by permission of Alfred A. Knopf, Co.

A series of articles in the *Chicago Tribune* about the Alcott School by Rich Soll. Reprinted, courtesy of the *Chicago Tribune.*

Edith West, *The Family of Man: A Social Studies Program,* 1971. Permission granted by Selective Educational Equipment.

Special material from the *World Book Dictionary,* © 1973 by Doubleday & Company, Inc. Used by permission of the publisher.

This book is one of the volumes commissioned as background information for A Study of Schooling in the United States. The Study is a large-scale examination of elementary, junior high, and senior high schools located throughout the United States. The Study focuses on the school as a whole including the curriculum, the student and adult life in the school, and relationships with the community. Results of the research are published separately.

John I. Goodlad
Principal Investigator

A STUDY OF SCHOOLING IN THE UNITED STATES

SUPPORTED BY

The Danforth Foundation
The JDR³ʳᵈ Fund
Martha Holden Jennings Foundation
Charles F. Kettering Foundation
Charles Stewart Mott Foundation
National Institute of Education
The Needmor Fund
The Rockefeller Foundation
The Spencer Foundation
U.S. Office of Education

Substudy on the teaching of global education in schools supported by an additional grant from the Charles F. Kettering Foundation

Conducted under the auspices of the Institute for Development of Educational Activities, Inc., |I|D|E|A|

The following persons assisted in the early planning for this volume and contributed valuable insights and directions. We wish to thank them for their time and effort. The resulting book, however, is the responsibility of the authors and the Study of Schooling and may not reflect the opinions of some of those listed below.

Lee Anderson
Northwestern University

James Becker
Indiana University

Irving Becker
Council on International
    Educational Exchange

James Bostain
Foreign Service Institute

Tom Collins
AFS/International/Intercultural
    Programs

M. A. Griffiths
Institute for Shipboard
    Education

Robert Leestma
U.S. Office of Education

Irving Morrisset
Social Science Consortium

Betty Reardon
Teachers College
Columbia University

Stephen Rhinesmith
AFS/International/Intercultural
    Programs

Judith V. Torney
University of Illinois, Chicago
    Circle

V. Lynn Tyler
Brigham Young University

Johannes Wilbert
University of California, Los
    Angeles

CONTENTS

GLOBAL AWARENESS: THE EDUCATIONAL OPPORTUNITY

Most of the world's educational systems, including those of the United States, have as one of their goals developing understanding and appreciation of other nations, other cultures, other peoples. Use of the word "other"—and it appears frequently—is revealing. It connotes a "we-they" kind of thinking that pervades most countries and their educational programs, in and out of schools. To speak of other nations or cultures is one thing; to speak of other peoples is quite another.

These programs promote nationalism and, to some degree, *internationalism* but rarely global awareness. The development of global perspectives, as defined and elaborated upon in this volume, is not an established educational goal in any country. The meaning and significance of such a goal can be described, at best, as only emerging. Gaining widespread acceptance of it and implementing what it implies will not be easy.

Fortunately, educators are perennial optimists, addressing themselves to the preparation of better persons for a better world. It probably would be difficult to proceed otherwise and remain an educator, at least a reasonably satisfied one. Not surprisingly, increasing numbers of educators, particularly those in leadership roles, have moved toward cross-national educational concerns, whatever they may be called: international, multicultural, comparative, global, or humankind education. Many are highly idealistic about what needs to be done and what education or schooling can contribute, probably naively so.

The fervor among some world-minded educators runs high here in the United States, so high that even global-minded scholars in this country brand what often is proposed for schools as impractical romanticism. Friendly critics here and abroad have difficulty squaring some proposals with the realities of rampant nationalism. Less friendly critics reject global awareness programs as inappropriate for schools, since "schools exist to strengthen understanding and appreciation of one's own country."

It must be recognized also that even when planned and carried out with the best intentions, education cannot offer immediate solutions to urgent global problems. Enlightened social engineering is required to face situations that demand global action now. Education is a long-term solution.

But let us assume that present and future conditions in the world and the need to prepare young people to live in and care for spaceship earth necessitate educating for a global perspective to a degree far surpassing anything attempted thus far. As James Becker points out in Chapter 2, we cannot wait for a worldwide consensus to be reached as to the need for promoting global perspectives. Indeed, we have a responsibility to help bring about that consensus. In short, we must respond educationally. The cultivation of global understanding and attitudes must begin with the soil of our backyard gardens.

However, to ignore the fact that there are strong inhibiting factors in the history of our national experience and in the environmental context where education must proceed would be dangerous to the point of assured failure. Factors in our heritage impinge significantly on our ability to become seriously involved in the processes of education required.* We have derived over the two centuries of our existence as a nation tremendous satisfaction from living with considerable self-sufficiency within our own boundaries. We have tended often to think of this nation as a unique experiment, not to be unduly influenced or, indeed, contaminated by the experience of others. This view, in turn, may have served to limit our horizons somewhat regarding the existence, needs, and potential contributions of the rest of the world.

This tendency toward ethnocentrism has been reinforced by our industrial and commercial orientation, agricultural self-sufficiency, military power, and religious and educational institutions. In commerce and industry, we have tended to place our enterprising character above a richness of resources as the key factor in our success. As in agriculture, we saw little to be learned from abroad. Even the trade union movement kept itself surprisingly autonomous, paying scant attention to the longer history of other industrialized nations. Our religious beliefs became closely associated with American beliefs and stimulated a missionary impulse to convert and instruct, not to share and learn. Our educational system, designed to educate the masses as never before attempted anywhere, became our special contribution to be given to the rest of the world whenever the opportunity arose. We showed it off proudly to the many who came to see, sometimes becoming angry when insightful visitors pointed to shortcomings, the gap between rhetoric and practices, inevitable and understandable in such a large and ambitious undertaking. Nonetheless, we have taken pride in the desire of educators abroad to emulate many of our innovations.

---

*In the discussion of these factors that follows, I draw from remarks made by John Richardson, former Assistant Secretary of State, at a conference sponsored by Global Perspectives in Education, Inc., July 7–9, 1976, Aspen, Colorado. However, the interpretations and elaborations presented here are my own.

Turning to another part of our character, only in recent years has volunteerism in this country begun to extend significantly to other countries, the Peace Corps being a case in point. The attentions of civic organizations have been very parochial, usually extending to the nation only as a response to some charismatic leader and a cause of local as well as broader appeal, such as President Roosevelt and the March of Dimes. Many philanthropic foundations created out of local industrial genius still support only projects limited to their own environs, even when the goods were sold and profits providing foundation funds were derived worldwide.

Until recently, the ideal of a single, national language and a blending of differences into a relatively common mold were not seriously challenged. The "melting pot" concept prevailed. The influx of people from other countries, people who immediately sought to acquire the "American" language and customs and divest themselves of their own, added to our sense of national self-esteem.

For a long period of time, we applied the Horatio Alger dictum— any American can make it in this great land if he only tries—to our view of both the individual and the nation. That we became both prosperous and strong inclined us to the position that we were more industrious and, therefore, given the work ethic, more righteous. People in other lands might come close to our affluence and well-being if they emulated our ways and tried hard enough. These and other illusions have been shattered in recent decades by growing awareness of problems—especially in the cities—that remain unsolved, problems as least as serious as those we've managed to do something about. Meanwhile, we increasingly realize that this nation and its people are inextricably intertwined with the rest of the world.

It will not be easy to turn from our past inward orientation to the outward awareness and involvement we must acquire. But the traits we see as constituting a significant part of our national heritage could be some of those that will serve us well in a drive toward a global perspective. Elsewhere in this volume, several authors refer to the self-transcendence that must take place in the person if the individual is to reach out to others in ways that are not self-serving. The concept of self-transcendence could apply to nations as well.

The philosophy of self-transcendence argues that strong feelings of self-worth are prerequisite to and perhaps instrumental in acquiring close identification with others. There is evidence to suggest that school programs designed to develop pride in one's own country succeed very well. There is no evidence to suggest that one loses this pride in also acquiring a rich appreciation of the whole of humankind. In fact, the more parochial appreciations may be the first step in a maturing process in which one moves from preoccupation with self and family to a perspective embracing community, nation, and humankind. Global awareness programs, then, need to accompany or be added to these other learnings, not replace them.

If this thesis has any validity, then our considerable sense of security and identity may be precisely what is required for national self-transcendence. The ecumenical process involved would strengthen, not weaken, our appreciation of and respect for this nation. In effect, we would have everything to gain and nothing to lose in turning part of our considerable energy and assets toward the present and future well-being of spaceship earth.

There are now clear signs of such an effort beginning. Citizens in many walks of life are realizing, sometimes to their astonishment, that we are far from self-sufficient. Families and communities are finding out, often stimulated by school programs, that scarcely a segment of our daily life proceeds without use of some element from abroad. Exchange programs of many kinds have helped, often resulting in communication networks among individuals, businesses, institutions, and cities. Global awareness, not always at more than a rather superficial level, has penetrated virtually all government agencies. There are now dozens of organizations, some of them with our most prestigious citizens on their boards, actively promoting goals and activities designed to raise our consciousness of the world in which we live. Many national educational organizations representing teachers, administrators, and policy makers have explicitly committed themselves to furthering the aims of global education. The local, state, and national context for global education grows more promising.

EDUCATIONAL DILEMMAS: THE CONTRIBUTION OF THIS VOLUME

Serious problems remain to be dealt with before the promise can be turned into reality. The target groups to be reached are many and massive. Although large numbers of teachers, administrators, and other educators are committed to the global perspective, others must be convinced of its necessity and given the opportunity to acquire the knowledge and skills needed to foster it in students.

Better curricular materials are needed, but experience with curricular reform shows that the ideas contained in books, films, film strips, and the like are easily subverted if teachers do not understand or support them. The tacit or contextual is often more significant than the explicit. Parents and the general public must be reached also. Otherwise, children and youth enrolled in globally oriented programs may find themselves in conflict with values assumed in the home. And then the educational institution frequently comes under scrutiny and must pull back.

The pedagogical problems are many and complex. Some studies show that well-meaning social studies programs focused on other cultures simply reinforce the attitude that the differences reveal inferior "others." How does one move simultaneously toward a deeper sense of cultural relativity and one's own sense of values? How does one come to acquire a worldwide moral landscape? How can we be assured that positive attitudes will emerge from personal contact with persons from other cultures, especially when these contacts usually are of short duration? What we know about developing empathy for the whole of humankind is dwarfed beside our ignorance.

Earlier, I stated that the goals of most educational systems say something about understanding and appreciating others—other nations, other cultures, other peoples—but that the goal of understanding and appreciating the whole of humankind as one has not yet been firmly established as a sociopolitical goal for educational systems. This is true, also, for the United States. In any list of a dozen major goals for our schools, several will refer to fundamental processes, several to civic responsibilities and the national heritage, and one to concerns extending beyond our own boundaries. This one almost always is phrased, approximately, "understanding and appreciating other people." The very use of the word "other" is jarring here, implying divisiveness rather than stressing the unity of humankind.

Because concern for global matters is an emerging and not an established goal for educational systems, there are no readily available, comprehensive, self-contained definitions, descriptions, and analyses of what global education is, how it differs from traditional studies of other countries, what its objectives should be, what is now worth endorsing as likely to contribute to these objectives, and so on. There is, of course, a substantial but rather scattered speculative body of literature describing what various individuals and groups would like to see done. This volume seeks to integrate some of this extant material and, in particular, to describe actual schools and classrooms in which some of these programs have taken form. The Annotated Bibliography lists other programs and materials.

Preparation of this volume was supported by a grant from the Kettering Foundation. The Foundation has a long-standing interest in worldwide issues and problems and encourages greater attention to world affairs here in the United States. For example, it provided financial support to the project, "Columbus in the World: The World in Columbus," in which residents of Columbus, Ohio, became actively involved in, among other things, documenting the international contacts of various segments of the city.

This book and several others are part of the background materials assembled for A Study of Schooling in the United States.* In addition to the Kettering Foundation, support for various stages of the Study has been provided by the Danforth, Jennings, Mott, Needmor, Rockefeller, and Spencer Foundations and by the JDR 3rd Fund, the National Institute of Education, and the U. S. Office of Education. Findings of the Study will be reported subsequently in a series of publications.

Our purpose in initiating this book was to compile the current thinking in the field of global education, to discuss what we know about learning and teaching for improved global understanding, and to describe both promising practices and directions for the future. To do so, we sought out several of those persons whose contributions already are known and respected. With James M. Becker of Indiana University chairing, they met in Los Angeles to determine the desirability and feasibility of what my colleagues and I desired. They then laid out the initial outline of this volume and proposed a list of authors to be invited; several subsequently became contributors. William Shaw provided the link with the Kettering Foundation; Kenneth Tye represented the interests of the global education segment of A Study of Schooling in the United States. Judith Golub attended the initial meeting, made suggestions throughout for revising both the outline and chapters, and edited the whole.

I believe this to be a realistic appraisal of the field and a sober, constructive approach to what should and can be done through education. A group of writers such as this, committed personally and professionally to the promotion of global awareness, might be

---

*For a discussion of the Study, see John I. Goodlad, "What Goes On in Our Schools?" *Educational Researcher,* vol. 6, no. 3, March 1977, pp. 3–6.

expected to present Utopian dreams. Their sense of urgency and cautious optimism come through but they are, for the most part, almost painstakingly careful to point out the roadblocks, pitfalls, and underbrush likely to be encountered in endeavoring to move millions of people from their present parochialism to an enlarged, appreciative sense of the world and its human family. The specialist should find much that is useful in what follows. Most educators and lay citizens will discover here new information and a great deal of food for thought, as I did. Some readers will revise their concept of community and perhaps their orientation toward daily life.

On behalf of the supporting foundations and the Kettering Foundation, in particular, I extend thanks to all those who contributed in various ways to the preparation of this volume.

John I. Goodlad
October 1978

SCHOOLING FOR A GLOBAL AGE

CHAPTER ONE

A Visit to Middleston's World-Centered Schools: A Scenario

Lee Anderson and Charlotte Anderson
Northwestern University

W hen I received the invitation from Middleston's superintendent of schools to come and observe what he called their world-centered schools, my initial impulse was to reply with a polite but firm, "No thank you." As a former teacher and principal who had left the schools to become a journalist specializing in education, I felt that I had already visited my share of schools. Besides, I had come to resent publicity-hungry educators who, after installing some new "educational fad" in their system, wanted me to portray their schools as "lighthouses" pointing the way to the salvation of American education. But the more I read of the superintendent's letter, the more I warmed up to the idea of visiting District 209.

The superintendent's letter informed me that Middleston has a unified K–12 district comprised of six elementary schools (K–5), three middle schools (6–8), and one large high school subdivided into three "schools within a school," each with its own name, administrative staff, and faculty. The schools fall into three alternative types, and parents can choose the type of school their children attend. The superintendent described one type of school as emphasizing "back to basics" and a second as leaning toward a more open type of structure.

The third type of school—the one I was invited to visit—was characterized as world-centered. I learned that two of the six elementary schools and one of the three middle schools were of this type, and at the high school level one of the three schools within a school was a world-centered school. "The world-centered schools," the superintendent wrote, "endeavor to furnish their students with the best possible global education that the district is capable of providing." He went on to explain to me that by global education the staff of the world-centered schools meant education for responsible participation in an interdependent global society.

By this time my curiosity was aroused. What does the process of teaching and learning for participation in a global society look like? What do students study? How is the curriculum organized? What kind of climate characterizes a school devoted to global education? What do teachers do? What role does the community play? These were the questions that came to mind as I dictated a letter informing the superintendent that I would be delighted to visit Middleston's world-centered schools. I indicated that, if convenient for them, I would like to come during the week of October 17.

THE CITY OF MIDDLESTON

On Sunday morning, I arrived at the airport serving the metropolitan area in which Middleston is located and drove a rented car the

25 miles to the city whose schools I had come to see. That afternoon I spent touring the city.

Middleston is a community of about 80,000 that can best be described as a rich mixture of urban and suburban USA. A variety of residential neighborhoods cluster around five commercial areas of differing size and economic function. On the periphery of the city, encircling the residential neighborhoods and commercial areas, are a dozen or so small manufacturing plants specializing in the production of office equipment and lightweight industrial goods.

Demographically, the city is about 65 percent white. The "non-white" residents are mostly blacks, many of whose families have lived in Middleston for three or more generations. A growing number of Hispanics are migrating to Middleston, most of them first- or second-generation families from Mexico or Puerto Rico. There is a sizable college-student population attending a university, two small colleges, and a theological seminary. The student population includes several hundred foreign students, most of whom are working on advanced degrees at the university.

Sociologically, Middleston is a middle- to upper-middle-class community. Nearly 65 percent of the labor force is employed in skilled and semiprofessional occupations. Approximately 15 percent of the population is professional and the remaining 20 percent of the labor force is made up of unskilled and semiskilled workers.

AN EVENING BRIEFING

The superintendent had invited me to his home for dinner that night. Besides myself, the guests consisted of two members of the board of education, the principals and several teachers from the world-centered schools, four or five individuals associated with community organizations and business firms, and about a dozen children and teen-agers. At first, I assumed they were the children of the adult guests. But when introduced, I learned they were students in the world-centered schools and, like the adults, guests of the superintendent. The composition of the group struck me as being somewhat unusual, but I refrained from either question or comment. Soon I was to discover that the mixing of individuals of differing ages and positions is very common in the life of the world-centered schools.

Early in the evening's conversation I was given an account of how Middleston had come to develop a system of alternative schools. "Like so many educational changes," the superintendent observed, "our system evolved in response to political conflict in the community." One of the board members went on to explain that for several years District 209 had had a Committee on Curriculum Review and Planning. This group, composed of representatives from the teachers' union, the administration, and the community, met throughout each school year to review particular areas of the curriculum. One year the math program would be examined; another year, the reading program; another year, the science program; and so on. "About eight years ago," one of the principals noted, "the curriculum committee decided to look at international education. After completing the study, it set forth a number of recommendations. I don't recall all of them now, but they included such things as a call for elementary schools to teach more about people outside of the United States and the creation of non-Western area studies programs in the middle schools. The committee recommended a course in world history at the high school level that did not focus exclusively on the development of the West. The committee suggested that a course in comparative government and politics replace the traditional ninth-grade civics course. It recommended that a class in international relations be added to the elective courses available to high school students. Oh, yes, the committee also suggested that language classes in Russian and Chinese be added to the traditional foreign language offerings at the high school."

"On their own merits, the committee's recommendations were relatively innocuous," one of the teachers continued. "But, in the context of the time in which they were put forward, they tapped a conflict that had been building up for some time. A sizable fraction of the community seized upon the committee's recommendations as an issue around which to organize a traditionalist attack on the schools. This group felt that the schools had already departed too much from solid, traditional education with its emphasis on the three R's combined with the study of American geography and the glorification of United States's history. On the other side of the fence was a group of parents and community leaders who felt school reform was coming too slowly. They believed that the committee's recommendations didn't go far enough. This group launched a campaign for a more humanized and world-centered educational program. Between these two camps stood another portion of the community and, I should add, of the school staff. This faction was generally content with the district's educational program as it stood and was opposed to the demands of the other factions."

I learned that this turmoil went on for nearly two years and that finally the board, in collaboration with several community leaders, was able to negotiate what came to be called "The Peace Treaty of Middleston." This was the agreement to establish within the district

5

the system of alternative schools that the superintendent had told me about in his letter.

Then, the conversation shifted to a discussion of the world-centered schools that I had come to observe. Some of the guests who had been instrumental in the initial creation of these schools described the rationale behind their efforts. One of the businessmen noted that the schools' founders believed a watershed had been reached in human history. He cited Rene Dubos's observation that humankind had reached a planetary stage in its evolution and now each person had two countries—his own and planet Earth. "All of us involved in the creation of the world-centered schools," one of the community leaders went on, "believed that schools should be transformed from an agent of nation-states into instruments of human survival and welfare." One of the high school students pointed out that the students now in school would live out most of their adult lives in the twenty-first century: "If our species does not commit suicide before then, this will be the global age of human history. We believe it is imperative that we begin to learn what it means to be a citizen of the world."

The rest of the evening's conversation focused directly on the world-centered schools. The children and the teen-agers took an active part in the discussion. They described for me some of the things they did in their schools and told me about what they felt were the strengths and weaknesses of the education they were getting. By the end of the evening it was clear to me that whatever else the world-centered schools did, they encouraged students to be reflective observers of, as well as active participants in, their own education. As I walked to my car for the drive back to the motel, I remarked to one of the teachers that the students were better philosophers of education than many adults I had met. Her response was simple. "We believe that if children and young people do not learn to think critically and creatively about their everyday lives, they will never learn to think this way about the problems that confront our nation and our planet."

A DAY AT TERRA SCHOOL

On Monday morning I drove to Terra School, one of the two world-centered elementary schools. Upon entering the school, I immediately noticed the rich diversity of artwork that decorated the halls and stairwells. Paintings, drawings, photographs, and small sculptures representative of human art in different parts of the world and from different historical eras were on display throughout the school.

A good deal, but not all, of the art was the work of children. I found out also that the children at Terra School were responsible for the selection, the organization, and the mounting of the art.

Walking down the hallway, I saw that the children were a mixture of racial and ethnic groups. There was an unusually large number of adults, older children, and teen-agers in evidence. As I wandered by one room, I saw a group of preschool children grouped around two students that looked to be of high school age. In another room, I noticed a circle of seven- to nine-year-olds involved in a discussion with a boy of twelve or thirteen. In still another area, I observed an elderly man and woman responding to questions from a group of nine- or ten-year-old students.

After ten or fifteen minutes of wandering, I came to an office in which three children were working. One child was answering the telephone while a boy of about ten or eleven was putting forms in a filing cabinet. A girl of about the same age was speaking to a smaller child and typing the information he gave her on a form. I asked these children where I could find the principal's office and was told that this was it. The boy at the telephone introduced himself and ushered me into the principal's quarters.

After I had settled into a very comfortable chair and happily accepted the offer of a cup of coffee, the principal asked me where I would like to begin. I said that I had already begun my observation of the school and would like to inquire about some of the things I had noticed on my way to her office. I mentioned the display of artwork and the wide range of people that I had seen in the school as well as the fact that her office staff appeared to consist of children. She informed me that everything I had noted was part of an overall strategy designed to implement the educational philosophy of the world-centered schools.

A PHILOSOPHY OF EDUCATION FOR WORLD CITIZENSHIP

I told her that I had picked up bits and pieces of this philosophy in last evening's discussion but that my comprehension of it was far from complete. The principal told me that the philosophy of the world-centered schools is most succinctly expressed in a position paper that had been prepared by the board of education. The relevant portion of the paper reads:

> The staff associated with the world-centered schools believes that to prepare children and young people for participation in a global society, two things must be done. First, we must help students understand their identities as individuals, as mem-

bers of the human species, as inhabitants and dependents of planet Earth, and as participants in a global society. Second, we must help students develop the competencies needed to cope with the problems, tensions, and tasks inherent in these identities and in conflicts among them. From this belief flow five major overarching purposes:

- To develop students' understanding of themselves as individuals
- To develop students' understanding of themselves as members of the human species
- To develop students' understanding of themselves as inhabitants and dependents of planet Earth
- To develop students' understanding of themselves as participants in global society
- To develop within students the competencies required to live intelligently and responsibly as individuals, human beings, earthlings, and members of global society

The staff of the world-centered schools believes that in order to accomplish these purposes we must be concerned with our schools as total institutions since a student's preparation for global citizenship is affected by the informal, as well as the formal, curriculum. Thus, we endeavor to create in world-centered schools the kind of social order, the organizational climate, the physical environment, and the formal curriculum that support and further the purposes of global education. Furthermore, we realize that schools working alone cannot achieve the goals we seek since students learn outside of schools as well as within them. Accordingly, the world-centered schools try to break down boundaries separating school, families, and the larger society. We strive to create an educational commonwealth in which the community is part of the schools and the schools are a part of the community.

THE INSTRUCTIONAL STAFF
"We take this philosophy seriously," the principal told me. "We try to implement it in every aspect of the operation of Terra School. You saw some evidence of this on your way to my office. You saw people of differing ages. In Terra, as in each of our other world-centered schools, there is a good deal of cross-age teaching. Indeed, we look upon teaching as an important learning process in the lives of people of all ages. Thus, in the world-centered schools older children work with younger children. You will see a good number of students from the middle school and the high school working with our children. The high school students work with preschool children as part of their study of human development.

"The adults in Terra School as well as in the other schools you will visit fall into three major groups. The world-centered schools are staffed by what we call *learning managers*. They are equivalent to teachers in other schools, work full time, and are paid by the school district. Supplementing the learning managers are *instructional specialists,* who work part-time with students as part of their regular job with one of the private or public institutions in the community. Sometimes these people come to the schools, but very often students go to them. For example, the banks, several business firms, the labor unions, and the university in Middleston have worked out an arrangement whereby some ten to fifteen people associated with the city's economic life instruct in the general area of economic education. The political parties in Middleston along with the university, the city council, and several political action groups support the part-time efforts of about five people who work with students in the area of political education. Over the years this program has grown, and there are now in the neighborhood of two hundred instructional specialists in various fields associated with our schools.

"Then there is a third group of adults deeply involved with the world-centered schools. These are volunteers that range in age from college students to senior citizens. This corps of volunteers is linked to the schools in several ways. Some work within the school as tutors; others serve as resource personnel for the Learning Managers. For example, the two elderly people you saw on your way to my office are lifelong Middleston residents and experts in local history. They frequently come to the school to be interviewed by students, and they take small groups of children into the community to visit sites of historical interest. Together with some of their friends and with the assistance of some high school students, they also are developing a small museum and library of local history.

"Still other volunteers are linked to the schools through a learning exchange program. The individuals in this program advertise skills or other things they are willing to teach children and young people. Interested students arrange to work with them in the late afternoon, evening, or on weekends. Conversely, we encourage our students to reciprocate by advertising things that they are able to teach adults or other children. The large chart behind my desk shows the learning exchanges in which Terra students are currently involved either as teachers or learners."

WORK AND SERVICE

I noticed on the chart that typing was one of the skills being taught, and I remembered the children I had seen working in the principal's outer office. I asked her about them. "What you saw," she informed me, "is but one example of many kinds of work that Terra students do around the school. We believe it is very important for children to develop a sense of responsibility for the welfare of the groups in which they are citizens. Since the school is one of the most salient of these in the lives of the children, we involve children extensively in the ongoing operation of Terra School, as both a social system and a physical plant. During my own school days, many of us worked as crossing guards. In our world-centered schools we have simply tried to extend the logic of responsible involvement to many more aspects of the school's operation. Older children participate regularly in the school's routine clerical work. Children of all ages assume a good deal of responsibility for day-to-day janitorial work. As you walk around the world-centered schools you will also see a lot of furniture and equipment that was made or reconstructed by students. In fact, the chair you are sitting in was an old discard that two Terra students refurbished with the help of a volunteer. He is an old gentleman who used to work in the furniture repair business and now spends a good deal of time working with students in the school's production shop."

"Is all of this emphasis on student work and on the use of refurbished equipment part of the school's educational philosophy or is it just a way of saving money?" I inquired. "It's both," the principal said. She went on to explain that Middleston had moved to its system of alternative schools when the era of constantly expanding school budgets was coming to an end. But as far as she was concerned, the budget squeeze turned out to be a blessing in disguise. "One of our hopes is that in developing an understanding of themselves as inhabitants of Earth, our students will come to see that they are passengers on a small cosmic spaceship whose limited resources must be carefully utilized. Moreover, many of us anticipate that scarcity rather than expanding affluence will be a hallmark of the future that our students will inherit. Thus, we feel very strongly that the schools should be models of how both individuals and organizations can creatively deal with problems of scarcity and limited resources."

THE CURRICULUM IN THE ELEMENTARY SCHOOLS

When I inquired about the curriculum in the world-centered schools, the principal told me that at the elementary level the curriculum is structured around the five overarching purposes stated in the world-centered schools' philosophy. There is an instructional program designed to implement each of the purposes.

These programs operate out of what the schools call "control centers."

"For example," she noted, "in the control center for helping children understand themselves as human beings, children are guided through specific learning experiences designed to develop that understanding. In addition to the learning experiences provided within the center, the center's staff is responsible for identifying opportunities in the rest of the school and larger community for children to continue their exploration of their human identity."

THE ME AND YOU ROOM

"Probably the best way for you to understand all of this is to visit the different control centers," I was told. I readily agreed, and the principal asked a couple of Terra School students to serve as my guides. They led me down a hall to a room labeled the Me and You Room, the control center for the program to develop students' understanding of themselves as individuals.

In the room a mixed-age instructional staff was working with several small groups of children. In one corner a half-dozen five- and six-year-olds were sorting pictures. The teenager working with them asked, "Okay, you all have your pictures in the order you want them to stay? Remember, put the thing you would like to do best on a Saturday morning first, the thing you would like to do next best second, and so on until your least favorite thing is last. All of you had the same six pictures to work with. Let's see if you all put the same picture first."

As I watched, a child of about ten came up and explained to me that this was one of the ways younger children began to identify their own attitudes and to see that others may not feel the same way that they do. "After they've discussed the reasons for their different choices, they'll probably watch that new tape that came in today," he said. "This week it's my job to take care of the films, tapes, and other media that come into the Me and You Room. The new tape is from a school in Sydney, Australia, and is labeled 'Some Sydney Children Tell about Their Favorite Things.' What do you want to bet that these kids find out that some kids in Australia like some of the things they like but that some Australian kids like some things they don't?"

I grinned but refused to take the bet, for that was just what I figured, too. The idea of having a videotape of other children in another part of the world exploring the same dimensions of their identity intrigued me. I asked one of the adults who was sorting through some books about it.

"Oh, yes," she said. "We make a concerted effort to help our children relate to other people around the world. It's not really so hard to make contact with schools around the world today. In a community like ours there are several hundred people who either regularly travel abroad or have friends and relatives living abroad. We simply describe the type of contact and exchange we would like to make and these people act as the liaison between us and our sister schools around the globe. You may have missed the camera focused on that group of children," she said as she pointed to a spot just above and to the side of the group. "These children are being videotaped as they do their attitude analysis. In this particular case, the tape will be carried by a local banker to Sydney this Friday. So the kids on the Sydney tape we see today will be watching our kids on tape next week. Of course, we can't afford to make videotapes all the time, but we do it as often as we can."

THE HUMAN BEING ROOM

As I stepped out of the Me and You Room, I was taken in tow by my young guides. "We decided to take you to the Human Being Room next," they said as they led me upstairs to the control center for developing children's understanding of themselves as members of the human species. When I entered, I was once again struck by the variety of people. The children were obviously of various ethnic backgrounds. Some were involved in mixed-age groups. Others appeared to be working mostly with children of similar age. It was not easy to distinguish the "teachers" from the "students." But those who were obviously assuming the teacher role ranged from a quite elderly gentleman to a girl who wasn't much older than the "students" around her.

Children were busy at one wall assembling a chart entitled "Tools Help the Human Body." One section was headed by a silhouette of a hand. Under the hand were scattered pictures including a typewriter, a hammer, a pencil, a shovel, a bulldozer, a globe, a mitten, a bucket, and a screwdriver. The children had just put up a large pair of eyes. Under it they had begun to place tools associated with human eyes. So far they had a microscope, a telescope, and a TV. A heated discussion was going on about a picture of a camera. The issue seemed to be whether to put it here under the eyes or to save it to put under the brain. The argument for the brain seemed to be that, like the brain, the camera stored information. Finally, one child found another picture of a camera, and it was agreed to put one picture under the eyes and save the other for the brain section.

As I watched, a learning manager stepped up to me. "As you can see, most of the tools the children have identified so far are ones they are fairly familiar with. Over the next week, each child is supposed to find out about a tool that is used in another part of the world. They will report on this tool and add a picture of it to the appropriate category on the chart."

She then indicated another group of children sitting around a large table. "This week those children are exploring the needs common to human beings and other living things," she told me. "Right now they are matching pictures of other animals engaged in protective behaviors with pictures of human beings of varying ages and in different cultural settings who are also engaged in protective behavior." I saw that one girl had a picture of a baby elephant walking under the belly of its mother. Lurking on the periphery of the elephant herd was a tiger. Next to this picture she had placed a picture of an adult human holding a child's hand as they crossed the street. Another picture showed a human mother holding her child while he was getting an inoculation. I asked why she had put this picture here. She told me this human mother was protecting her child from germs and sickness just as the elephant mother was protecting her child from the tiger.

As I was leaving the room, the learning manager directed my attention to a large illustrated chart that flanked the left side of the door.

WHAT DO YOU KNOW ABOUT BEING HUMAN?

1. How are human beings like all other living things?

2. How are human beings more like some living things than others?
Are you more like animals than plants?
Are you more like a jellyfish or a bird?
Are you more like a bear or a lizard?
Are you more like a monkey or a cow?

3. How are human beings unlike all other living things?

The learning manager explained, "Here you see the three basic questions children explore in this program. The two activities you observed this morning were related to questions two and three. In seeking answers to those questions, the children are guided to study themselves and to search for data across the total spectrum of human life on this planet. Through such processes we hope children will learn to see themselves as members of the family of humankind."

By this time the afternoon had ended. Many of the children in Terra School were heading for home. Those who were part of Monday's clean-up detail stayed to begin their work. Several other children who were involved in learning exchange activities at the school also lingered behind. When I returned to the principal's office, she asked if I would like to stay and look at some of the learning exchange activities. I thanked her but said no. I needed to get back to my motel room and put in order my notes and reflections on the day's experiences.

A DAY BEGINS AT FUTURA SCHOOL

I was scheduled to spend Tuesday visiting Futura School, the other world-centered elementary school. When I arrived, a few children were raising the flags in front of the building. Besides the United States flag, there was a United Nations flag, a flag displaying an ecology emblem, and two others that I did not recognize. The children told me that the blue-and-white flag was Middleston's flag and the orange-and-brown one was Futura School's flag.

As the principal of Futura School approached, I asked him about the flags and was told that the world-centered schools try to symbolize in as many ways as possible the multiple loyalties of their students. "We strongly believe," he told me, "that global citizenship entails loyalty to many kinds of human groups besides the global community itself. An active concern for the welfare of one's nation, community, family, religious group, school, or professional association is very much a part of being a good world citizen."

When we entered the school, the principal asked me what I would like to do first. I told him that I would like to visit the control center for the instructional program concerned with developing children's understanding of themselves as inhabitants of Earth.

THE PLANET EARTH ROOM

He took me to a room called the Planet Earth Room. When we entered, children were singing. As I listened, I discovered that all the songs were about water. The principal informed me that these students were studying water as part of humankind's natural environment. Currently, the children were looking at the feelings human beings have about water as expressed in music from different parts of the world.

As we listened, we quietly wandered about the room. It was virtually a "water museum." Maps, charts, graphs, and pictures dealing with water and its human uses (and misuses) covered the walls. On the tables were models, clearly constructed by children, of a variety of tools used by human beings around the world in relation to water. There were canals, many kinds of boats, fountains, sewage disposal systems, steam engines, and hydraulic generators. I was particularly attracted to one picture display. A large bulletin board entitled "Water and Human Needs" was divided into columns with each column headed by a particular human need such as "The Need for Beauty," "The Need for Fun," "The Need for Protection," and so on. Each column consisted of a collage of photos, magazine pictures, and children's drawings that depicted ways human beings around the world used water in meeting the particular need. "The Need for Beauty" collage contained pictures showing the use of water in Moslem temples, ice sculpture, ponds in urban areas, mountain streams, rainbows, cloud formations, fountains, colorfully lighted aquariums, and so on. I was also impressed by a large diagram of the global hydrologic system that covered almost a full wall.

The principal interrupted my observation to note that if I were to come later in the year I would see comparable displays dealing with air, with land, with plant and animal life, and with the earth's energy resources.

A learning manager joined us and I asked him about the rationale behind the program. "The purpose of this part of the curriculum is essentially fourfold," he informed me. "We try to show our kids how we humans depend on the planet's natural resources for gratifying all our needs. These include psychological needs such as our need for affection, beauty, self-actualization, and learning, as well as biological needs for food, water, air, and protection. Closely related to this is our effort to foster children's respect for nature and their sense of ecological responsibility. Also, at the elementary level we begin to develop students' understanding that the earth's biosphere is a global system.

"You might be interested in looking at these projects. They were done by some nine-year-old students." He pointed out two projects. One was a set of thank-you cards children had written to the rain forests in Brazil expressing appreciation for the oxygen the forests had contributed to the air. The other was a combination map and story depicting the trials and tribulations of a drop of water as it made its round-the-world journey through the planet's hydrologic system.

"Also in this program," he concluded, "the children are exposed to a bit of earth history and astronomy in an effort to start them on their way toward an understanding of their own place in the vast reaches of cosmic time and space. In this connection, a group of our students is going to a local observatory tonight as part of a project directed by three undergraduate student volunteers from the university."

The principal told me he had to leave to attend a staff meeting and offered to direct me to the control center of another program before leaving. I accepted his offer and we proceeded to another part of the building where he pointed out a room labeled the World Community Room.

THE WORLD COMMUNITY ROOM

I entered the room with a group of children of about six or seven. Each was carrying one or two toys. They went to one end of the room where a large plastic world map covered the floor and put their toys down on different places on the map. A girl of middle-school age who was directing this particular project told me that the children were studying where their toys had been made. "For the past three days the kids have been bringing from home one or more toys they no longer play with," she told me. "After we have located their place of origin on this map, the children box the toys and a couple of the group's members take them to a day care center where the toys are used by younger children."

Elsewhere in the World Community Room another group of students was working on a scrapbook of photos and letters. One of the children told me that his group had visited a local factory that manufactured office equipment. In an interview with the sales manager they found out the names of firms in different parts of the world that were using equipment made in Middleston. Then they wrote these firms for information on the products the firms produced as well as for photographs of people using the Middleston equipment. The group was organizing the information in a scrapbook they had entitled "Middleston's Machines in Offices around the World."

I spotted an elderly man who seemed to have a free moment, and so I approached him. The introductions revealed that he had been, until his retirement, an officer in a small multinational corporation whose main office was located in Middleston. Now, he spent a good deal of his time as one of the instructional specialists associated with the world-centered schools. He informed me that he was particularly interested in the effort to develop students' understanding of themselves as participants in global society. I asked him about the two projects I had just observed. "What you saw," he explained, "were small parts of a large, ongoing project operated jointly out of the World Community control centers of Terra and Futura Schools. The project is named 'The World in Middleston and Middleston in the World'[1] Beginning with the youngest children and going through to the oldest, Terra and Futura Schools involve their students in a continuous exploration of all the ways they are linked to people in all parts of the world." He went on to explain that one of the university professors, who was also a volunteer in the project, calls it a study of the international relations of everyday life. "I think this is a good description," he said. "For like all of the educational programs in the world-centered schools, our efforts to develop students' understanding of themselves as participants in global society is grounded in the child's everyday world. We try to enhance each child's awareness of how he or she personally, along with family, friends, and other people in Middleston, is affected by and in turn affects the remainder of the planet's four-plus billion human beings."

At this point he directed my attention to a group of students who were getting ready to leave the school and suggested that I might enjoy going with them. I asked one of the group where they were headed and was told they were off to interview the ministers in three local churches. The students explained that the interview was part of a study they were doing of how the churches in Middleston linked their congregations to the world outside of the United States.

Riding in two cars, one driven by a high school student and the other by a middle-aged woman who was the chairperson of the World Affairs Committee of the Middleston League of Women Voters, we soon arrived at the Middleston Community Church. After the introductions were completed, I stepped into the background and watched the students interview the church's minister.

"How many people from outside of the United States visited your church last year? Where did they come from?" one of the children asked. Another inquired, "Did any members of the church travel outside of the United States on church-related business?" "Are any members of your church from other countries?" a third asked. Another child asked a series of questions about money and goods that the church sends abroad. Still another student questioned the minister as to whether there were any groups within the church that study world problems like war and peace, hunger, or pollution. When the interview was over, one of the students asked the minister if she could borrow a copy of the hymnal used by the church. She explained that she was doing a special study of where the composers of the music used in local churches had lived.

The interviews in the other two Middleston churches went much the same way. On the way back to Futura School, the children told me about some of the other things they had done in the Middleston and the World project. The month before, a group of Futura and Terra students, with the help of undergraduate students from one of the local colleges, had constructed a random sample of Middleston families and sent questionnaires to this sample inquiring about the ways these families were linked by relatives, friends, and acquaintances to people elsewhere in the world. I also discovered that another group of students was currently engaged in a study of how books in the Middleston Children's Library linked their readers to the global community. Another group was constructing an inventory of imported goods sold in Middleston stores. Still another group, equipped with a list of the 200 largest multinational corporations, was identifying the goods and services produced by these firms that were used by Middleston residents.

When we arrived back at Futura School, I asked the high school student who had accompanied the children on their field trip how she happened to be involved in this particular project. She told me she was working with the children as part of a seminar called "The Individual and Global Society" that she was taking at the high school.

Upon entering the school building, I was greeted by some children who invited me to join them in a vegetarian lunch. While eating a cold and very tasty casserole dish, I found out that the meal had been prepared by some members of the Vegetarian Cooking Club. This club, which was run as part of the learning exchange program, taught children about vegetarian diets from different parts of the world.

The sole adult at the lunch table, besides myself, was a young agricultural economist from Jordan who was spending several months in the United States. She told me she had started the club as one step in her efforts to educate Americans to the adverse consequences of their excessive reliance on meats. She informed me that the club was preparing a slide-tape show they could use in presentations to adult groups. The show was entitled "What We Eat Can Make Other People Hungry."

THE COMPETENCY CENTER

After lunch I rejoined the principal and we chatted a bit about all the things I had seen in the elementary schools these past two days. "This afternoon," he said, "I imagine you will want to visit our control center for competency development." He explained that there was a unified competency development program for all world-centered schools, kindergarten through high school, in the district. "This program," he said, "is designed to foster skill growth in four major areas. One area consists of the three R's. Like all schools in Middleston, the world-centered schools are strongly committed to the development of children's reading, math, and writing skills.

Another area consists of what we've termed information-acquisition and thinking skills. A third focuses on affective skills, such as role taking and the ability to empathize. The fourth area focuses on those skills which probably best fit under the umbrella term 'political skills.' For example, these include decision-making and conflict management skills. The final area is language study. This is what we used to call foreign languages."

As an afterthought he added, "Of course, you understand we place a heavy emphasis on skill development in each of our other control centers. Our competency center is, in a way, our skill insurance policy. There, skill development can be reinforced in a systematic way. Children who are having difficulty with any skill can get help and, finally, skill development in the other parts of the educational program can be extended and enriched." With that he asked a girl to show me the way to Futura's competency center.

She guided me to a cluster of three large rooms adjoined by some smaller ones and a maze of what I learned were individual study carrels. A large sign dominated this section of the building. It read, "You Can Do It."

In one of the small rooms, children were working with all sorts of maps, charts, graphs, and tables. My attention was drawn to an array of world maps on one wall. Something about them puzzled me but at first I couldn't figure out what. Then I realized that when I had last sat in a student's desk the world map facing me had been a projection that placed the United States in the center or near-center of the world. In contrast, these maps were more often polar projections than equatorial and included both eastern-hemisphere-centered and western-centered. It was then I saw that each of the five globes in the room was set at a differing angle and the printing was shifted to accommodate each angle. The children seemed quite at home with what for me was an "upside-down" world and could as easily identify the silhouette of a "sideways" Australia as a "right-side-up" one.

While I was still puzzling over an "upside-down" globe, a boy of about ten came up to me. "Do you think that globe is as strange as my father does?" he asked. When I admitted that I was a bit confused by it, he led me over to a box in the corner and told me to look through the peephole. A little shiver went up my spine. There, suspended in the center of a black void, a miniature replica of planet Earth spun like an iridescent blue jewel. As I watched, a minuscule spacecraft came into view and passed over Earth and out of sight once again. When I finally tore my eyes away, my beaming guide explained that he and some classmates had constructed the model.

"Now," he said, "if you saw Earth from that spaceship, do you think it would have an up or a down and do you think the United States would look like it was in the center of the world?" He called my attention to the quote on the Earth box. At that point, I began to grasp the full significance of the world map projections and globes in this room. They, too, carried the message, "You are a rider on spaceship Earth."

As I wandered through the rest of the competency laboratories, I saw that the kind of learning that was encouraged in the map room pervaded all other skill development areas. Whenever it was natural to do so, skills were taught in the context of a global perspective.

That night I fell asleep trying to identify all the ways my perception of the world had been inadvertently distorted by the maps that had dominated my childhood. When sleep finally came, I was trying to convince myself, but to no avail, that the South Pole was just as much "up" as it was "down."

WORLD MIDDLE SCHOOL

The next day was Wednesday and I was scheduled to spend it at the World Middle School. When I arrived, I was politely stopped at the door by a girl who handed me a card. "My name is Carol," she said. "I wonder if you would mind taking a few minutes to fill out this card before you leave the school. Please drop it in a box you will see by the door when you leave." When I inquired about the card, she elaborated. "A few other students and I are doing a survey this month of adults who come into our school. The information we get from these cards will tell us where the adults come from, why they've come to our school, what they did while here, and so forth. This project will help me fulfill part of this month's 'Institutions' contract." I said that I'd be happy to help and asked to be directed to the principal's office.

Here, as in the elementary schools, students were working side-by-side with adults keeping the central office functioning. The principal escorted me into his office and introduced me to a boy of about thirteen who was sitting behind the second desk in the room. "Tom is the student principal for this month," the principal explained. "We feel that one of the best ways our students can learn how an institution such as this school works is to experience different roles within the institution. We have found that the student needs at least a month in the role of student principal to really begin to get a 'feel' for the principalship. Unfortunately, this means only a few students can experience this role. The student council has the responsibility of naming the student principals from the members of each year's graduating class. Two student vice-principals are chosen in the same way, as is the student head custodian."

Tom, the student principal, asked me what my impressions were of world-centered schools now that I was beginning my third day in them. I responded that I was still sorting it all out and was very anxious to see how a world-centered middle school functioned. After a brief exchange between themselves, the two principals agreed on the best way to initiate me. They pulled a large chart down from a wall.

HUMAN CULTURE				
APPROACHES	INSTITUTIONS	LANGUAGE	BELIEFS	TECHNOLOGY
STUDY				
SKILLS				
SOCIAL ACTION/ SERVICE				

"The major focus of the World Middle School program is on human culture," the principal explained. "You will recall from the philosophy behind the world-centered schools that one of the overarching purposes of our schools is to develop children's understanding of what it means to be a human being. The single most salient answer to the question 'How are human beings unlike all other living things?' is—humans create culture."

When I asked for clarification of the terms on the chart, I was given these working definitions. *Institutions* are defined as long-lasting ways of doing things. They include everything from a fire drill in a middle school to an organization like the United Nations. *Language* includes all the ways humans have invented to communicate with one another, with other animals, and with machines like computers. In addition to the systems of sounds and symbols we conventionally call language, human languages include music, dance, and other art forms; man-machine languages like Fortran; mathematics; and the silent languages of facial expressions and body motions. *Beliefs* are threefold, including empirical beliefs, moral or ethical beliefs, and aesthetic beliefs. *Technology* is defined as tools and the skills to make and use them. Tools, incidentally, include every concrete thing humans make to satisfy their needs— glasses, books, clothes, buildings, implements, and so on.

The principal next directed my attention to the vertical axis of the chart. "We have identified what we call three basic approaches to the development of the children's understanding of human culture," he noted. "As you can see, these are study, skills, and social action/ service. When children first enter World Middle School, major emphasis is put on the study of human culture as it is manifested around the world. For almost a whole school term these children are immersed in our program called 'The Human Way of Living.' Of course, skills or competencies are a part of this study, but our major concern is to develop our students' understanding that human beings everywhere and in all times share a common way of living— that is, culture."

THE CONTRACT SYSTEM
"At the close of this study," he continued, "children move into our contract system that they will follow for the remainder of their time at World Middle School."

The mention of contracts reminded me of my encounter with Carol. So that was what she meant by a contract. The principal went on to say that through the contract system each child was exposed to each component of culture every month. Students were free to choose the approach they wanted as they focused on each of the four components.

At this point Tom commented, "This month the part of my contract dealing with Institutions calls for me to work alongside the principal. While I learn about the school from this perspective, I am gaining administrative skills and, at the same time, serving my school. Thus, sometimes the different 'approaches' really happen all at once."

I asked if it would be possible to get a copy of a student contract and was given a replica (see below).

RESOURCE CENTERS
I was told that the physical organization of the school reflected and facilitated the focus on human culture. The school has six major resource centers—one for each of the four components of culture, one for skill or competency development, and one for learning through social action/service activities.

The rest of the day was spent visiting these resource centers and watching the children and staff in action. I learned that the personnel in each resource center are responsible for developing a basic structured program for all students at WMS. For example, in the Institutions resource center, I observed a class studying sex roles in various societies. In a competencies lab one group of students was

MY CONTRACT FOR OCTOBER
NAME: *Terri J. Williams*

FOCUS ON HUMAN CULTURE

	INSTITUTIONS	LANGUAGE	BELIEFS	TECHNOLOGY
STUDY	Study World Middle School (*WMS*): —Write history of school's founding.	Take an inventory of the languages used in WMS that can be understood by others around the world: —mathematics —music —smiles		
SKILLS	Ask questions clearly. Make a survey of visitors. Who visits our school? What do they learn? How do they feel about it? (see Beliefs) Use facts and information about past events. Interview witnesses and participants: —people involved in the creation of WMS	Work with my dance group to develop a dance interpretation of how people are alike and different at the same time.	Analyze visitor survey to see what people think about our school.	Construct a map showing major world transportation arteries which connect WMC to Asia. Will begin map with street in front of school, on to Highway 10 leading out of town, to Interstate 66, etc. Will include roads, airways, waterways.
SOCIAL ACTION/ SERVICE	Participate in orientation program for foreign visitors. 1. (see Language) 2. Seek visitors' help in setting up communication between WMS and a school in visitors' home cities. Write letter to that school and give to visitor for delivery.	1. Identify languages visitors speak. Locate needed interpreters.		Work with a group of five other students and adults at WMS to identify public body responsible for traffic in front of school and take action to get a traffic light installed.

practicing interviewing techniques. A group in the technology resource center was studying the effect of fuel-powered machines on the global water system. In addition to providing these structured courses, the personnel in the resource center serve students' individual needs as they go about fulfilling their monthly contracts.

At the end of the day I returned to the principal's office and thanked my hosts for the full and informative day. As I left the building I dropped my card in the box as Carol had requested that morning. I made a mental note to check with Carol and her colleagues at the end of the month. Their study of the World Middle School should prove a valuable item in my growing file on world-centered schools.

21ST CENTURY HIGH SCHOOL

Wednesday night I dined with the co-principals of the world-centered high school. We chatted about many things including the school's name, 21st Century High School. When they told me that the name symbolized the future-oriented education to which the school was dedicated, I remembered the high school students I had met my first night in Middleston and their acute awareness of the fact that most of their lives would be lived in the twenty-first century.

When the dinner ended, I was given a brief brochure describing 21st Century's curriculum, which I read before going to bed. I discovered that the high school's curriculum was organized around six major programs:

- The Program for Studies of Individual Development and Behavior

- The Program for Studies of the Human Species

- The Program for Studies of Humankind's Planetary and Cosmic Environments

- The Program for Studies of Global Society

- The Program for the Development of Human Competencies

- The Program for Social Service, Political Action, and Work Study

The brochure informed me that during their first two years in high school, all students took an intensive year-long lecture/seminar/lab course in each of the first four programs. Following the year-long course, each of the programs offered a rich array of minicourses, independent study projects, student-initiated and -directed seminars, and field experience projects of varying lengths and levels of sophistication. At the start of every three-month period, students would construct for themselves a program of study comprised of "modules" which they selected from one or more of the program areas. The only requirement was that in submitting their program of study, all students were required to accompany it by a statement which set forth their personal educational philosophy and a rationale explaining why their self-designed program did, in fact, further the educational goals they had set for themselves. A system of advisory committees comprised of students, school staff, and adults from the community reviewed each student's study program and statement of educational philosophy. If a committee felt that a student's program was unsound in light of his educational aspirations and/or that these aspirations were ambiguously formulated, the student would meet with an adviser from his committee and discuss the matter. Following the discussion, the student had the option of proceeding with the program he had proposed or modifying it in light of insights or information acquired in the course of the discussion.

In addition to work in the first four programs, 21st Century High expected each student to engage in activities provided by both the Program for the Development of Human Competencies and the Program for Social Service, Political Action, and Work-Study. The brochure pointed out that normally students elected activities that related directly or indirectly to one or more of the "academic" topics they were studying or, conversely, students elected to take a particular module because it related directly to a competency or action activity in which they had a particular interest. For example, a student who was learning a language such as Spanish or Russian might couple this with a minicourse or seminar or independent study project in linguistics offered by the Program for Studies of the Human Species. A student who was involved in a work-study project in the international division of a bank might combine this experience with a study of economic institutions. Similarly, students working part time in a photography shop in the city and doing photography skill development activities might combine this work and skill development with a minicourse on the physics of light offered by the Program for Studies of Humankind's Planetary and Cosmic Environments and an independent study project in the psychology of visual perception available under the auspices of the Program for Studies of Individual Development and Behavior.

A DAY IN THE LIFE OF A 21ST CENTURY HIGH STUDENT

After reading about the educational programs at 21st Century High School, I decided that perhaps I could best get a flavor of the school by spending my time observing how one student spent his or her day. When I arrived at the school, I asked one of the co-principals if this would be acceptable. She graciously told me that the school was mine to visit as I wished and called Nobu Tanaka, a third-year student, to ask if she would be willing to spend the day with me. I discovered that Nobu had spent the last six years in Middleston's world-centered schools. Her father was a United States sales representative for a Japanese electronics firm. I asked her if there were many non-American students in the school and was told that counting exchange students who usually spend a year at 21st Century, about 100 members from a student body of 750 were citizens of other nations.

Nobu told me she had about twenty minutes before she was due at one of her minicourses and asked if I would like to join her for coffee in the student/staff lounge. I took the opportunity to ask her about her first two years at 21st Century High. She told me that in the first year she took the basic courses offered by the Program for Studies of Individual Development and Behavior and the Program for Studies of the Human Species. Then in the next year she took the two basic courses offered by the Program for Studies of Humankind's Planetary and Cosmic Environments and the Program for Studies of Global Society.

I inquired about the general content of these courses. She told me that the course dealing with individual growth and development was an interdisciplinary mixture of material from biology, the health sciences, and the social sciences. One part of the course focused on the biological, cognitive, and emotional processes involved in human growth, development, and change from conception to death with an emphasis on the influence of environmental factors on the development of individuals. Nobu reported that one of the highlights for her of this part of the course was the time she spent in a cross-societal study of infancy. For the field experience component of this study she spent her late afternoons babysitting for a family that had a six-month-old boy and a girl just turning two. At the same time she took a short independent reading project on the methodology of participant observation. "Just the other day," she remarked, "I looked at the notes I made on my observations of those children. I am still proud of them." I discovered that the other part of the course dealt with a variety of basic human behaviors including attitude formation, the psychology of prejudice and stereotyping, social learning, hostility and aggression, and the ethics of interpersonal relations.

Nobu then described her course in the Program for Studies of the Human Species. It was roughly divided into three parts of varying durations. The course began with an overview of the place of the human species in the taxonomy of life. Nobu pointed out that an emphasis was placed on students personally identifying their own physical features, biological functions, and psychological and social behaviors that can be traced to different parts of their prehuman biological heritage. This part of the course was followed by a period in which students engaged in a comparative study of the behavior of human beings and other animals. Particular attention was focused on learning, communication, and social organization. Nobu had done an observational study of play among kittens and human children. The rest of the course, Nobu informed me, focused on the global history of humankind. She indicated that the students' work was organized around the study of points of revolutionary change in the human condition and long-term historical trends. She had been particularly interested in studying the agricultural revolution and trends in world population growth.

The basic course Nobu had taken in the program for Studies of Humankind's Planetary and Cosmic Environments combined and mixed studies of topics drawn from the earth sciences, ecology, and astronomy. I detected from her description that this course, like the other basic courses she had taken, succeeded in personalizing the subject matter to a much greater degree than is true of most high school courses that I had observed over the years. In addition to the knowledge it imparted, the course had obviously enhanced Nobu's awareness of her identity as a part of the fragile life-support system of one small planet adrift in a universe of awesome size and eternal mystery.

Our coffee break at an end, Nobu and I left for one of the school's resource centers. As we walked, she briefly described the course she had taken the previous year in the Program for Studies in Global Society. They had begun the year by studying about the sociopolitical organizations characteristic of human history prior to the rise of nation-states. They had looked at hunting and gathering bands, ancient empires, city-states, and various forms of feudal organizations. Attention then turned to the evolution of the nation-state system in Europe and its subsequent diffusion to the rest of the planet. She told me the class had spent a good deal of time constructing a simulation depicting the structural characteristics of the classical nation-state system and then systematically modifying and changing the model to illustrate the historical innovations that were transforming the classical system into a global society. Nobu, I learned, had been responsible for adding global corporations and the growth of international organizations to the simulation while some of her classmates worked on modifying the simulation to represent such changes as the growing permeability of nations to the diffusion of beliefs, information, people, and goods from other nations; the impact of nuclear and missile technology on doctrines of warfare; the decline in the ideologies of sovereignty, national loyalty, and nonintervention; and the development of global systems of rapid communication and transportation. Then, after an overview of some of the major problems confronting contemporary global society such as the war system, runaway population growth, resource depletion, environmental pollution, and economic inequalities, the course ended with an exploration of alternative planetary futures.

The minicourse Nobu was headed for turned out to be an extension of the latter feature of the global society course she had been describing. I discovered that the particular course she was taking was part of a cluster of minicourses and independent study projects all sharing a common task, the construction of a social planetarium. When completed the planetarium would enable students and townspeople to immerse themselves in a bombardment of visual and auditory stimuli depicting alternative world futures that ranged along a continuum from highly desirable to highly undesirable. The planetarium was being constructed in a large abandoned warehouse on loan to 21st Century High from one of Middleston's manufacturing firms.

The particular minicourse Nobu was taking concerned the problem of social justice. Specifically, I learned that the students were constructing two alternative slide/tape shows. One depicted a world in which a network of small political elites scattered across the globe systematically discriminated against the mass of humankind. The other depicted a world in which most of humanity enjoyed a high level of respect in relations with governments as well as in relations with one another. The students in the seminar informed me that they had been working on the project for a month and expected to complete it in the next four weeks. They also told me that ten or twelve other minicourses were involved in the social planetarium project along with about thirty-five independent study projects.

Following the minicourse, Nobu took me with her to a seminar she was taking. The seminar, also offered under the auspices of the Program for Studies in Global Society, focused on the intellectual history of the ideas of global community and world citizenship. This particular Thursday morning, the students in the seminar were discussing the idea of world community implied in the United States Declaration of Independence. At the end of the class I was introduced to the adult who had led the discussion. I learned he was a local lawyer specializing in international law and one of the instructional specialists who worked with 21st Century High.

When noon came, Nobu told me she would have to leave me to my own devices as far as lunch was concerned. This was her week to work the lunch period in the school's cafeteria. She suggested that I meet her at the student/staff lounge at 1:30 and she would take me to an afternoon class on world literature.

Left on my own, I took the opportunity to wander about the school plant. I saw that like the lower schools I had visited, the physical environment of 21st Century High School had been designed to further the philosophy of the world-centered schools. I was particularly attracted to the photographic display along one of the hallways. The wall was lined with photos showing human faces, some revealing happiness and joy and others grief and sadness. The display, I learned from reading a plaque, was entitled "The Language of Smiles and Tears" and had been created by a student photography club. What the students had done, I discovered, was to match pictures of Middleston residents with pictures of individuals elsewhere in the world whose faces expressed the same emotion.

Later I met Nobu and we proceeded to her world literature course. I saw from a copy of the syllabus she loaned me that the course was organized around topics relating to the cycle of life with the students studying short stories, poems, novels, myths, folk tales, and films dealing with the different "crises" of life. On this particular day, they were ending the section of the course that dealt with birth. One of the students had written a short essay dealing with similarities and differences in attitudes toward the birth of children revealed in the literature the students had read, and today the class discussed and criticized the young man's essay.

The world literature class ended Nobu's afternoon in the 21st Century School as such. The rest of her afternoon was devoted to a work-study job in the pediatrics ward of a nearby hospital. I accompanied her and two other students who were also working in the same hospital on the short bus ride. I discovered that, like Nobu, these students had a particular interest in children and planned to follow some kind of career that involved work with children.

I also learned that Nobu's school day continued into the evening. As part of its career education effort, 21st Century High ran a program entitled "Jobs and World Citizenship." As its name implied, the program focused on the concrete ways different people in various occupations could constructively participate in global society. That week the program was dealing with child-care-related occupations, and Thursday's session was a discussion led by three nurses. They described ways in which they could participate as individuals, as members of their professional associations, as citizens of the city, state, and nation, and as participants in transnational institutions in efforts to enhance the quality of the health care enjoyed by the world's children. In the course of the evening's discussion, I counted no less than twenty alternative ways that a professional in child health care could become involved in local, national, and transnational activities aimed at improving the health of the planet's next generation.

DEPARTING MIDDLESTON

The next morning I called upon the superintendent to wish him good-bye and to thank him for the opportunity to visit the world-centered schools. I expressed regret that I could not stay on and visit the other types of schools in the district. He said that he, too, was sorry that I could not since I would undoubtedly find the others of interest. "The three types of schools in Middleston are by no means islands unto themselves," he informed me. "To the contrary, there is a great deal of interaction among the three types." In the course of the conversation I discovered that as a part of the district's staff development program, the permanent instructional staff regularly engaged in a teacher exchange program. For example, each year a few members of the staff of the world-centered schools spent three to six months in the traditional schools and staff members from the latter worked in the world-centered schools. "In this way," the superintendent said, "we assure that good ideas adaptable to the different kinds of schools are diffused throughout the district. For example, the reading program used in the two elementary world-centered schools was borrowed with some modification from the traditional schools. On the other hand many features of the multi-disciplinary culture study program you observed in the world-centered middle school have been picked up and used in Middleston's other middle schools. In this sense, the system of alternative schools in Middleston is more than a political solution to a political problem. It is a good way of assuring high-quality education in all our schools. Good ideas and sound educational practices pioneered in one type of school spread to other schools. This is as it should be in a society dedicated to the support of diversity and pluralism."

NOTES

1. The program described here is adapted from "Columbus in the World, the World in Columbus," a project of the Transnational Intellectual Cooperation Program, directed by Chadwick F. Alger, Ohio State University, with financial assistance from the Kettering Foundation. For further information write: Transnational Intellectual Cooperation Program, 199 West Tenth Avenue, Columbus, Ohio, 43201.

CHAPTER TWO

The World and the School: A Case for World-Centered Education

James M. Becker

Mid-America Program for Global Perspectives in Education

T ravel, newspaper headlines, trade missions, exchange students, multinational corporations, and television provide millions of Americans with information and experiences which twenty years ago would have seemed unreal or impossible. Volkswagens, Toyotas, radios, tea, bananas, Rotary clubs, churches, and a host of other products and organizations provide links between our hometowns and cities and towns the world over.

Many of our states sponsor trade missions; some have promotion offices overseas. There are few grocery stores these days without foreign products on the shelves. Foreign cars, motorcycles, cameras, radios, and television sets have become so common as to go largely unnoticed. Entertainment, sports, and a host of cultural events include performers from other countries. Renewed interest in ethnic and national origins results in many Americans tracing their heritage back to another country or area of the world.

These developments in hometowns everywhere, like the networks of jet airplane routes, oil pipelines, giant ships, and instantaneous global communication, have largely eliminated the cushion of space that once separated nations and peoples. But being closer does not necessarily mean that improved understanding or a sense of world community is inevitable. Proximity contains not only the potential for integration, but also the potential for increased conflict. These conditions demand new concepts and practices of worldwide sharing of responsibilities and a readiness to see the world as an interdependent community.

The increasing impact of world events on the everyday lives of more and more people is stimulating changes in the ways individuals view themselves, other human beings, and planet Earth. There is increasing awareness that we are all inhabitants of a single planet and share a common fate as members of a single species. As a nation and as a people we may not yet be ready for planetwide discussion or involvement. Other nations and peoples probably are not ready either, but as a powerful nation, our shortcomings may count more.

The situation does suggest that we need to develop further our capacities to benefit from diversity, to communicate with others who do not share our values, to recognize the need to identify with human beings everywhere, to manage conflict, and to tolerate ambiguity. It also suggests that opportunities for participation in the social and economic processes of our increasingly interdependent world must be made more visible and that more attention should be paid to developing the understandings and skills needed for such participation. Reischauer argues:

We need a profound reshaping of education if mankind is to survive in the sort of world that is fast evolving. . . . Before long humanity will face grave difficulties that can only be solved on a global scale. Education . . . is not moving rapidly enough to provide the knowledge about the outside world and the attitudes toward other people that may be essential for human survival within a generation or two.[1]

But what kind of educational responses do these world trends and looming global problems require? How can education help people perceive what is happening? What changes are needed in our schools? How can the needed changes be brought about? What research, what knowledge, what experience can best serve these ends? What civic attitudes and skills are needed for responsible participation in an increasingly interdependent world?

In this volume we are concerned about how education, at the precollegiate level, can help people understand the nature of the emerging global society and develop the identities, attitudes, and competencies needed for responsible participation. Questions which help provide a focus for the volume include:

1. What kind of experiences are likely to help youth develop the competencies and insights needed to gain some understanding of and control over the global events and processes in which they are involved?

2. What resources, talents, and instructional materials are available and appropriate for such efforts?

3. What agencies, school programs, and special projects offer promising programs in the area of world studies?

4. How can schools and communities design and manage programs which are likely to help youth develop the skills and identities needed for responsible participation in an interdependent world?

We began this book, in Chapter 1, with a vision. The Andersons were asked to imagine what the program of an ideal school dedicated to promoting global perspectives would look like. Middleston, unfortunately, does not exist. However, many, if not most, of the activities, programs, and materials described can be found in some form in some schools. Later chapters in this book will make this explicit. This chapter focuses on analyzing what the process of teaching and learning looks like in the Middleston world-centered schools, that is, what students study, how the curriculum is organized, what teachers do, what the role of the community is, and what characterizes the climate of a school committed to preparing citizens for responsible participation in a global society.

THE WORLD-CENTERED ALTERNATIVE

Increasing interdependence and rapid change are facts of life in the late twentieth century. We assume that a complex society requires diversity of character and competence in order to deal with new and changing situations. The world-centered school can be an important element in the effort to develop pluralism in outlook, competence, and approaches to action.

Although respect for diversity is one of the noblest traditions of American society, American schools have not always been guided by this principle. Instead, the focus has often been on teaching the "American way" and presenting students with an uncritical chauvinistic view of our society. New patterns of education can strengthen our commitment to pluralism. But it seems unlikely that such a condition will be fostered in a single setting or a unitary school program.

We believe that it is not enough to be exposed to only one set of values, however perfect they may seem. Growing up with a single set of values can be imprisoning. A diversity of settings and experiences and exposure to many different values are better than imposed accommodation. The focus must always be on the ability to adapt—to understand, to participate in, to cope with social and technological change.

To foster global perspectives, a chance to see beyond the local group and to experience a variety of social and cultural settings should be provided for every child. In Middleston, these experiences are provided through activities such as exchange programs involving students, materials, and artifacts from several countries and through the use of foreign visitors as teachers or resource persons. Within the world-centered schools, the same experiences are provided through activities such as role taking, simulation, and use of culturally diverse sources and materials.

A second cornerstone of the world-centered philosophy is community. While we believe that the choices available to students should be basic enough to produce significant differences in attitudes and views, those differences should not be so divisive that they seriously threaten the notion of community. A great deal of the effort of a world-centered school must be devoted to awakening in students an awareness of their membership in the global human community and in all other communities to which they belong. Learning situations and classroom practices, whatever the subject matter or grade level, must be deliberately shaped so that they contain, as elements of the learning process, certain important components of community.

Among the sources of capacity for consensus which are apparent in the Middleston world-centered program are:

1. A strong feeling of shared membership in human culture—American, Western, world

2. A concern for traditions, heroes, and critical events in human history

3. Ethical concerns as represented by notions of what is praised, blamed, or ignored

4. Language and arts, especially as they relate to mutual comprehension and communication

5. Ways of knowing, especially as they relate to problems which have no single correct answer

It is important to recognize that in Middleston, the world-centered schools are only one *alternative*. Because of value conflicts within the community, a series of alternative schools was set up to give parents and students a choice. The fact that alternatives exist is in itself an important lesson in pluralism and respect for diversity. Even if parents and students do not choose the world-centered alternative, they have at least been exposed to the notion that different ways of thinking and different approaches to problems can coexist.

The idea of public alternative schools—a modification of regular patterns of schooling within public schools through plural education—has spread rapidly over the last decade. The alternative school trend, as demonstrated at its best by the Middleston example, seems promising. By emphasizing variety in education rather than the "one right way," such efforts seek to provide appropriate learning experiences for the various life and learning styles of their students. However, care must be taken in setting up optional patterns not to undermine the existing pattern as a legitimate choice. Most parents, teachers, and students still prefer it and should have such an option in public schools of choice.[2]

In addition to providing alternatives in education, efforts in Middleston generally seek to include smaller, more diverse, cross-age and community-related school programs which are characterized by both academic and action learning and involve alternative paths to adulthood, including work and social involvement in the community. These conditions also provide a strategy for constructive change which enables various segments of the community to participate in meaningful ways. The world-centered school is part of an alternative program that can be not only a means of accommodating diverse views in a community but also a viable strategy for change.

With increasing acceptance of the alternative school approach, some supporters of the idea are seeking to demonstrate not only the viability of the idea but also the benefits which the larger community derives from such a notion. Among the benefits they frequently cite are increased participation in educational activities by parents and other adults; more public discussion of the purposes and objectives of education; more effective use of a great variety of community resources for educational purposes; and a growing recognition on the part of citizens that education is a community responsibility in which schools play an important role.

Using the alternative school approach as a change strategy is based on the notion that the way schools actually operate at any given time is a result of an accumulation of thousands of day-to-day decisions. Therefore, in order to change the reality of schooling, careful attention must be paid to the host of natural and ordinary events which occur in the district—textbook selection; hiring, promoting, and retiring of personnel; curriculum review and revision; faculty meetings; accreditation; budgeting—and all the situations and conditions which shape the way the schools actually operate. Knowledge of these occasions for decisions and good working relationships with those individuals and agencies most involved in these decisions are basic to such a strategy.

Another assumption which guides those who see the alternative approach as part of a strategy for change holds that the images of the world people have provide the environment for individual action and are capable of being influenced by persuasion, examination, and confrontation. Thus, if the natural occurrences within the school system are seen as occasions to help shape people's images of reality, they can be important in creating acceptance of pluralism in education as a social value. This means that participation in the events of the community-school complex is a must because it helps all those involved, whether they support or oppose the alternative approach, to get a better grip on the social reality in which the schools operate and a better understanding of how the world works, which is an essential element in all efforts to shape a better world. While no one has a complete grip on the social realities of our time, sharing our impressions of those realities can help us perceive them more accurately and completely and help in shaping them more to our liking.

Many supporters of alternatives in education are supporters of the notion that schools have an important role to play in helping to create and maintain a learning society. They feel that neither the school nor any other institution can alone furnish the kinds of comprehensive educational experiences needed. Living in an increasingly interdependent world poses problems for which school and nonschool experiences are needed to find solutions. Furthermore, the issues are so intertwined that neither school nor nonschool institutions can alone furnish the wide range of educational experiences needed. Therefore, they seek to deal with the issues of world-centered education in a way that not only draws on but expands the capabilities of the schools and other institutions to furnish the comprehensive educational experiences needed. Examples of how schools and other institutions can work together are found in later chapters of this book.

DESIGNING WORLD-CENTERED PROGRAMS: GOALS AND OBJECTIVES

The learning environment provided in the world-centered school is based on a number of assumptions about the kinds of knowledge, attitudes, and skills which best serve students. Just as there are different views of the world, so there are differing opinions about the goals of global or international education. While consensus may seldom occur, there is considerable agreement among educators and lay persons alike that school curricula should help students develop the capacities to lead productive, meaningful lives. Guiding those who make decisions in these areas are assumptions not only about how people learn but also about the nature of the problems today's students will deal with as adults, the type of experiences most likely to enable them to develop the capacities to deal with these problems, and the most effective and appropriate ways to provide these experiences.

An important concern in establishing goals and objectives for world-centered schools is the concept of citizenship, not in the narrow sense of serving the state but rather in the sense of encompassing whatever individuals do that affects the welfare of others. Reviews of goals for education in schools in the United States reveal that effective citizenship along with the development of ethical values and "thinking abilities" have been persistent concerns of educators throughout the last century.[3] Broadly defined, this had meant education to prepare citizens for membership in particular societies.

In this sense the responsibility for citizenship training has a long history in American education. The next step must be to broaden citizen or civic education to include global dimensions.

We start with the assumption that citizens must be prepared to participate in a variety of groups—family, local community, nation, and transnational—and accept the notion that individuals enjoy rights and privileges as well as obligations and responsibilities as a result of being members of these groups. A world-centered program should provide experiences and settings which enable students to develop identities and competencies for participation in the complex world of today.

These assumptions and beliefs provide the basis for the five major goals of the schools described by the Andersons.

1. *To develop students' understanding of themselves as individuals.* This is most apparent in the activities associated with the Me and You Room.

2. *To develop understanding of themselves as members of the human species.* Exercises such as "What do you know about being human?" and "Tools to help the human body" are examples of efforts to implement this goal.

3. *To develop students' understanding of themselves as inhabitants and dependents of planet Earth.* The Planet Earth Room is the focus of many activities associated with this goal.

4. *To develop students' understanding of themselves as participants in global society.* The "Middleston in the World/The World in Middleston" project seeks to help students see how participation in global society is a fact of life in hometown, USA.

5. *To develop within students the competencies required to live intelligently and responsibly as individuals, human beings, earthlings, and members of global society.* While all aspects of the world-centered school deal with this goal, the competency center has a major responsibility for competency development.

Identities, loyalties, and competencies as well as rights, duties, obligations, and privileges are associated with each of these goals. For example, students might explore the issues involved and discuss the rights one has by virtue of being a member of the human species. The Universal Declaration of Human Rights, the Humanist Manifesto, and "UNICEF and the Rights of the Child" are among many documents and other materials which can be used in considering this question. As Torney points out in Chapter 3, many American students believe that ours is the only country which protects human rights and that people in other countries do not care about having such rights. An important element in dealing with this topic is helping students understand that all human beings are born into the "nation of persons" and therefore are entitled to respect, dignity, love, and life as members of the human species. The other side of the coin is that as members of the species each of us assumes responsibilities and obligations. The struggle for human rights is thus more likely to be viewed as a worldwide struggle in which each of us plays a part.

The same is true regarding the study of our rights and obligations as inhabitants of planet Earth. Each person is entitled to some share of the beauty and material benefits which the planet provides; in turn, each has obligations regarding the care and feeding of the planet. There is a strong feeling among many proponents of global education that merely having knowledge about and concern for world issues is insufficient, that students must become active. For example, understanding the energy crisis is of little consequence if one does not turn down the thermostat or use less fuel or take whatever action the student believes will help the situation. The school is seldom seen as an appropriate proponent of specific kinds of action the individual should take but rather as a developer of action-oriented individuals. But the school must, at least, offer alternative courses of action or opportunities for students to develop their own alternatives.

No list of competencies or other objectives is likely to be complete. Changes in technology and developments in learning theory as well as developments in the social sciences and in the way the world works require constant review and redefinition of objectives and goals. The objectives listed here are among those which world-centered schools strive to maintain.

1. Provide learning experiences that give the student the ability to view the world as a planetwide society

2. Teach skills and attitudes that will enable the individual to learn inside and outside of school throughout his or her life

3. Avoid the ethnocentrism common in sharp divisions drawn between the study of us and them (America and the rest of the world)

4. Integrate world studies with developments in other disciplines and fields of study

5. Teach the interrelatedness of human beings rather than simply identify uniqueness or differences

6. Explore future alternatives

7. Recognize in the experiences provided for students the likelihood of continued change, conflict, ambiguity, and increasing interdependence

That each of us lives in a world community, that it is possible to maintain harmonious membership in family, church, local community groups, the nation, transnational groups, and in humankind generally may seem self-evident to some people, but in many communities they are matters of great controversy. If we are to avoid world conflict and solve global problems, many more people must hold these views. The world-centered school with its emphasis on helping children and youth understand themselves as individuals, as members of a single species, and as participants in a great variety of local, national, and transnational groups, together with its emphasis on the "oneness" of the modern world, can help students and other members of the community grapple with these complex and controversial issues. The school should make no pretense that it has the answers, but it can seek to help children and youth develop the identities and competencies needed to participate in today's world.

ORGANIZING THE PROGRAM

Informed by general goals and objectives such as those stated here, the designers of the settings and experiences in world-centered schools must next consider questions such as these: What aspects of the world—that is, what phenomena or objects—should one seek to help students understand? What are the qualities, characteristics, or capacities one should seek to have students develop? And what experiences, approaches, processes, and techniques are most appropriate and useful?

Ultimately, a combination of community concerns, school policies, student orientations, and teacher preferences determine how the resources, opportunities, and experiences available to the schools are used to fashion specific programs. Each of these factors is complicated. For example, just as a student's attitudes reflect a composite of influences, so a teacher's preferences grow out of a variety of factors including accumulated experiences in the field, differing views of the world, and awareness of research findings, alternative strategies of instruction, and theories of learning. Sensitivity to societal needs and problems and concern about various pressures from the community also play a part in decisions about what to teach. The point here is that the program or curriculum in a school often reflects the assumptions, preferences, priorities, and understandings of those who make the decisions. Involving more people in the process complicates the problem, but it also increases the likelihood that the needs of the larger community will be served. Making the preferences of various groups known can help in the discussion of alternatives and in the process of reaching agreement and consensus; more importantly, it can contribute to self-awareness, an important ingredient in situations involving human communication. Instead of smoothing over differences in outlook, educators and lay persons alike need to be open to each other's views and perspectives as they work to define the goals and purposes of world studies and to implement them in programs.

At least three different views exist about how international or world studies should be organized. One view holds that the most important goal of such a program should be to help students become intelligent, loyal supporters of the national interest. Proponents argue that good citizenship education should result in greater student understanding of and support for the foreign policies of our national leaders. The supporters of this view feel that the study of diplomatic history, current foreign policy issues, the organization and functions of the Department of State, and America's role in the world should be the focus of international or world studies.

Another view advocated by some supporters of international education holds that intercultural understanding should be the central focus of international education. The supporters of this position favor a strong emphasis on language and area studies. The geography, language, and culture of various areas and peoples around the world provide a focus in this approach. Asian, African, and Latin American cultures and areas are generally given special attention.

A third group argues that while foreign policy issues and language and area studies are important, a world view—that is, seeing oneself and human beings generally as members of a single species on a small planet—is what is most needed today. For the most part, the authors of this volume speak from this position. We hold, with the Andersons, that global education means "education for responsible participation in an interdependent global society."

This is not merely an "academic" argument. How a field or area of study is defined largely determines not only what resources will be viewed as available for use in designing programs but also how they will be used in fashioning the programs. For example, if foreign policy is a major area of study, then students should be familiar with Department of State bulletins and a wide variety of sources of information on the making of foreign policy and on foreign policy issues. If international education includes the transnational interactions of business, professional associations, civic and educational agencies, and individuals, then local newspapers, clubs, business concerns, and individuals with transnational ties are all potential sources of information in developing projects, programs, and activities on world studies.

To further clarify and explain these contrasting views, Table 1 offers a summary. These characterizations are of course overdrawn and simplified. They can be cumulative. That is, studying the world as nations or as cultures or regions does not rule out studying the world as a society and as a single planet. But such distinctions are useful in efforts to clarify what we mean by world-centered education. To summarize, world-centered education seeks to help students understand themselves as individuals, as members of the human species, as inhabitants of planet Earth, and as participants in a world society. Further, it seeks to help students develop the competencies needed to live intelligently and responsibly as individual earthlings and members of a world society.

The world-centered school also represents shifts in other aspects of the educational process such as a shift from information-centered education—wherein discrete bits of inert information are passed on from generation to generation—to problem or value-centered emphases wherein the available store of information is used by young people as they grow in their power to analyze, to develop alternative policies, and to engage in decision making regarding the problems of humanity. The program seeks to help students transcend their local culture and to be sensitive to the moral and ethical conditions associated with such complex issues as hunger, poverty, violence, and resource depletion. Another shift evident in the world-centered school is from spectator-centered to participatory education. World affairs is increasingly seen not only as something that one can observe or worry about but also as an arena in which individuals can participate through personal and group political action.

We consider basic skills of reading, writing, and arithmetic to be essential to citizenship development for participation in a global society. In the world-centered schools described in Chapter 1, these skills are taught and practiced in conjunction with an emphasis on a variety of civic competencies and human relations skills which all citizens need. Among these are:

1. The skills of comparison, analysis, inquiry, and the capacity to make rational judgments. This skill includes learning modes of

TABLE 1. THREE VIEWS OF GLOBAL EDUCATION

WORLD-CENTERED EDUCATION	WORLD AFFAIRS OR FOREIGN POLICY STUDIES	WORLD CULTURES OR AREA STUDIES
1. A variety of units of analysis is used in examining social events and situations, including individuals, nongovernment organizations, multinational corporations, Rotary clubs, professional associations, as well as nations and international organizations (UN, NATO, OPEC, OECD).	1. The nation is a unit of analysis for examining social events on the world scene. It is viewed as the chief or sole actor in all international transactions.	1. Cultural or geographic areas are the main units for examining the world scene. They are viewed as the most significant elements in understanding the nature of the modern world.
2. A great variety of transnational ties, links, and connections between individuals, organizations, and nations—tourism, trade, education, scientific exchange, military aid, economic aid, foreign policy, etc.—are studied.	2. Government-to-government relations—treaties, executive agreements, summit conferences, foreign policy, diplomacy, etc.—are the focus for studying international transactions.	2. The history and development within cultures or areas receive special attention; ties, links, or connections between areas or regions are viewed largely in terms of their impact on the areas or cultures being studied.
3. The planet or global system is seen as the physical and social environment in which individuals and many groups, including nations, interact.	3. The nation is seen as the center of people's concerns, with the environment for action being composed of other individual nations.	3. Cultures or areas are seen as the center of people's concern; the environment for action is other cultures and areas.
4. The involvement by individuals in international transactions by virtue of their roles as consumers, citizens, workers, producers, etc., is considered to be important.	4. Little attention is given to individual involvement in world affairs except in the role of a national citizen: American soldier, voter, or taxpayer.	4. The extent and manner of individual participation in world affairs is determined largely by the cultural group and world region one lives in or identifies with.
5. Humankind or the human species is emphasized as a unit of analysis or focus for study.	5. Nations and areas of the world as well as comparisons among these units receive heavy emphasis.	5. World cultures or world regions are the focus for study.
6 Models or patterns of human interactions dealing with individuals and their well-being in political, social, and economic settings make interdisciplinary and multidisciplinary study more likely.	6 Social science patterns emphasizing individual disciplines make multidisciplinary approaches more difficult.	6. A variety of disciplines is used to provide insights into cultural patterns or regional developments.

TABLE 1. THREE VIEWS OF GLOBAL EDUCATION (*Continued*)

WORLD-CENTERED EDUCATION	WORLD AFFAIRS OR FOREIGN POLICY STUDIES	WORLD CULTURES OR AREA STUDIES
7. The world is seen as the arena or laboratory for studying human experience and for generating subject matter or knowledge.	7. Accidents of history such as the existence of particular nations are used to organize and create knowledge.	7. Geographic areas or cultures are used as a basis for organizing and creating knowledge.
8. Membership in the world and an important identity are seen as stemming from being a member of the human species and an inhabitant of a single planet.	8. Membership in the world and identity are seen largely as the result of being a member of a particular nation.	8. One's membership in the world and one's identity are seen largely as the result of being a member of a particular culture or region.
9. The individual is seen as participating in world society in a multiplicity of ways—as an individual and through the groups one works with or is a member of; the individual is viewed as a member of the species and a citizen of the planet as well as a citizen of a particular nation.	9. The opportunities for participation in the world are seen largely as limited to working through the nation one lives in.	9. Opportunities for participation in the world are seen largely as limited to the role one's cultural group or world region plays in today's world.
10. The interaction between the natural environment—the planet—and the social environment—human relationships—is stressed. The care and feeding of the planet are seen as everyone's concern.	10. The planet is seen as something to be exploited by all. Human-to-human relationships are stressed. The relationships between humans and the physical environment are largely ignored.	10. The planet is viewed as made up of distinct regions and the social environment as made up of distinct cultures. The relationships between humans comprising a particular culture and the region in which they live are stressed.

thinking that are relatively free from egocentric and ethnocentric perceptions.

2. The ability to understand, analyze, and make judgments about the policies and actions of governmental and nongovernmental actors on the world stage. For example, students can study how a multinational corporation affects the job market in a particular industry, or how foreign policy decisions are made, or how churches affect world food or population policies.

3. The capacity to observe intelligently and critically current developments and trends in the world system.

For example, a unit which focuses on the role of the media could incorporate these competencies by stressing the following abilities:

1. The ability to detect typical biases in the various media

2. The ability to piece together fragmentary information from different sources in order to arrive at a plausible explanation of an international issue or event

3. The ability to list the uses, limitations, and liabilities of various sources of information including the media

4. The ability to "read" public statements of governments, official denials, announcements attributed to official sources, and public relations messages

5. The ability to identify the various steps in the process of news gathering and distribution and to cite examples of ways in which certain biases are built into the process

6. The ability to detect cultural contexts which may help explain the justification offered for the actions being observed

The same unit could also pay a great deal of attention to basic reading and writing skills.

DEVELOPING CURRICULA

Despite the recognition that schools are a reflection of the larger society of which they are a part, there has always been the simultaneous belief in the United States that education is the most powerful tool available for shaping young minds. Hence, the strong emphasis given to the development of curricular materials—textbooks, filmstrips, maps, workbooks, exercises—as a means of bringing about changes in the attitudes or skills of children and youth.

Most of the time and in most places, curricular materials tend to be traditional in format, concentrating on textbooks and stressing the learning of facts or basic skills. Supplementary materials or additional activities are usually associated with special projects or experimental efforts and are used by a small percentage of the teachers, often on their own initiative. University professors are heavily involved in the production of formal curricula, generally by working with the large publishing companies.

The actual content of materials, however, is not determined solely by these producers but rather by a variety of influences, agencies, and processes including pressure groups, textbook screening committees, and a variety of local and state agencies responsible for public education. Ward Morehouse has complained that the decentralized nature of education makes it difficult for internationally focused programs to be implemented and promoted.[4] The fact that the selection of curricular materials is a state and local responsibility also results in greater variety in content and focus and creates numerous opportunities for experimental efforts, though they may well be limited, fragmentary, and piecemeal.

Whatever the strengths and weaknesses of the curriculum change process, world affairs and international concerns have appeared in curricula throughout the United States to a greater or lesser extent at least since the early 1900s.[5] There was much activity in this country in this field during the 1930s. *International Understanding through the Public School Curriculum*[6] was one of the important documents which served to focus attention on the issues involved in education for peace and world understanding at that time.

The establishment of UNESCO in 1945 is generally regarded as the most important event in the field of international education during the post-World War II era. The UNESCO Associated Schools program—a network of secondary schools established in 1953 and now including more than 1,000 schools in over sixty countries (in 1977 some forty United States schools located in eight different states were involved in this effort)—has sponsored numerous conferences for teachers. The East-West Major Project, concerned with the improvement of textbooks, and the UNESCO geography series are among UNESCO's other major contributions to the improvement of international and intercultural education at the precollegiate level.

The 1960s saw the passage by the U.S. Congress of Title VI of the National Defense Education Act (NDEA), which provided federal funds to stimulate language and area studies at the postsecondary level. The U.S. Office of Education funded a major study in goals, needs, and priorities in international education at the elementary and secondary level in 1966.[7] Known as the Anderson/Becker report, it called for a new definition of international education emphasizing the need to prepare children and youth to live in a global society.

The UNESCO Recommendation concerning Education for International Understanding, Cooperation and Peace and Education relating to Human Rights and Fundamental Freedoms adopted by the General Conference in November 1974 builds upon the progress made during the last twenty-five years in UNESCO member states. It also is in keeping with perspectives on international and global education espoused by social scientists and educators in the United

States. The Recommendation offers an excellent set of guiding principles for educational policy in the field of international education. They include:

1. An international dimension and a global perspective in education at all levels in all its forms

2. Understanding and respect for all peoples, their cultures, civilizations, values, and ways of life, including domestic ethnic cultures and cultures of other nations

3. Awareness of the increasing global interdependence between peoples and nations

4. Ability to communicate with others

5. Awareness not only of the rights but also of the duties incumbent upon individuals, social groups, and nations toward each other

6. Understanding of the necessity for international solidarity and cooperation

7. Readiness on the part of the individual to participate in solving the problems of his or her community, country, and the world at large

Like the Andersons' world-centered approach, these guiding principles with their focus on problem-centered education, active participation by individuals, and the importance of international cooperation might well serve to provide some common focus to the great variety of approaches found in United States schools. In 1976, an Amendment to Title VI of NDEA was passed authorizing support for the development of international programs at the precollegiate level. These recent developments suggest that prospects for improvement in this area are probably somewhat better than heretofore.

In spite of such developments, much of elementary and secondary school offerings in this field still tend to convey the impression that the West is and always has been superior to all other civilizations. However, the past two decades have seen many attempts to correct this parochial and dangerous outlook. There is a growing feeling that students need to know and understand more about other peoples and cultures and about challenges humankind faces in an increasingly interdependent world. Furthermore, intergroup tensions in the United States have sparked numerous efforts and programs designed to help students develop the capacity for understanding and working with people whose lives and background may be very different from their own. The need for schools to reflect and perpetuate cultural diversity as well as teach a commitment to and respect for values such as justice, equality, and human dignity is more widely recognized today.[8]

Current events, world history, the study of other languages, international relations courses, world problems units, and the study of other nations have long been used to insert international and intercultural content into the curriculum. During the 1960s, area studies became a popular method of expanding international and intercultural awareness. Within these various approaches there has been a growing recognition that technology has extended the boundaries of occupations, cultural activities, and other human endeavors. This acceleration of human mobility and communication greatly increases cross-cultural and cross-national contact, thereby speeding up and making more complex the process of cultural change. Today all of us are affected by and, in turn, have some opportunities to influence global affairs. Increasing interaction on a worldwide scale has sparked a number of new approaches emphasizing increasing interdependence, the universality of human needs, the growing similarity of human experience, and the necessity of facing up to threats to human survival on a global scale.

While schools use a great variety of labels to identify courses and units in international and intercultural studies—bilingual education, ethnic origins, multicultural studies, world affairs, area studies, and many others—the context for many of these programs increasingly recognizes that we are all members of a single species living on a single planet and sharing a common fate. There is growing recognition that patterns of transnational contacts are becoming more influential in setting the direction of human affairs.

However, the diversity of humankind is not being ignored. Efforts are being made to recognize that the world is composed of many nations, cultures, and peoples unequally endowed with the good things of the earth and holding different ideas about society and that the general necessities for survival often conflict with the achievement or preservation of justice and dignity of actual people and society. Such efforts are based on the belief that identities, loyalties, rights, and responsibilities are multiple and associated with humankind as well as with smaller and more intimate groups.

While it probably is true that most schools give some attention to world problems and issues and that there is an array of materials conveying some information or insight into some aspects of world or intercultural understanding, programs reflecting a comprehensive world or mankind view are rare. Despite this fact, numerous successful efforts at the local and regional level can be found.

The California Task Force for Global Perspectives in Education, for example, is a loose-knit association of fifteen school districts and the San Francisco State University. The development of more sensitive curricular materials is one long-range goal of the group, as is the active participation of community groups presently uninvolved in school activities. Member districts design their own world-centered programs and components, with the task force providing assistance in the form of periodic review conferences and the consulting services of such groups as the Bay Area China Education Project, the Center for Global Perspectives, and the San Francisco United Nations Association.

The Los Angeles Unified School District, a member of the task force, has used part of its ESEA Title I funds to implement an Intergroup Cultural Program of the Performing Arts. Aimed primarily at inner-city schools, the program offers a variety of live dance and music presentations from which teachers can select according to the interests of the students or the needs of a particular academic unit in progress. Each of the more than two dozen offerings—traditional American folk singers, Latin American dance troupes, classical guitars, jazz, modern dance, Asian-American drama—is accompanied by a teacher's guide that outlines the historical and social backgrounds of the presentations. In addition, students are given a number of learning activities to broaden their understanding of artistic expression as common to all cultures.

The Los Angeles arts program is representative of one trend in the field of world-centered education. The emphasis is first placed on the ethnic and cultural diversity within the school district or community. Thus children become acquainted with and may come to accept the value of different groups within the same society. When such experience is designed to create greater self-awareness as well as familiarity with variety in human culture, it can contribute to better intercultural understanding. The group this program serves, like the school-age population of any multicultural urban center has special needs:

> Children in Watts or the East Los Angeles barrio desperately need inspiration for their success as individuals in not one society, but in several different societies living side-by-side. Because they exist in such a diffusion of cultures . . . our

program . . . will help these children develop an understanding for other minorities and for peoples of the world in general.[9]

The massive amounts of data available, new research findings, and the constantly shifting areas of public concern make it unlikely that there can ever be one "best" program in world studies. Learning to sift and sort through this mass of data in order to separate the significant from the trivial and developing a sensitivity to important world trends are crucial. A continuing review of goals and objectives and an awareness of available resources are necessary parts of the process. Intelligent participation in an increasingly complex society requires that students have a great diversity of experience in order that they may develop the competencies and knowledge needed. A world-centered school is an important part of a community effort to provide ample opportunities for students to acquire such experience.

THE ENVIRONMENT FOR LEARNING

Three other factors should be discussed briefly as we consider the implications of establishing world-centered programs. In the Middleston schools described in Chapter 1 and in many of the programs described in other chapters in this book, the setting and climate for learning and the attitude and roles of teachers are somewhat different from traditional programs. On the other hand, most of these programs can be financed within the same budgets as existing programs.

A wide range of activities and settings for learning—classroom, factory, business, office, community agency, playground, and, on occasion, street corners—is important. Schools which open their doors and expand their outlook can engage a wide range of talents and resources in the service of educational goals. They also improve their ability to provide youth with a diversity of settings, experiences, and opportunities to develop the competencies needed to learn to participate intelligently and responsibly in the twenty-first century.

The extent to which the traditional notions of the learning environment, the distribution of authority and responsibility, the division of labor, and the roles of teacher, student, and administrator have been expanded and made more flexible in the Middleston schools is evident in the involvement of students in the maintenance and governance of the school and in cross-age teaching both within and outside the school; in the learner exchange program involving both students and adults other than teachers; and in the fact that students serve as volunteers in the community. The students' role in helping arrange and maintain the physical environment and assisting in the management of the school, as well as their work in various community projects, not only helps students to understand how the world works but also provides them with opportunities to develop and practice the human relations skills of bargaining, negotiating, cooperating, influencing, and compromising. Even more important is the fact that such participation provides them with some sense of efficacy. Thus, student involvement helps them develop the competencies needed to participate more responsibly and effectively in the life of the school and community—which is seen as part of a global society. At the same time, they gain a better understanding of and some degree of control over the social processes which affect their lives.

"Teachers" in Middleston include a number of part-time or occasional teachers who make their living in other occupations. Students are also involved in teaching. The full-time staff members of these schools are seen largely as resource managers, coordinators of experiences, and resources for students and learners. Teachers in Middleston and in programs described in later chapters appear to have more tolerance for ambiguity and unfinished tasks and a greater willingness to take risks than the staff of more traditional schools. Flexibility, patience, ability to improvise, and tolerance of noise level are also traits likely to be found in these teachers. Furthermore, recognizing that students learn outside of school as well as within the school, they make an effort to work with families, local groups, and community agencies. These new roles and desirable characteristics raise questions and challenges for pre-service training and teacher selection.

It is a fact of life today that the tax-paying citizens who support the schools are cost-conscious. Faced with tight budgets and increasing demands for other tax-supported services, the schools, like other public-supported institutions, are increasingly expected to justify any increases in expenditures.

A world-centered school can manage to provide an unusually broad and varied program at about the same cost as other schools with different orientations. The Middleston example demonstrates that if a community is willing to engage in a careful reallocation of existing resources along with a reappraisal of priorities, major shifts in structure, organization, content, and methodology can take place in schools without undue financial dislocations. The use of volunteers and community settings, the practice of cost-sharing with a number of community agencies, and contributions of time and materials by numerous individuals and institutions can all play a part in keeping costs down without curtailing the program. Multinational corporations with local offices can be a resource to a school, contributing personnel, in-service opportunities, and even funding for special projects. But by and large a world-centered school's budget can come from the same sources and exist within the same parameters as that of any other school.

A brief note about terminology is in order before this chapter is brought to a close. For the most part, throughout this chapter and the rest of the book, we have adopted the Andersons' term *world-centered education* to describe our goal of establishing programs to educate students for responsible participation in an interdependent global society. Many other terms, some with very different connotations for some people, are also used, such as *global education, global perspectives, international education, global studies,* and on and on. We have made no attempt to restrict the authors of this book to using only one term, but unless otherwise indicated (for example in Table 1), all these terms are meant to imply the definition given here.

SUMMARY AND CONCLUSIONS

Devising an educational system capable of responding to society's needs in the late twentieth century is one of humankind's most challenging problems. Education has become a major means of informing people of the need for change and for stimulating acceptance of new attitudes. The need to understand the consequences of growing pressures of human activity on the ecosystem, the input of technological forces weaving all humankind into a single planetary society, and the consequences of the accelerating pace of change put heavy burdens on the educational system. To date, the dramatic changes in society since 1900 have not resulted in significant changes in our schools or in our colleges and universities. Many American children today receive much the same education their grandparents received. In the view of some critics, efforts to use the schools to bring about needed changes in society relating to world affairs have not always met with success. "After 40 years of exposure to world cultures, world politics, world geography, we have turned restless and, on the world scene, more chauvinistic and militaristic than at any previous time in our history," wrote Commager in 1975.[10]

Even those who point to our success in changing some aspects of public education are left with a question: Does the preparation we provide our students assure the socially responsible action required in larger measure than we seem to have displayed in recent years? How do we prepare Americans for responsible involvement in planetary discussions and decisions?

A realistic look at the challenges and obstacles involved in devising educational programs for today's youth is needed. The remainder of this volume seeks to provide such an analysis. It includes a number of examples of activities, projects, and school programs which provide hope for the future of world-centered education.

NOTES

1. Edwin Reischauer, *Toward the 21st Century: Education for a Changing World,* Knopf, New York, 1973, p. 4.

2. For a discussion of alternatives within public schools see Mario D. Fantini, *Public Schools of Choice,* Simon & Schuster, New York, 1974.

3. Roy A. Price, "Goals for the Social Studies," in *Social Studies Curriculum Development: Prospects and Problems,* 39th yearbook of the National Council for the Social Studies, Washington, D.C., 1969.

4. *American Education and Global Interdependence: Scaling the Shoulders of Atlas,* No. 3, Interdependence Series, Aspen Institute, Fall 1975.

5. D. C. Scanlon, *International Education: A Documentary History,* Columbia, New York, 1960.

6. I. L. Kandel (chmn.), *International Understanding through the Public-School Curriculum,* 36th Yearbook of the National Society for the Study of Education, Part II, University of Chicago Press, Chicago, 1937.

7. J. M. Becker, "An Examination of Objectives, Needs, and Priorities in International Education in the United States' Elementary and Secondary Schools," report to the U.S. Office of Education on Project 6-2908, ERIC Document Reproduction Service, Bethesda, Maryland, 1969.

8. For a statement regarding cultural pluralism and the schools, see James A. Banks, "Cultural Pluralism and the Schools," *Educational Leadership,* December 1974, pp. 163–166.

9. *The Performing Arts: Teacher's Guide,* Los Angeles School District, 1974.

10. Henry Commager, "The Schools as Surrogate Conscience," *Saturday Review,* Jan. 11, 1975, p. 56.

CHAPTER THREE

Psychological and Institutional Obstacles to the Global Perspective in Education

Judith V. Torney

University of Illinois at Chicago Circle

I f it were natural for children to adopt and retain a global perspective, it would be superfluous to consider obstacles; likewise, if the full interdependence of nations in the international system could be explained as concretely to students as the effect of the cost of raw materials upon prices in the United States, we might speak with less urgency about those things which stand in the way of a world-centered orientation. It is possible to distinguish two types of barriers. One set may be thought of as having its source *within the individual student* and the other as originating *outside the individual student* in the society or socializing agents. Because of the particular concern in this volume for the effect of schools, that institution will be of primary concern—though the family, certain aspects of governmental policy, and the media will also be considered.

OBSTACLES WITHIN INDIVIDUALS

Many obstacles within the individual are related to developmental processes, and a knowledge of these processes will allow more effective design of programs for young people of various ages. Concrete facts that adults believe to be beyond dispute may be perceived in quite unpredictable ways by children. Cognitive structures change with age, but the adoption of a global perspective is not an inevitable result of development. Attitudinal assumptions or motivational predispositions also may markedly affect certain students' preexisting level of awareness or knowledge and the relative effectiveness of specific programs in reshaping or influencing their attitudes. Programs may have to be tailored to the needs of particular groups or individuals.

This chapter will consider four types of within-individual obstacles to the attainment of a global perspective: cognitive, attitudinal, personal, and communication barriers. In some sense all these kinds of handicaps to global education have a developmental aspect and an individual difference aspect since in each there is some change with age (not necessarily in the direction of surmounting the obstacles) and the obstacles existing within any given individual will be somewhat different from those in other individuals.

It is probably not possible to construct a school program that is adequate to deal with all the obstacles existing in every student. Some ways in which the world-centered schools described in Chapter 1 attempt to overcome some of these barriers are indicated here, however.

COGNITIVE OBSTACLES

About fifteen years ago, political scientists began to study political socialization and to measure civic attitudes as well as knowledge. They sought to understand how established political systems ensured the development of supportive attitudes in future generations. It became clear from a variety of research conducted during the 1960s that the process of political learning begins early in life as children participate in authority relationships, make decisions, and deal with interpersonal as well as intergroup conflict or cooperation. Public political issues or elections are only part of this process.

The knowledge and attitudes about social systems that children acquire during elementary school influence what they will learn and believe during later school years. Remy, Nathan, Becker, and Torney concluded a discussion of the way in which international learning takes place in elementary students as follows:

> By the time elementary school students reach the intermediate grades they have developed a sense of national identity, a set of attitudes, beliefs and values about their own and other nations as international actors and about such international processes as war and peace. Children's international learning is cumulative. What children learn about the world at one age builds upon and is influenced by what they have previously learned.[1]

A few political socialization studies have paid explicit attention to the influence of cognitive level. Hess and Torney surveyed 12,000 American elementary school students and found that those of high intelligence were accelerated in their political attitude development.[2] Connell, in an interview study of Australian children, described the influence of cognitive factors even more precisely:

> Children do not simply reproduce the communications that reach them from the adult world. They work them over, detach them from their original contexts, and assimilate them to a general conception of what the government is about. . . . The development through these stages, the construction of more and more elaborate interpretations of politics, and the gradual approach to political action, is basically due to the activity of the children themselves. The children selectively appropriate the material provided by schools, by mass media, by parents, and build of them individual structures.[3]

Connell and others who hold a developmental view of political socialization processes identify stages of thought that children go through. Age boundaries should not be attached too firmly to these stages, however, in order to avoid the incorrect assumption that children grow naturally into mature political attitudes. If attitudes developed like the ability to walk or sit, primarily as a result of neural maturation, one might conclude that environmental or educational support was unnecessary. However, according to Piaget, all development is a process of interaction between maturational level and the environment which presents new information. The child may either assimilate new data into current schema and concepts or he may change or accommodate the schema. Ten-year-olds not only have more mature neural structures, they also have had more experience than six-year-olds; this experience is reflected in the complexity and type of mental schema which they commonly employ. A true developmental theory with regard to social and political attitudes recognizes the constantly shifting equilibrium between assimilation and accommodation and between inner and outer events.

The observable results of these developmental changes may be categorized along several dimensions. Generally the movement with increasing age is from a lesser to a greater degree of organization. For example, Connell describes the young child's political orientations:

> Nationality apart, political consciousness at these ages [five and six] is a collection of scraps of information, unrelated to each other and with no special status to distinguish them from other bits and pieces of the world; there is no conception of politics as a distinct sphere of activity. We may note the arguments (at this intuitive stage) that leap so suddenly from topic to topic . . . the seizing on odd and irrelevant details, and the apparently random juxtapositions of details, the repeated bending of reality to the demands of a momentary stream of thought. These children lack a conception of political structure not because they lack sources of information about it, but because they lack the cognitive equipment to represent it. About the age of 7, as many psychologists have observed, there is an important and relatively sudden change in the character of children's thinking. This change is great enough to mark off the period which goes before it as a distinct stage, a kind of prologue to politics.[4]

The chaos and disorganization characteristic of young children's political understanding has also been noted by others describing the ages from five through adolescence:

Older age students find politics more salient as well as more comprehensible. They have developed the cognitive skills and motivation to pay attention to, to understand and retain political knowledge. . . . Moreover, their perceptions show a movement from personalism, parochialism, and concreteness toward greater impersonalism, universalism, and abstractness.[5]

Adelson and O'Neill point to similar patterns of movement during adolescence—from personalism to impersonalism; from a present, concrete, specific orientation to a more future, abstract, and general orientation; from a concern with one's own individual needs to a greater responsiveness to community needs; and from an authoritarian response pattern to a less authoritarian orientation.[6] The young child tends to be either labile or rigid in his attitudes while the slightly older child is flexible.

Studies based on Piaget's work have found that younger children are characterized by *perceptual centration*. They are overwhelmed by one aspect of a visual situation (usually the most perceptually obvious one) and are unable to focus on other aspects, especially contradictory points of view. This centration phenomenon may help explain the narrowness of children's political conceptions. It may be especially important to give children practice in directing their attention to many aspects of a situation. It may also be possible to identify the particular aspect of a situation to which a child is paying attention and thereby to understand what holds prominence for that child.

Piaget studied *perceptual role taking,* the child's ability to view a concrete perceptual situation from a perspective other than his own. Flavell moved the concept of role taking into the realm of social relationships and related it to the child's ability to communicate with others (by comprehending the perspective of the listener, for example).[7] Feffer found in a social perception task that there was an increase in what he called "balanced decentering" between eight-to-nine- and ten-to-eleven-year-old children, followed by some decline in this ability in the years after eleven.[8]

The increase in social-role-taking ability and the overcoming of cognitive egocentrism are among the most important psychological landmarks during middle childhood. Experience with the physical and personal environment rather than direct tutelage is thought to be the most important influence upon the ability to see other people's perspective. Certain characteristics of personal or social experience seem to make an especially important contribution to a decline in cognitive egocentrism. Chandler[9] studied a group of forty-five chronically delinquent boys (aged eleven to thirteen), first demonstrating that they were deficient in social-cognitive role-taking skills when compared with a similar group of nondelinquents. The delinquents were particularly likely to assume that others were in possession of information to which only they had access. The author took an experimental group of delinquents and arranged for them to spend half an hour a week for ten weeks participating in training in role-taking skills. They made videotapes of skits involving characters of their own age and observed their own performances in different roles in these skits. One control group of delinquents in this study made animated cartoons or films about their neighborhood in which they neither performed different roles nor watched their performances. A second control group was simply tested preceding the ten-week period and following it. The delinquents who participated in the videotaped social-role-taking skits improved in their role-taking ability more than those in either control group. Practice in performing different roles and viewing one's performance apparently is helpful in beginning to understand others. In the world-centered schools described in Chapter 1, role-taking competency is fostered by providing the opportunity for students to take a variety of roles (teacher, student, secretary, or custodian) and view the school environment from a variety of perspectives.

There is also some evidence about important changes in social perception and cognition which take place during middle childhood. Gollin found a rapid increase between an eight-to-nine-year-old group and a ten- and eleven-year-old group in the ability to reflect conflicting themes in the perception of persons.[10] A number of studies have also indicated changes during middle childhood in the way audiovisual media, an important source of social attitudes, are viewed. Flapan investigated the interpretations girls placed upon a simple story presented in a movie.[11] By the age of nine, these children were able to report communication fairly accurately and to project feelings and thoughts onto adults whose actions they had observed. A similar study was conducted in the Federal Republic of Germany, France, Great Britain, Czechoslovakia, and the United States.[12] The researchers contrasted the behavior of eight-to-nine-year-old children with that of ten-to-twelve-year-olds after each group was shown two films. The younger children appeared to concentrate on the story line at the cost of retaining details. The older group not only remembered the details but used them as clues to the meaning of the story.

Neither cognitive nor affective factors operate in isolation, and so it is important to consider their interplay. There is evidence that beginning at about the age of seven the child enters into a period of rapid cognitive development, especially related to the area of perspective and role taking, which continues into adolescence. Affectively speaking, middle childhood is a period of relatively fluid attitudes, particularly with regard to feelings about other people, groups, and countries. At about the age of fourteen there appears to be a loss of attitudinal plasticity; opinions seem to become a way of expressing peer group solidarity and excluding those who are different.

Lambert and Klineberg in the late 1950s conducted an interview study of 3,000 children at three age levels (six, ten, and fourteen) from eleven parts of the world.[13] Among their most important conclusions about American children was that those of about ten years of age were particularly receptive to approaches to and information about foreign people; they were interested in individuals seen as dissimilar to themselves as well as in those seen as similar. By the age of fourteen, American young people appeared less open to positive views about foreign nations.

The role of stereotyping was discussed at some length by these authors:

> The first signs of stereotyped thinking turned up in the descriptions children gave of their own group rather than of foreign people; even at the six year age level many different national groups of children made over-generalized statements about the personality traits of their own group at the same time as they described foreign people in more factual objective terms. . . . From ten years of age . . . children start stereotyping foreign people.[14]

Jahoda also found that attitudes about other countries shifted in Scottish children beginning at about ten or twelve years of age.[15] A study of 3,000 American seventh and twelfth graders using a map-related technique found that stereotypic concepts associated with Africa (natives, tribes, cannibals) and with Russia (enemy, dictatorship) increased from the seventh to the twelfth grade.[16]

Stereotypes may be seen as a kind of concept which children use to organize masses of information. Although educators may believe that stereotypes are major barriers to a world perspective, as long as educational efforts are based on teaching children quantities of information about the unique characteristics of a collection of nation-states rather than teaching them to look at dynamic interrelationships in the world community, stereotypes may be the best device available to young people to organize this information. Substituting human culture as an organizing framework is one viable alternative (see Chapter 2).

Allport developed a three-stage theory of prejudice[17] which is a good example of the relationship between cognitive and affective processes in childhood. During the first stage, pregeneralization, children seem aware of group differences but do not categorize or have strong negative feelings toward different groups. The second stage is total rejection and is thought to reach its peak in early puberty (the same period identified in empirical studies such as those listed above). In the third stage, in adolescence, greater differentiation and less generalized prejudice are expected to be characteristic of young people's approach to ethnic and national groups. Allport's theory leads to the prediction of the maximum intensity of negative attitudes in early adolescence with more positive attitudes in middle childhood and later adolescence.

Four European psychologists tested the theory on a group of Dutch students; they showed a clear preference for the Netherlands when asked to compare pairs of countries and show which they liked best.[18] The intensity of this preference increased between grades two and six, and the total amount of differentiation between preferences for these countries also increased. With regard to the cognitive judgment of similarity between one's own country and other countries, there was a change from second grade (where one's own country was seen as different from others but other countries were seen as relatively similar) to the structure at grade five (where differences among all countries were commonly perceived). Some of the measures used in this study showed the kind of relationship with age which Allport's theory had predicted. For example, the correlation between preference for the five other countries and the cognitive distance of these countries from the Netherlands reached a peak at grade four and declined thereafter. The authors' final conclusion was as follows:

> The child's own country is preferred to other countries, and the more a country is perceived as similar to one's own country, the more it is liked. . . . People who are perceived as one's countrymen are liked more than people who are perceived as foreigners. There is a significant relationship between the attitude

toward other countries and the attitude toward foreigners. Some of the results are in apparent contradiction to our expectations. The discrepancy could be explained by making the assumption . . . that equivalent stages in the developmental process are reached at ages which differ according to the complexity of the task. Thus, the peak of ethnocentricity displayed by the younger children in the photography study would be equivalent to that found in children of intermediate age for the more complex cognitive tasks.[19]

The period of middle childhood (before the onset of puberty) has thus been identified by many studies as a time of relatively low rejection of groups and relatively high attitudinal flexibility. We might even go so far as to call this a critical period in attitudinal development.

The term *critical period* was originally used by psychologists and ethologists to describe an age-bounded period during which the social behavior and learning of young animals demonstrates a high degree of plasticity. Once the end of this period is reached, behavior organized in a given pattern is extraordinarily difficult to reorganize.[20] It may be appropriate to consider middle childhood as an optimal or perhaps even critical period for development of world-centered attitudes and a global perspective, given the evidence of cognitive and attitudinal changes during this period, peaks of certain functions which later decline, and especially the existence of attitudinal flexibility followed by later rigidity. Even if one does not accept the "critical" nature of this period, however, middle childhood is a time of important developmental changes in many attitudes and a period during which certain barriers to a global perspective have not yet been erected. The stress of the world-centered elementary school upon human differences and variations is an attempt to reach children during this critical period.

Children cope with new information and attitudes according to the cognitive processes available to them. They have particular cognitive (and also affective) prisms through which they view the world. In some cases the limitations of the framework or prism may constitute a complete obstacle to the achievement of educational aims. In other cases the process of education can aid in the development of more advanced structures and cause the prism itself to change at the same time global awareness is fostered. Alternatively, a new educational technique may circumvent the barrier by presenting material in a more concrete form or tailoring the presentation to the child's level of understanding.

ATTITUDINAL OBSTACLES

Some attitudinal characteristics of individuals are not modified extensively by development but are stable from the child's early years. These qualities may nevertheless be impediments to students' international socialization. In many cases there are considerable individual differences in these attitudes.

The first set of potential attitudinal obstacles is a very strong sense of national community as an in-group. Connell points out that young children's ideas about potential external enemies that pose a threat to their country are related to primitive and diffuse fears that the nice and safe places of their own lives will be disturbed.[21] This often causes an intensification of support for one's own national system and the status quo. He found that as a result of these basic fears, the threat schema and nationalism are very strong and resistant to change from early childhood on in Australia. It is probable that these same processes are operating in the United States.

Positive attachment to a national community is established early, largely with the aid of national symbols. Since the child's initial identification with his country is associated with little information about it, these symbols provide important concrete links. The link between prominent symbols and abstract terms like liberty and freedom is illustrated by this interview with a second grader:

I: What does the Statue of Liberty do?

R: Well, it keeps liberty.

I: How does it do that?

R: Well, it doesn't do it, but there are some other guys that do it.

I: Some other guys do it for the Statue of Liberty?

R: The statue is not alive.

I: Well, what does it do?

R: It has this torch in its hand, and sometimes they light up the torch. If the statue were gone, there wouldn't be any liberty.[22]

When children were asked (in the same study) to select from a set of pictures "the two best pictures to show what *our country* is," the Statue of Liberty and the American flag were the most popular choices at grades three through eight. When children were given the same set of pictures but asked to choose the two that best depicted *our government,* the statue and flag were seldom chosen; pictures of the President, Congress, and voting were much more popular.

Elementary schoolchildren's sense of belonging to a national political community is established and reinforced by many symbols.

The global political community lacks such readily available symbols; the UN flag, for example, is known to only a small proportion of young children. The ecology flag and the photograph showing the world as it appeared to the astronauts from outer space are becoming more commonly displayed symbols. Recall also the several flags displayed in Middleston's world-centered schools. However, for most children membership in a world community is not fostered with the same intensity or consensus by socialization agents as is membership in the national community.

Another reason that socialization to the national political community is so effective is that the child tends to perceive the world in terms of undifferentiated evaluations—America is good while communist countries are bad. Linkage between good-bad judgments and other attitudes is characteristic of younger children. The child's fantasy appears to be that everything must remain just as it is or the whole system is in danger of falling apart. Young children tend to believe that all laws were made long ago and that they should not be changed. Some children believe that any conflict of opinion poses a basic threat to society and that any criticism of government is a threat to overthrow it. For a child who makes such assumptions, any political dissent is a failure of the system to hold total consensus and is therefore bad. Adelson and O'Neill concluded from a study of ten-year-olds that they have a "pervasive incapacity to speak from a coherent view of the political order," finding it difficult to grasp exceptions to rules, for example.[23] Lack of the ability to grasp alternatives to the current organization of nation-states may also result from the belief that the system as a whole will fail if changed in any part. The school undoubtedly bears some of the responsibility for failures of socialization in this area. Elementary schoolchildren require a great deal of help in understanding what a pluralistic system is, in learning to value diversity of points of view, and in comprehending how the global system operates, persists, and changes over time.

The continuation into later childhood of belief in a domestic or global system which cannot tolerate change or criticism without collapse may be traced to adults who believe that any criticism of the status quo allowed in a school text or by a teacher is likely to warp children's values (especially nationalism). However, the research indicates that the strength of nationalistic feeling is already so strong by the age of seven or eight that discussions of controversial national policy will not disturb it. And for brighter children, denial of the existence of conflict and criticism may actually convey the latent message that something must be wrong with the system since everyone is so eager to expose only safe facts. One responsibility of the elementary school should be to teach children not only the maintenance functions of a system but also how the global system changes through accommodation and diverse pressures. An overlearned fear of the threat to the political system implied by change, coupled with misunderstanding of accommodation processes, is an obstacle to a global orientation in children.

PERSONAL AND MOTIVATIONAL OBSTACLES

The attitudinal barriers previously discussed have their origin in orientations to social objects outside the individual. The individual's self-orientation and motivation may also constitute a kind of obstacle. A frequently voiced but as yet untested assumption is that a high level of personal self-esteem is a necessary prerequisite to fruitful experiences in an intercultural context. Programs to raise ethnic consciousness and pride make the assumption that a high level of self-esteem within individuals will lead them to a willingness to accept others. Some research on personality inventories answered by adults is quoted in support of this relationship,[24] but this assumption has not as yet been subjected to rigorous empirical testing.

One difficulty is that programs intended to foster cultural pride may sometimes generate a defensively high level of self-esteem which denigrates other individuals or groups. Perhaps the ideal would be a moderate level of self-esteem—not so high that individuals become convinced of the unique value of their own experience and the inferiority of others, nor so low that the individual sees little of value in himself or his cultural heritage. The same may hold true at the level of allegiance to country. An individual who has a chauvinistically high level of national self-esteem may use it to downgrade other nations and cultures, while an individual with a moderate level of such feelings may be more open to international contacts. Self-esteem and national esteem as either potential prerequisites or obstacles to successful global education programs need considerable further study.

Another aspect of individual differences in motivation is the need for novelty and diversity in contrast to a preference for sameness. Some individuals are obviously happiest when they are confronting new experiences; others prefer an environment of sameness and predictability. Some attempts have been made (primarily with adults) to measure this need for stimulus variation and the challenge of environmental novelty. Social psychologists have studied the relationship of preference for similarity to personal attraction. Byrne and his associates have demonstrated that when individuals are asked to rate the attractiveness of a stranger described in terms of attitudes and opinions, the raters are more attracted to someone described as holding attitudes similar to theirs than to a stranger described as different from them.[25] Although this preference for similarity over diversity has been demonstrated for a variety of groups (children as well as adults), no one has considered what kinds of experience might modify this similarity-preference obstacle to intercultural experience.

A third personal characteristic which may serve as either a barrier to or a facilitator of education is the basic activity or passivity of an individual. A number of political attitude studies have shown that children who were active in nonpolitical school organizations were also more likely to be active in political matters.[26] Tempo has also been shown to be an important individual difference in cognitive style. The individual who is active rather than passive in his or her approach may be easier to involve in global education activities. As Chapter 2 indicates, active participation is an important component of citizenship in the context of the world-centered school.

These three aspects of personal individual differences—self-esteem (and group or national esteem), preference for similarity or difference, and an active or passive approach to life—are basic characteristics which must be taken into account in the design of global education programs. Children who have low self-esteem, a preference for sameness, and a passive approach (to take the most extreme example) may need to feel more personally secure or to learn more active coping styles before they can be educated to a world-centered view. On the other hand, it may be that successful global education programs can incorporate techniques designed to modify these basic predispositions at the same time a world-centered view is fostered.

COMMUNICATION OBSTACLES

A fourth kind of intraindividual impediment is what we might call a perceptual or communication obstacle. The most obvious example is spoken language. A striking discovery in a previous interview study was that children, when asked how other countries differed from their own country, placed great stress upon language. This factor was mentioned spontaneously by more than 70 percent of the children interviewed at all ages from six through twelve. For example, these responses were given by an eight-year-old boy:

I: How are people in other countries different from you?

R: Most talk Mexican.

I: Anything else?

R: Most talk different from us.

I: Do you think it would be better if everyone in the world were American?

R: Yes, because I want them to talk normal, the way we do.

This example of ethnocentrism shows a child who feels that his group's way of speaking is the only normal one. He is unable to take the perspective of those who belong to different linguistic communities. Children perceive various reasons for diversity in language. Some attribute such differences to authority, divine or mortal: "Well, it's probably because of their first ruler, how he spoke," or "I suppose God made it that way to be more of a challenge to people on earth."

The development of language ability in children has been extensively linked to the development of cognitive processes. Speaking and hearing language also appear to have an influence on socialization. Perhaps children need to have exposure to a language other than their mother tongue in order to be globally or interculturally competent. Riestra and Johnson report that the study of another language appears to increase positive attitudes toward speakers of that language and the culture it serves.[27] The early years of education may be a particularly important time to begin integrated cultural and language study.

Although the influence of language on children's attitudes has not been fully explored, some psychologists have studied the reactions of children to speakers of different languages. The phenomenon is of particular interest in countries where bilingualism or polylingualism is a national problem, such as Canada, Israel, and the Philippines. The technique, called *matched guise,* uses tape recordings of bilingual speakers, speaking first in one language, then another; they are rated by subjects who have been instructed to look for personality traits reflected in the voices. This assessment seems to elicit facets of attitudes and stereotypes which differ from those brought out by standard attitude rating forms. Some authors suggest that language ratings index a more private reaction than direct questioning about national characteristics. For example, speakers with Scottish accents were rated in one study as more generous than those with English accents, in spite of the common stereotype derived from other attitudinal measures that the Scots are tighter with money.[28]

Lambert's findings about language are important to the study of attitude development and education in middle childhood. He found that preference for English over French is characteristic of English-Canadians of all ages but only of older French-Canadians. Among French-speaking subjects there are important shifts occurring at about age twelve toward "feelings of ethno-linguistic inferiority."[29] Language is clearly more than a communication mode; it is also in some sense a socialization mode. Belief that one's own language is the only truly human way of communicating can be a barrier to understanding between cultures.

Nonverbal styles of communication as well as verbal communication may also constitute an impediment to global education. Erickson, in a study of filmed interactions between junior college counselors and students from black, Chicano, Polish-American, and Italian-American groups, discovered that when counselors were dealing with students from ethnic backgrounds different from their own, implicit messages were often misunderstood; the interaction made each party uncomfortable because of the lack of rhythmic behavioral symmetry.[30] Rist also showed that patterns of nonverbal communication in a kindergarten classroom were important in the relationship between students and teachers of different ethnic backgrounds.[31] In the world-centered schools, the attempt is made to make students more sensitive to nonverbal as well as verbal communication. For example, facial expressions and body stances were examined in one activity described by the Andersons.

In summary, even if we are quite clear about the type of global awareness or understanding to be created, we may nevertheless be unable to foster it effectively because of the existence of cognitive, attitudinal, personal, or communication obstacles existing within the individual. Some of these impediments may be lowered either permanently or for the duration of the programs we wish to implement. According to developmental logic, some obstacles may disappear as the child's level of cognitive development becomes higher. Others may remain intact but may be circumvented by particular methods or approaches. Attention to these barriers is important in improving the effectiveness of global education programs.

OBSTACLES IN SOCIALIZING AGENTS

The previous section suggested how it would be possible to maximize the effectiveness of programs for children by taking better account of levels of cognitive development and particular individual differences. However, obstacles to effective international socialization may also exist within those persons and institutions responsible for socializing children—examples are the parent answering questions when the child inquires about what "Red China" means, the school board choosing a social studies text, government policy in dealing with issues of human rights, or television programming. The effects of these socializing agents cannot be discounted. Levine provides a perspective on the role of socialization agents when he notes that:

> Every adult individual . . . notices to some degree the evaluative and distributive operations of the socio-cultural system. From observations of individual instances of conformity and nonconformity . . . success and failure, social reward and punishment—in a process equivalent to the vicarious trial-and-error or observational learning of reinforcement theorists—he draws conclusions about which behavioral dispositions are favored and which disfavored. These inductive conclusions become part of his cognitive structure, joining attitudes, beliefs, and values already there, and become consistent with them to some degree. From this cognitive structure . . . comes his definition of the situation in which he sees his children growing up and his prescriptions and proscriptions for their adaptive performance. . . .[32]

The socializing agent, in this view, serves as far more than a reflector of sociocultural policy. An important barrier to the child's international awareness in some cases may be the experience and perception of the parent, teacher, or television producer.

Levine also addresses a second important dimension of socialization—slippage in the socializing process resulting in unplanned and often undesired processes and outcomes:

> The explicit goals of socializing agents are frequently not recognized in the behavior of those they train. First, the socializers are at best imperfect psychological engineers (they do not command the necessary but as yet ill-known laws of behavior acquisition); second, they must operate within the limits set by

their trainees' pre-existing behavioral dispositions acquired genetically and through "accidental" events of early experience. . . .[33]

He continues:

Recognition of this slippage . . . brings to our attention two major sets of variables related to socialization: the conscious aims, concepts, and knowledge of the socializers and the relationship between unplanned and deliberate influences in the child's behavior development. . . . The most urgent objective for empirical research on socialization is to understand the relation between the planned and unplanned aspects of social learning.[34]

Unanticipated *influences* and *outcomes* of practices are important in the socialization of a global orientation. A given educational practice, for example a school policy limiting the discussion of controversial issues, may have a series of planned outcomes such as less conflict in the classroom but also unintended outcomes such as a belief by students that freedom to express one's opinion is not a universal or important principle. A map on the schoolroom wall which presents the North American continent in the middle with other countries as borders will teach geography. It may also transmit the relative importance of one part of the world in relation to others. Most socialization agents do not intend to discourage children from learning about other nations or acquiring a planetary level of awareness. The barriers to that learning and awareness, however, are often the unplanned and even unrecognized consequence of some of these practices.

In addition to understanding unplanned consequences of socialization practices, a cross-national perspective on these obstacles is needed. Important clues to what stands in the way of the acquisition of global awareness by United States children comes from comparing civic education practices in the United States with those in other nations and from examining common themes of education for international understanding as it exists in our country and other nations. It is ironic that although American educators have become very familiar with the phrases *global education* and *international education,* many of them are unaware of similar programs taking place in other countries around the world. Two very important pieces of work in this area contribute to understanding both obstacles and facilitators which have their origin outside the student.

RECOMMENDATION ON EDUCATION FOR INTERNATIONAL UNDERSTANDING AND HUMAN RIGHTS

In 1974 at its General Conference, UNESCO adopted the Recommendation concerning Education for International Understanding, Cooperation and Peace, and Education relating to Human Rights and Fundamental Freedoms.[35] It represents a consensus of governments regarding the role of education in this area and requires a report at specified intervals on action taken in each member state (including the United States) to implement the Recommendation. Two articles from the guiding principles of the Recommendation set forth a full agenda for international education.

Education should be infused with the aims and purposes set forth in the Charter of the United Nations, the Constitution of UNESCO and the Universal Declaration of Human Rights, particularly Article 26, paragraph 2, of the last-named, which states: "Education shall be directed to the full development of the human personality and to the strengthening of respect for human rights and fundamental freedoms. It shall promote understanding, tolerance and friendship among all nations, racial or religious groups, and shall further the activities of the United Nations for the maintenance of peace." [para. 3]

In order to enable every person to contribute actively to the fulfillment of the aims referred to in paragraph 3, and promote international solidarity and co-operation, which are necessary in solving the world problems affecting the individuals' and communities' life and exercise of fundamental rights and freedoms, the following objectives should be regarded as major guiding principles of educational policy:

(a) an international dimension and a global perspective in education at all levels and in all its forms;
(b) understanding and respect for all peoples, their cultures, civilizations, values and ways of life, including domestic ethnic cultures and cultures of other nations;
(c) awareness of the increasing global interdependence between peoples and nations;
(d) abilities to communicate with others;
(e) awareness not only of the rights but also of the duties incumbent upon individuals, social groups and nations towards each other;
(f) understanding of the necessity for international solidarity and co-operation;
(g) readiness on the part of the individual to participate in

solving the problems of his community, his country and the world at large. [para. 4][36]

Several significant characteristics of these guiding principles and the manner in which they were formulated need to be highlighted. First and most important is the explicit connection between education for peace and education relating to human rights and fundamental freedoms. The recognition that in education there is an important relationship between international understanding and human rights is a major breakthrough. In many places in the document, the centrality of the Universal Declaration of Human Rights and the International Human Rights Convenants is noted. The Recommendation stresses internalization by students of the principles of these documents and proposes that students should be aware of violations of human rights and familiar with United Nations institutions which attempt to protect them.

American students may be prone to special difficulties in understanding the international protection of human rights, even though President Carter's human-rights-oriented foreign policy made these issues front-page news. Some of the obstacles may in fact be unintended outcomes of otherwise successful social studies programs. Terms like "rights and freedoms" have been discussed in American civic education almost exclusively when studying the U.S. Constitution and Bill of Rights. There is a certain natiocentrism among Americans when they think of human rights that limits their conception to rights and freedoms guaranteed to American citizens in those documents and leads to the belief that ours is the only country which protects fair trial or peaceful assembly. Many Americans believe that people in other countries neither have nor care about having such rights and freedoms—a belief which might be changed significantly if the Universal Declaration of Human Rights and other instruments which express an international consensus were discussed in social studies classes along with the U.S. Constitution.

Other institutional barriers to achieving a high level of public awareness for adults and to adequate education for preadults have existed in the United States government's policy toward the international protection of human rights. Buergenthal, reviewing American action on this subject, noted that in 1953 John Foster Dulles, then Secretary of State, formally advised the United Nations that the United States did not intend to become a party to any international human rights covenants. Buergenthal continued to assess the situation in 1974 as follows:

We read daily about individuals who demonstrate their readiness to sacrifice their lives, to be tortured, imprisoned, deprived of their livelihoods, buried alive in mental institutions, all because they believe that freedom of expression, freedom of religion, equality of treatment, due process of Law, the right to emigrate, and many other basic human rights, are values for which no sacrifice is too great. The courage of Messrs. Sakharov and Solzhenitsyn is by no means unique, it is only better known. Despite the fact that, in a world dominated by equally powerful super-states, the historic commitment of the U.S. to human rights is a foreign policy asset of immense importance, the international promotion of human rights is a low priority item for our policy-makers. As a result, we have done relatively little in the last two decades to promote international protection of human rights. . . .[37]

This country's past neglect of United Nations human rights efforts may be thought of as constituting an obstacle to understanding human rights issues and problems by American adults and young people.

In the recent past American policy has been changing in this area. Statements by Secretary Kissinger and other representatives of the Department of State during 1974 and 1975 indicated that the United States government considered human rights violations matters of international concern and that the government would support efforts to deal with violations of rights. President Carter even more recently has emphasized international human rights in American foreign policy, making it still more important that the public be informed about these issues.

In many respects international human rights is an ideal topic to be treated in a global education program because it illustrates so well the existence of international agreement about basic human characteristics, qualities, and rights and is closely associated with major international organizations. The UNESCO Recommendation addresses these issues explicitly from an educational perspective and provides an international base to launch such efforts. To the extent that the United States as a member state of UNESCO is bound to promote its aims, the Recommendation may aid in overcoming past obstacles to international human rights education.

A second characteristic of the guiding principles of the Recommendation is their explicit statement that an international dimension and global perspective are meant to be realized at all educational levels. There was basic agreement on the meaning of the term "global perspective and international dimension" among the large majority of delegations at the Committee of Experts representing the member states of UNESCO which drafted the Recommendation. Work done in the United States on these topics was familiar to many.

A third characteristic of the revised Recommendation is the inclusion of "intercultural education" through the study of domestic ethnic cultures as well as foreign cultures. The intended positive outcomes of this approach include empathy, the ability to take the role or viewpoint of another person, acceptance and trust of those from other cultural groups, and the ability to interpret customs and nonverbal behavior in differing cultural styles. The potential role of the school in intercultural education has been summarized as follows:

> In particular we find much evidence to recommend school efforts to create an *intercultural dimension* in childhood education. We define the term "intercultural" generically to include international as well as domestic second culture experience, since many of the objectives are identical. . . . By the term "dimension" we mean more than adding a few units on Africa and Asia, Mexican-Americans and Polish Americans, while the regular curriculum remains monocultural. . . . In social studies and language arts, in music and art, the intercultural dimensions are created by incorporating data and experience from appropriate domestic and "foreign" cultures.[38]

Amendments to the UNESCO Recommendation introduced by the United States delegation explicitly referred to intercultural education and to domestic ethnic cultures; these amendments were actively supported by countries which themselves are culturally pluralistic.

Obstacles to international understanding in the form of world problems were also noted in the Recommendation. It requires an in-depth treatment not only of the existence of problems but also of possible solutions. Unwillingness on the part of educators to deal with problems such as war and overpopulation may be an obstacle to the achievement of a global perspective among young people.

The importance of the citizen's active involvement was noted several times, and it was also recognized that both knowledge and attitudes must be the focus of educational attention.

Many educators in the United States have taken a leading role in the development of material and methods for world-centered education. The commitment of some United States educators to international education has been weakened by a belief which might be phrased as follows, "It is all very well for us in the United States to educate our young people about peace, but what if we're the only country doing this?" The UNESCO Recommendation should be of some value in answering that objection. At the same time it should stimulate international cooperation in international education and action by the United States as called for in the provision that declares: "Member States by their own actions, should demonstrate that implementing this recommendation is itself an exercise in international understanding and cooperation [para. 43]."

THE IEA CIVIC EDUCATION SURVEY

Evaluation of the characteristics of effective educational programs in different nations is another source for the identification of obstacles to global education. The International Association for the Evaluation of Educational Achievement (IEA), with its headquarters in Stockholm, collected data on the outcomes of education in six subject areas. The civic education data include responses to cognitive tests and attitudinal questionnaires from more than 30,000 students (ten-year-olds, fourteen-year-olds, and preuniversity students) in nine countries (Finland, Federal Republic of Germany, Ireland, Israel, Italy, Netherlands, New Zealand, Sweden, and the United States).[39] Two-stage stratified probability sampling was employed. In the first stage, schools were selected from a nationally stratified frame with a probability proportional to their student-body size. In the second stage, students were selected randomly from within the chosen schools with probability inversely proportionate to the size of their school. Sampling errors were reduced by stratifying the schools by factors such as size of school, type of school, and region served by the school. The data were collected in 1971 and included information from teachers about pedagogical practices as well as student and principal questionnaires. A brief review of the general findings will put the study in perspective.

First, it was necessary to determine whether the outcomes of civic education are multidimensional or unidimensional and whether the structure or clustering of these attitudes is similar in different nations. This question was addressed by examining the the correlations and factor analyses of the outcomes of civic education separately in each age-by-country group. There were at least three clusters of such outcomes which were relatively independent of each other. These included a Support for Democratic Values factor, a Support for the National Government factor, and a Civic Interest/ Participation factor. A fourth factor differentiating the local from national government system also appeared in some groups. These results suggest that the outcomes of civic education in the affective or attitudinal domain are in fact multidimensional—there is not a simple prototype "good citizen" in these nations. The factor patterns were very similar in countries which have very dissimilar governmental and educational systems.

Since there are distinguishable independent dimensions of civic attitudes, the second question is whether educational systems are differentially successful in fostering these citizenship outcomes in students. A preliminary answer to this question was provided by comparing the *pattern* of civic attitudes in different nations. The most striking finding from this analysis was that those countries where students were above the mean for all countries on Support for Democratic Values were countries where Support for the National Government was below the mean for all countries. This was true for both fourteen-year-olds and preuniversity students. Likewise, countries where Support for the National Government was above the mean for all countries were countries where Support for Democratic Values was below the mean for all countries. Among the younger groups, high Civic Interest/Participation tended to accompany high Support for the National Government. These data indicate that a system which effectively educates its students toward support for democratic values may not be equally effective in promoting support for the national government, and vice versa.

There are several possible explanations for these patterns. It might be concluded that the resources which schools presently devote to civic education are not sufficient to foster all three of these attitudinal outcomes. The schools which effectively foster democratic values may have insufficient time remaining to encourage civic interest, for example. In partial support of this interpretation is the information that although teachers and experts on civics curriculum in these countries rated many potential topics in civic education as important for students to learn, the small amount of school time actually devoted to civic education seems insufficient to cover in depth all these topics.

A second possible explanation for the failure of the students of any given country to demonstrate uniformly high civic achievement is that there may be an actual incompatibility between these outcomes that constitutes a kind of barrier to the achievement of full democratic citizenship. For example, a stress on patriotism and nationalism in schools, which seems to contribute to adolescent support for the national government and active civic participation, may foster those outcomes at the expense of support for democratic values. The patterns of achievement in different countries support this interpretation. The regression analysis, based on student differences within countries, indicated that participation in patriotic ritual is positively related to authoritarian attitudes and also to participation in political discussion. If education practices in these nine nations increase one positively valued civic outcome at the expense of another, imaginative new approaches may be required.

The major kind of school-based variable which seemed to contribute in a positive direction to the students' achievement of all three desired outcomes was the indication that students were encouraged by teachers to express their opinions. Reports of this kind of classroom atmosphere were characteristic of the students in the IEA survey who were more knowledgeable, less authoritarian, and more participant. If the argument concerning incompatibility of outcomes is taken seriously, it becomes important to examine both the planned and unplanned effects of educational practices. From these data it appears that encouragement of student discussion and participation in the classroom is one practice in which both the intended and unintended effects might be called positive; in contrast, other aspects of school input may increase one intended outcome at the expense of another, creating one obstacle in the process of destroying another.[40]

The IEA analysis that related specific curricular topics to student attitudes indicated that including a study of non-Western cultures fosters democratic values and knowledge in some nations. In contrast, a very traditional approach to civic education, which stresses facts and memorization and includes a great deal of patriotic ritual, seemed to constitute an obstacle to democratic attitudinal development. Change in teacher behavior to foster a more open classroom atmosphere is probably one of the most difficult educational alterations to bring into effect, requiring reform of many aspects of teacher training. However, the general results of the IEA survey suggest that it is the most important element in the improvement of civic education.

The IEA Civic Education Survey also collected data about international orientations, allowing a comparison of American adolescents and those in other nations. Students were asked how frequently they discussed domestic and international politics with parents, friends, and teachers. Students in the United States ranked fairly high on total amount of discussion engaged in and on other aspects of active civic interest or participation. There were, however, considerable differences among countries in the topics that students reported discussing. On the average, fourteen-year-old students in the Federal Republic of Germany, Finland, Italy, the Netherlands, and New Zealand discussed with parents and friends the subject "what is happening in other countries" more frequently than "what is going on in our country in government and politics." National politics were of somewhat greater interest to Irish and Israeli students than international politics. The United States was the only country (of those eight) where there was substantially *less* interest among fourteen-year-olds in discussion of foreign politics with friends and parents than in the discussion of national political affairs. Similar patterns characterized the performance of preuniversity students.[41]

Although American adolescents did not report frequent international discussion with parents or friends, discussions of international topics with teachers were reported more frequently for American preuniversity students than for those in any other country. Fourteen-year-old American students were tied for second rank in frequency of their discussion with teachers. Students in the United States tended to have more of their political discussion and experience focused in the classroom than did the students in other nations. Thus, school programs such as those described in Chapter 1 and other chapters to follow bear a particularly important responsibility for international education in the United States.

The data collected from teachers concerning the importance of various civic education topics did not parallel the national differences among students reported above. National and international problems were seen by the teachers of fourteen-year-olds as being about equal in importance in the Federal Republic of Germany, Italy, and New Zealand. In Finland, Ireland, and the United States national problems were seen by teachers as somewhat more important; in the Netherlands international problems were somewhat more important. No data on teachers were available from Israel. The study of non-Western cultures was perceived as considerably less important than national and international problems in the opinions of teachers in all the nations surveyed. Some greater importance was attributed to this topic in New Zealand, Sweden, and the United States than in other nations. Those classrooms in which study of non-Western culture was stressed tended to have somewhat less authoritarian students.

The questionnaire used in the IEA survey included items to measure both cognitive and affective outcomes of civic education. Out of forty-seven multiple-choice questions administered to fourteen-year-olds, seven dealt with the United Nations. Among students in the United States, more than 65 percent knew that the

Universal Declaration of Human Rights does not guarantee the right to disobey national laws if one's family is in danger. Approximately 50 percent of the fourteen-year-olds knew that the Security Council (out of five listed UN units) is charged with major responsibility for keeping the peace.

In two of the seven questions, more students chose a single wrong alternative than chose the keyed correct answer. For example, more of the American students believed that the signers of the UN Charter promised to "stabilize the world economy" than believed that they promised to "prevent the use of armed force except in the common interest of member states."[42]

Scores summarizing students' knowledge of domestic and international politics were also available. The average American fourteen-year-old was more knowledgeable about domestic political institutions and processes than the average fourteen-year-old in any other country except Israel. In contrast, the average American fourteen-year-old was less knowledgeable about international institutions and processes than the fourteen-year-olds in any other nation except Ireland.

The National Case Study Questionnaire collected by IEA is helpful in understanding the finding that adolescents in the United States focus more on the national than on the international while those in countries like the Netherlands focus more on the international than on the national.[43] An index of foreign contact was formed for each nation. For example, of the countries testing in Civic Education, the Netherlands ranked the highest on percentage of the Gross National Product which entered world trade (40 percent) while the United States ranked the lowest (6 percent). Indices including percentage of films imported, textbooks imported, and international mail and telephone services also placed the Netherlands as the highest and the United States as the lowest in foreign contact. An important obstacle to the natural achievement of a global perspective may be a lack of international contact in the form of daily exposure, books, movies, and communication. Through projects like "Columbus in the World"[44] and other activities of the world-centered schools described in Chapter 1, it may be possible to maximize available international experience.

In addition to items in the cognitive test measuring knowledge of the UN, there were a series of ratings of the UN. Students were asked to indicate what effect each of ten listed institutions had on the realization of a series of values. Students in all participating nations rated the UN relatively high on achievements such as the following: "creates better understanding so that people can live and work together," and "settles arguments and disagreements." However, American fourteen-year-olds believe that other institutions are equally effective or more effective in promoting understanding and settling disagreements (police and laws). High school seniors in the United States tend to hold perceptions of the UN similar to those of fourteen-year-olds. If anything, the seniors are slightly *less* favorable. The attitudes toward the UN in the United States were neither consistently more positive nor consistently less positive than those of students in the other nations.

In summary, American fourteen-year-olds and seniors in high school perceive the major activities of the UN relatively accurately, but it is not an institution about which they have extensive knowledge, a clearly developed image, or strong positive feelings. There is a very small change between the fourteen-year-old and the high school senior level with regard to knowledge of and exposure to information about the UN or in clarity of attitudes toward it. This is further evidence that the years before age fourteen may be thought of as a kind of critical or optimal period in the acquisition of knowledge and attitudes about international organizations and processes.

It is important to encourage further study of international socialization not only in the United States but also in other countries. It is clear that the United States occupies a unique position even when compared to Western European countries. Educational programs in the United States may bear a particularly heavy responsibility in view of the relatively low level of naturally occurring international contact and the greater interest of American students in domestic rather than international politics.

SOURCES OF OBSTACLES COMMON TO SCHOOL CURRICULUM AND TELEVISION PROGRAMMING

Because television is widely acknowledged to be a source of many attitudes toward other nations, this section will examine the obstacles created by programming and parallel aspects of the school curriculum as it currently exists.

Both television programming and school curricula tend to emphasize the unusual or exotic elements of other countries and cultures. Beyer and Hicks found that in some items of a multiple choice test of factual knowledge, 45 percent or more of the seventh grade students selected a single wrong alternative. These widespread misconceptions included the following: most of Africa south of the Sahara is covered by jungles (correct answer—*by grassland*); in terms of dollar value the most important exports of Africa south of the Sahara are mineral products (correct answer—*agricultural products*). These authors criticized the mass media for not helping students to form a more realistic picture.

> The information that students have about Africa may come primarily from the popular media. Students may never have heard of Africa's Sudanic kingdoms, but they probably have heard of Tarzan. . . . If a student has seen numerous . . . animated cartoons of missionaries in the cooking pot with savages dancing around the fire, but has never seen a photograph of an African farmer or fisherman he will not have a balanced image of the region. . . . [45]

They described school curricula and practices in similar fashion:

> Lack of balance is especially noticeable in the elementary grades. Here instruction about Africa south of the Sahara tends to focus on the strange and bizarre. There are very few pygmies in Africa in relation to the total population: yet they are often the only Africans studied . . . as a result these [elementary] students get the impression that pygmies are a major segment of the population—or, in some cases, the total population. Since Pygmies live for the most part in rain forest areas, the image of Africa as a land covered by jungles is reinforced. [46]

Much of the study of Africa in secondary schools, according to these authors, consists of "twenty-one-day travelogues of a continent." Research indicates that student attitudes focus on the bizarre and the backward, reflected in comments such as those recently obtained from interviews with young children. When asked how people in other countries were different from themselves, such exotica as "people in Africa eat dogs and ants" or "in Japan they shape the children's feet" were mentioned.

The perception of one's own nation and one's own people as insiders and other nations as outsiders is common both in the mass media and in the schools. Morehouse commented on the extensive nationalistic focus in the United States:

> While no one would dispute the central importance of study of our national history and government in the school curriculum, it is frequently carried out . . . beyond legislative requirements. In New York State, one of the more progressive states

in international education matters ... most students in fact spend ... on U.S. and New York state history and government, close to 70 percent of their time, and give 85 per cent of their attention to Western civilization and its contemporary manifestation on the North American continent, leaving a scant 15 percent of the curriculum for the study of the rest of mankind.[47]

A similar nationalistic perspective characterizes the view of human rights in the school curriculum, according to Goldstein, who reviewed the content of elementary social studies texts and curriculum guides:

When personal freedom is discussed the content of the textbooks suggests that there are no personal liberties in Russia while there are virtually no limitations or conflict over civil liberties in the United States.[48]

According to a 1973 survey conducted by UNESCO, only from 1 to 2 percent of the average television week on commercial and public television in the United States is devoted to international programs—lower than in any of the other 100 countries surveyed.[49]

Television is potentially a very potent source for presenting cultural similarities and differences so as to increase two important abilities identified by Hanvey: "perspective consciousness" (understanding that our own view is not universal and that others view things differently) and "cross-cultural awareness" (awareness of diversity in ideas and practices).[50] A closer partnership between television and schools might allow awareness of other cultures' diversity in ideas and practices to be coupled with respect for that diversity, thus helping to overcome the obstacle of ethnocentric nationalism.

Hanvey has also pointed to a major assumption which schools and television programming share—a belief in the naturalness and goodness of both economic growth and technological innovation. What children learn in schools about other countries, according to Goldstein's review of curricula and texts, shows the same bias toward technology and industrialization and creates an obstacle to appreciation of cultures which do not value technology:

Many of the texts and guides ... stress that all people on the earth have the same basic needs, are interdependent, and need to cooperate ... yet when individual countries are discussed it is clear that an implicit, and sometimes explicit, standard of industrialization and democracy is used. ... Indiscriminate westernization is the standard used to measure the underdeveloped countries.[51]

Northwestern European countries and English-speaking countries (as well as countries like Israel and Japan which are highly industrialized democracies) are praised in the texts as "skillful," "energetic," and "freedom loving." The less industrialized nations of southern Europe and all less developed countries are presented as using inferior substitutes for modern technology, as being uneducated, and as suffering from many problems associated with poverty.

Some recent television programs have attempted to help students understand and value the perspective of people who live in nontechnological societies. Before students can fully benefit from these programs, however, they may need the help of parents or teachers to overcome their unconscious assumptions that technological innovations and diffusion are positive and folkways negative. On some topics there is considerable contrast in the communication which children receive from television and that which they get at school, but neither source may be adequate.

CONCLUSIONS

There exist in every nation, every school system, and every student factors conducive to world-centered education as well as obstacles which stand in the way. This chapter has taken the negative point of view—reviewing the way in which cognitive limitations, attitudinal rigidity, or inadequate motivation may stand in the way of the individual's full realization of a global perspective. The description of the UNESCO Recommendation called attention to the mutual interdependence of international education and human rights education and of domestic intercultural education and international education. It also highlighted the need for international exchange and cooperation in the process of implementing world-centered education. The comparative approach exemplified in the IEA Survey of Civic Education suggests that students in the United States may need to overcome certain political and geographical obstacles in order to reach full understanding of a worldwide perspective but that schools can make a difference in this area. Finally, the way current television programming and school curricula may contribute to obstacles was considered.

It is important to keep a dynamic rather than a static view of both barriers and facilitators of global education. Psychological obstacles, even more than physical ones, are capable of being surmounted, circumvented, or actually lowered by the process of education. Some of these obstacles may be interconnected so that circumventing one may lower another. In all cases, however, we need to know more about existing obstacles and facilitators in our quest for world-centered education and in our evaluation of its materials and methods.

.

NOTES

1. Richard C. Remy, James A. Nathan, James M. Becker, and Judith V. Torney, *International Learning and International Education in a Global Age,* Bulletin 47, National Council for the Social Studies, 1975, p. 39–40.

2. Robert D. Hess and Judith V. Torney, *The Development of Political Attitudes in Children,* Aldine, Chicago, 1967.

3. R. W. Connell, *The Child's Construction of Politics,* Melbourne University Press, Melbourne, 1971, p. 27.

4. Ibid., pp. 17–18.

5. Charles F. Andrain, *Children and Civic Awareness,* Charles E. Merrill, Columbus, Ohio, 1971, p. 89.

6. Joseph Adelson and R. P. O'Neill, "Growth of Political Ideas in Adolescence: The Sense of Community," *Journal of Personality and Social Psychology,* vol. 4, pp. 295–306, 1966.

7. John Flavell, Patricia Botkin, and C. L. Fry, *The Development of Role Taking and Communication Skills in Children,* Wiley, New York, 1968.

8. M. Feffer and V. Gourevitch, "Cognitive Aspects of Role Taking in Children," *Journal of Personality,* vol. 28, pp. 383–396, 1960.

9. Michael Chandler, "Egocentrism and Antisocial Behavior: The Assessment and Training of Social Perspective Taking Skills," *Developmental Psychology,* vol. 9, pp. 326–332, 1973.

10. Eugene S. Gollin, "Organizational Characteristics of Social Judgment: A Developmental Investigation," *Journal of Personality,* vol. 26, pp. 139–154, 1958.

11. Dorothy Flapan, *Children's Understanding of Social Interaction,* Teachers College, New York, 1968.

12. *Findings on the Television Perception and Cognition of Children and Young People,* Internationales Zentralinstitut fur das Jugend und Bildungsfernsehen, Munich, 1969.

13. Wallace E. Lambert and Otto Klineberg, *Children's Views of Foreign People,* Appleton-Century-Crofts, New York, 1967.

14. Ibid., pp. 223–224.

15. Gustav Jahoda, "Development of Scottish Children's Ideas and Attitudes about Other Countries," *Journal of Social Psychology,* vol. 58, pp. 91–108, 1962.

16. E. Hicks and Barry K. Beyer, "Images of Africa," *Journal of Negro Education,* vol. 39, pp. 155–170, 1970.

17. Gordon Allport, *The Nature of Prejudice,* Addison-Wesley, Cambridge, Mass., 1954.

18. J. M. F. Jaspars, J. P. Van de Geer, H. Tajfel, and N. B. Johnson, "On

the Development of National Attitudes," *European Journal of Social Psychology,* vol. 1, pp. 360–370, 1966.

19. Ibid., p. 368.

20. J. P. Scott, "Critical Periods in Behavior Development," *Science,* pp. 949–958, 1962.

21. Connell, op. cit.

22. The data and interviews cited in this section are taken from Hess and Torney, op. cit.

23. Adelson and O'Neill, op. cit.

24. K. T. Omwake, "The Relationship between Acceptance of Self and Acceptance of Others Shown by Three Personality Inventories," *Journal of Consulting Psychology,* vol. 18, pp. 443–446, 1954.

25. D. Byrne, *The Attraction Paradigm,* Academic, New York, 1971.

26. Hess and Torney, op. cit.

27. M. A. Riastra and C. E. Johnson, "Changes in Attitudes of Elementary School Pupils toward Foreign Speaking Peoples Resulting from the Study of Foreign Language," *Journal of Experimental Education,* vol. 32, pp. 65–73, 1964.

28. William M. Cheyne, "Stereotyped Reactions to Speakers with Scottish and English Regional Accents," *British Journal of Social and Clinical Psychology,* vol. 9, pp. 77–79, 1970.

29. Wallace Lambert, *Language, Psychology and Culture,* Stanford University Press, Stanford, Calif., 1972.

30. Frederick Erickson, "Gatekeeping," *Harvard Educational Review,* vol. 45, pp. 44–70, 1975.

31. R. Rist, "Student Social Class and Teacher Expectations," *Harvard Educational Review,* vol. 45, pp. 411–450, 1970.

32. Robert A. Levine, *Culture, Behavior and Personality,* Aldine, Chicago, 1973, p. 105.

33. Ibid., p. 106.

34. Ibid., pp. 106, 135.

35. For a full discussion of the UNESCO Recommendation see T. Buergenthal and J. V. Torney, *International Human Rights and International Education,* U.S. National Commission for UNESCO, Department of State, Washington, D.C., 1976, available from U.S. Government Printing Office.

36. Ibid., pp. 153–154.

37. Thomas Buergenthal, "International Human Rights: U.S. Policy and Priorities," *Virginia Journal of International Law,* vol. 14, 1974, p. 618.

38. John A. Carpenter and Judith V. Torney, "Beyond the Melting Pot to Cultural Pluralism," in *Children and Intercultural Education,* Annual Bulletin of the Association for Childhood Education International, 1973–74, p. 20.

39. The report of the findings briefly summarized here may be found in J. V. Torney, A. N. Oppenheim, and R. Farnen, *Civic Education in Ten Countries,* Almquist and Wiksell, Stockholm, and Wiley, New York, 1975.

40. This argument is paraphrased from the concluding chapter of Ibid.

41. These findings are presented in greater detail in J. V. Torney, "The International Attitudes and Knowledge of Adolescents in Nine Countries," *International Journal of Political Education,* vol. 1, pp. 3–20, 1977.

42. Ibid.

43. A. Harry Passow, Harold Noah, and Max Eckstein, *The National Case Study: An Empirical Comparative Study of Twenty-One Educational Systems,* Almquist and Wiksell, Stockholm, and Wiley, New York, 1975.

44. Chadwick Alger et al., "Columbus in the World, the World in Columbus," Brief Reports Nos. 1–16, Mershon Center, Ohio State University, Columbus, 1974–1976.

45. Hicks and Beyer, op. cit., p. 164–165.

46. Ibid.

47. Ward Morehouse, "A New Civic Literacy," Aspen Institute, Aspen, Colo., 1975.

48. R. J. Goldstein, "Elementary School Curriculum and Political Socialization," in B. Massialas, *Political Youth, Traditional Schools,* Prentice-Hall, Englewood Cliffs, N.J., 1972, p. 28.

49. Cited in *Education for Global Interdependence: A Report with Recommendations to the Government/Academic Interface Committee,* American Council on Education, Washington, D.C., 1975.

50. Robert Hanvey, *An Attainable Global Perspective,* Center for War/Peace Studies, New York, 1975.

51. Goldstein, op. cit., p. 26–27.

CHAPTER FOUR

Imperatives for Global Education

Bruce R. Joyce and Alexander M. Nicholson
Stanford University

L ater chapters in this book discuss and analyze the elements of school and community programs in global education and catalogue promising practices in global education already in use in schools around the country. What we propose in this chapter is to set the stage for discussion of these programs, both hypothetical and actual, by developing imperatives for global education today. What things must be done? What ideas must be followed so that today's schoolchildren will become responsible citizens in an interdependent world? What overriding concepts must guide our educators if we hope to bring the promise of global education to fulfillment?

TOWARD 2001 A.D.

As we approach the year 2001 A.D. and realize that today's schoolchildren will spend most of their lives in the twenty-first century, it occurs to us to speculate on what the number 2001 A.D. means. It refers to the first year of the third millenium of the Christian era, the Christian reckoning of years having been generally accepted as the world's standard over such alternative calendars as those of the Chinese, the Hebrews, the Muslims, or the Greeks. Although the world is not Christian, it adopts the Christian calendar. We recall that once, from the eleventh through the fourteenth centuries of its era, at least, Christendom *was* the world—or at least *a* world—not just a religion but a transnational culture that held together disparate ethnic and political entities spread over a large portion of the globe. We wonder whether a transnational culture of such scope is possible today, whether there can be any common ground for a world society in which the various nations and peoples participate while maintaining their separate identities.

Although both sides of the question can be argued, we believe the answer has to be yes. We want the answer to be yes; but the answer will be yes if, and only if, the imperatives for global education are carried out. Here, then, is the source of the imperatives: a conception—not substantive but procedural—of world society to which today's schoolchildren will relate on a variety of levels. It is likely, for example, that the future citizen will relate to many relatively local societal units, some national units including the nation-state, and to numerous arrangements for global problem solving. The meanings of local, national, and global citizenship will differ, but they are all likely to be present; how to prepare for each and how to integrate them all will assume increasing importance. A "multiple loyalties" concept of citizenship will be more complex than was simple national loyalty alone.

THE SEARCH FOR IMPERATIVES

The problem we set ourselves is to arrive at a philosophy of global education: a system or set of beliefs and values that is internally consistent and at the same time complete enough to inform all the widely divergent programs that are included under the rubric of global education. How shall we develop such a philosophy? There seem to be four approaches we can take. Let us explore each of them in a scenario.

SCENARIO 1

To arrive at a set of imperatives for global education, we can begin with a set of assumptions about the world's future. For example, we may postulate that certain natural resources will be depleted within a given amount of time and that the world economy and living conditions will have to adapt to that circumstance. The assumptions may be phrased as narrowly ("no fossil fuels available after 1994") or as broadly ("scarcity of natural resources") as desired. From these factual predictions, we infer the imperatives, that is, the things we think it necessary for children to be taught in order to live in that particular future.

The problem with Scenario 1 is the unpredictability of the future. What seems in any one time to be the indisputable truth may well become a quaint myth five years later. The belief in continuing abundance that was nurtured by the American boom economy of the fifties and sixties is a good example. This problem increases, furthermore, as the length of projection into the future increases, so that prognostications for about twenty years hence are almost totally worthless. To follow Scenario 1, then, would result at best in a picture of what in the 1970s seems likely to occur in the future and at worst in a future educational program doomed by the misconceptions of the past.

SCENARIO 2

If we accept, as it seems we must, the cogent criticism of Scenario 1, then Scenario 2 inevitably suggests itself. Let us consider alternative assumptions about the future and not tie ourselves down to a single set. We may then think about future f_1 based on premises A_1, B_1, C_1, etc., as well as any number of futures $f_2 \ldots f_n$ conditioned on premises A_n, B_n, $C_n \ldots$. We may criticize each set of assumptions and assign them relative probabilities of occurring.

This approach ameliorates the failing of Scenario 1 by taking an open-ended attitude toward the future. This approach has actually been used by the Club of Rome in its various computer-modeled predictions of the future.

Though this approach improves on Scenario 1, it still suffers from the same basic problem. No matter how many different predictions of the future are made, their sum is only a broader prediction of the future, constrained by the limits of present knowledge (and ignorance) and subject to the unknowable vicissitudes of the future. What is worse in Scenario 2, however, is the fatal flaw that the very notion that alternative factual assumptions about the future can be postulated renders inferring imperatives from them impossible.

SCENARIO 3

If from alternative assumptions we can draw no imperatives at all and if we cannot be sure what the future will be, then shall we suggest alternative imperatives for global education? This approach seems the next step in our progression. On reflection, however, the very idea of an alternative imperative is self-contradictory; saying, "Either you have to do X or you don't have to," implies that you don't have to. Our imperatives would no longer be very imperative.

SCENARIO 4

Suppose then that we make no factual assumptions about the future. Instead, we merely suggest logical alternative approaches to global education. This solution may satisfy the problems encountered in the previous scenarios, but, unfortunately, it leaves us with only suggestions—far short of our goal of arriving at imperatives.

Our logical meditations on the imperatives for global education lead us to conclude that we cannot reach any *substantive* imperatives. We cannot with any certainty say, "The world is going to be thus-and-so, and consequently children must be taught X-and-Y." We must instead turn our attention to the development of imperatives that deal with the social process of education. The basis for these imperatives is the Andersons' definition of global education as "education for responsible participation in an interdependent global society"—one in which we will have multiple loyalties depending on the level of issues involved. Some issues are purely local, some national, and some are nation-interdependent. Although it may draw upon current factual knowledge and various predictions of the future, this conception's validity does not depend upon whether any particular vision of the future does in fact turn out to be the case. The only imperatives for global education which can be worthy of the name are those which are inherently independent of concrete occurrences in the future, imperatives which enjoin us to action regardless of what the future holds and which prepare our children for whatever their future may be.

THREE ASPECTS OF GLOBAL EDUCATION

The goals of education in general may be thought of as belonging to one of three domains: the personal, the social, and the academic. Personal goals are those which deal with the development of a healthy, integrated personality and a sense of individual worth and meaning. Social goals are those which spring from humanitarian interests and from the need to function in a world of other people. These goals include preparation for citizenship and for participation in the various political, economic, and social systems in which people may find themselves. Academic goals serve at times to facilitate the achievement of personal and social goals but also hold a value in themselves. They represent the attempt to make available to the student the constructs and ways of thinking which are the product of reflective, scholarly thought.

All three domains of educational goals are clearly relevant to any program of global education and should be kept in mind throughout the ensuing discussion of global education's imperatives. In the personal context, it is becoming more and more important that everyone understand himself or herself not only as an individual but also as a member of the human species and as an earthling. International events and processes swirl about us, and without an understanding of these events and processes we may well be cut off from an important portion of ourselves. In the social sphere, there is the growing realization that all human beings are members of a society that is now global in scope and as such are subject to the vicissitudes of political, economic, and social orders that extend beyond local and even national bounds. The academic pursuit is even more clearly necessary in the global sense: the task of the scholar is to comprehend the awful complexity of the world and translate it into ways of thinking and inquiring that will facilitate personal meaning and social action.

TWO CAVEATS ON GLOBAL EDUCATION

The primary purpose of this chapter is to arrive at a reasoned set of imperatives for global education that will guide the construction of school curricula. Against this end there are two impediments that must be mentioned before we proceed to elaborate the imperatives themselves.

The first of these is that this particular area of curriculum is tinged with ideological overtones that are lacking in other less controversial areas. Although it may be disputed as to which is the best way to teach mathematics—by traditional methods or innovative ones, by textbooks or programmed materials, and so on—it is not generally disputed as to what is true in mathematics or as to what should be taught. Such is not the case in global education. Hard-and-fast facts or formulas are simply not available. Ideological strains such as isolationism, jingoism, and chauvinism militate not only against much of what is being taught in global education but even against teaching it at all.

The other special impediment to global education is the lack of a global government and other appropriate institutions to carry it out. Although there are a number of agreed-on domains of international action in such fields as health, postal service, air traffic, weather observation, and international communications, most issues must be negotiated specifically in the absence of general policy. There is no universal language of learning comparable to Latin in the Middle Ages. The problem of creating international institutions, moreover, involves much more difficulty than merely extending existing national institutions to international dimensions. The deficiencies of the international monetary and legal systems point up this fact only too well. Added to this inherent difficulty are the differences in perceived self-interest among nations. For the purposes of this book, we must be content to limit our discussion primarily to global education in our own national context.

GLOBAL SOCIETY AND IMPERATIVES FOR THE FUTURE

Having rejected the possibility of substantive imperatives for global education and having reflected on the hindrances we face and the goals we must keep in mind, we can now proceed to elicit the imperatives from our conception—a conception of social process—of global society. From knowing *how* we want things in the future to work, we derive what things are imperative for global education today.

We have in mind an international social system that combines relative order and stability with social progress. This aspect of our conception is the first of two overriding values, that is, values that must come before all other ideologies, orientations, and persuasions simply because these values are necessary so that all other competing, even conflicting, values may exist simultaneously. The need for world stability with progress is a precondition for the continuing interaction of the world's nations, religions, ideologies, economies, and other entities and institutions. The problem with creating and maintaining such a situation is the conflicting interests of individuals and entities comprising the world and the reluctance of all to restrain self-interest. Here we face a classical ethical dilemma: "Why should I restrain myself in the interest of the common good when I cannot be sure that others will do so as well?"

Our first imperatives derive from this problem: (1) *Provide perspectives which reconcile the various conflicting interests of individuals and entities who necessarily share the same earth,* for which purpose it is necessary to (2) *render the immensely complex global scene comprehensible in terms faithful to reality.*

The number of different interests to be reconciled may be as large as the number of possible relations among persons and groups of persons in the world. That number is too great to imagine. Almost all the types of conflicts, however, can be subsumed under a single description: the conflict of interest of a smaller unit (however defined) against that of a larger unit of which it is a part. These are true conflicts of interest, wherein a person or group is pulled in opposite directions according to whether it views its own good in the narrower or the broader context.

Consider first an example on the level of a primary group. Mr. Thomas, an industrialist living in a beautiful lakeside town and owning undeveloped property there, wishes to develop the site into a glue factory. The factory would produce income for its owner and would create jobs and generate tax revenue for the town. The factory would also, on the other hand, seriously impair the rustic beauty of the town and would pollute the lake. The owner of the land has a conflict of interest (not to be understood here, of course, in the same sense in which the term is used in law or in professional ethics). As an individual industrialist, he stands to gain profits by developing the land; as a citizen of the town, he stands to lose the ambience which makes the town a desirable place in which to live. Whichever way the question of the glue factory is resolved, the decision process should include input of both his and the town's interests and some sort of balancing mechanism whereby the conflict (if any) among such interests would be resolved. For this purpose, of course, it would be necessary to gather factual data and to have the scientific constructs with which to draw conclusions from the data.

The essential point of this example is that the conflict is not to be understood as between industrialist and town, but rather between Mr. Thomas as industrialist and Mr. Thomas as town resident. This latter identity includes him in a group larger than himself, even though he retains his individualistic interests as industrialist. The significance of the example may be thought to be nullified by having

Mr. Thomas move to another town; in that case he would no longer share the interests of his former fellow townspeople. But if his new home is in the same state, then as a citizen of the state he has an interest in not despoiling one of its beautiful towns and lakes. Or if his new home is not in the same state, it is in another state in the same country; and so the same argument, *mutatis mutandis,* applies again. The planet is, after all, finite. This idea is the essential message behind the concept of Spaceship Earth.

The example described above involves only the most simple kind of conflict of interest. When we move beyond the realm of primary groups to larger entities—community, state, nation, hemisphere, planet, species—the number and complexity of competing interests increase exponentially. It becomes clear that the need for comprehension of realities on the global scale is the most pressing imperative for educating tomorrow's citizens. Knowledge and comprehension are the first step in sorting out our various loyalties and ordering the priorities among them. The greatest challenge in this area is to render the global system comprehensible in a manner that is not excessively tinged with ideology. An isolationist approach, for example, offers a compact way of dealing with world problems: simply ignore them, a strain of thought derived from a certain interpretation of Washington's admonition to "avoid foreign entanglements" in his Farewell Address. This approach is too easy, and the dangers of its use are too great. "Foreign entanglements" are inevitable on Spaceship Earth.

It is only if we can perceive all of our true loyalties, including those to entities broader in space and time than we have been accustomed to think in terms of, and reconcile the possible conflicts among them that world order with progress will be possible.

The second great overriding value with which we are concerned is the preservation and promotion of cultural pluralism. The danger in this area is the threat that the technetronic revolution the world is currently experiencing may result in the eventual homogenization (that is to say, the loss) of culture worldwide. The standardization of language patterns and of other human institutions—especially through the proliferation of the mass media and of modern techniques of production, packaging, and marketing—confers a mixed blessing on the peoples of the world. On the one hand, standards of living are being raised and poverty is being lessened through the introduction of Western technology and its concomitant values. The richness of individual cultural differences, on the other hand, is being rapidly impoverished at the same time.

Our third imperative addresses itself to this problem: (3) *Promote the kind of pluralism that will allow individual cultures to flourish and enrich one another and people everywhere.* The prospect of a sterile, monocultural (though materially satisfied) world of the future gives impetus to this imperative. The theme of pluralism is closely related to the final two imperatives and will be reiterated below.

As the effective temporal and spatial dimensions of the world continue to shrink because of advances in communication and transportation, and as all parts of the world become consequently more interdependent, a serious problem to global society arises in the affective domain. Citizenship and morality have traditionally been rooted in our involvement in primary groups: face-to-face relationships with family and neighbors. We learn to feel moral empathy with those with whom we interact daily. As the size of the collectivities of which we are a part increases, however, relations become increasingly impersonal, and morality and bonds of citizenship break down. This is not always the case, though, as evidenced by observed strong loyalties to one's nation in times of war or to one's ethnic group under persecution.

The problem on the global level is how to foster true citizenship among the world's peoples. Hence our next imperative: (4) *Encourage international citizenship based on a global perspective through achieving moral empathy with those remote in space and different in culture.* The strategy is to find some method of infusing students with the same moral perspective toward other peoples that they have acquired toward members of their own primary groups. It is a difficult task requiring a projection of morality into international dimensions. To the values of the technetronic revolution (clarification, rational decision making) must be added the moral direction provided by feelings of empathy for our fellow human beings.

A first step in achieving moral empathy on a global scale is the elimination or reduction of three divisive factors. The first of these is poverty, perhaps the most serious divider of all. The poor of the world are isolated from other socioeconomic classes and also from other poor people. The spread of modern technology has alleviated some poverty but has at the same time exacerbated the problem by widening the gap between the poor and the highly participatory middle class. What is needed in the developing nations and in developing areas of the well-off nations is a more localized or regionalized technology that aims toward self-sufficiency rather than dependence.

The second divisive factor is ethnicity. Although loyalty to an ethnic group provides a sense of identity and of morality, it also cuts groups of people off from others and thereby impoverishes everyone socially and culturally. When combined with poverty, ethnicity may be especially divisive.

Nationalism is the third divisive factor. Again, like ethnicity, it has a positive aspect: it offers identity and unity to large groups of people with otherwise divergent interests. By so doing, however, it also alienates one people from another and leads to the creation of stereotypes. National loyalty, however, need not have this effect.

By fostering moral empathy on a global scale and by reducing the above-mentioned globally divisive factors, new types of empathic relationships can arise. We envision a new pluralism based on affiliation groups (social, political, professional, avocational, economic) and other interests, technologies, and commitments.

A related problem caused by the complexity of the global scene is that of finding a way of being efficacious on a global level. It is often difficult enough to be efficacious in a primary group. With even our closest intimates we are often unable to have influence in many domains. Being influential on an international scale appears almost ridiculous to most people. At this point we can state the imperative as: (5) *Create a sense of meaningfulness on a global scale and a belief that one's efforts can be efficacious in the improvement of the world context.*

Both efficacy and morality traditionally come from our involvement in primary groups. In the face-to-face human groups of our families and our villages we need reciprocal relations with others and we know other human beings well enough to have considerable empathy with their needs and interests. Out of this rises our ability to act in a social situation in such a way as to be morally effective. We feel the need to be moral in some kind of sense with those whom we interact with daily because we understand the common good in a small group and we understand the needs of the other individuals with whom we interact. In large collectivities, it is more difficult to have a sense of morality. However, the human being has many times shown himself capable of finding identity and moral meaning in larger collectivities. Loyalty to one's nation, for example, and to one's ethnic group transcend the primary group considerably. And people feel a sense of kinship with the huge mass of people that make up their particular subculture. The technocratic or technetronic dimension of modern society does not by itself have any particular morality except that it is based on the scientist's desire for clarification and understanding of the real nature of things. The technetronic values of clarification and rational decision making are not without merit, but they are insufficient to provide a moral direction unless they are combined with the same kind of empathic urges which cause us to have regard for our fellow humans and to act in communal interest in primary groups. The answer seems to be to create a global humanitarian point of view, and there are some signs that this is taking place. People appear very ready to engage in drives to alleviate the problems of persons in many places where they have not been themselves. By no means do all citizens feel the same degree of humanitarian urges at the present time, but the fact that substantial numbers do indicates that it is possible for members of our species to feel empathy for people far removed from them in time and distance. The answer may lie in a magnification of the concept which McLuhan expressed as the global village[1] in which the electronic media have brought all parts of the world much closer together and we are able to see, as it were, other people's difficulties in our own terms. There does not appear to be much doubt that many Americans developed a tremendous sympathy for the Vietnamese people and for our own citizens who were serving there as soldiers. During the Vietnam war, people in America, and indeed all over the world, actually saw soldiers dying, citizens being displaced—in short, all the horrors of war—on the screens of our living rooms. Gradually, as a consequence of this, many United States citizens began to project the kind of morality which is ordinarily reserved for primary groups into the international arena. They began to feel sympathetic to the Vietnamese people, upset about the involvement of American soldiers in such a situation, and even began to understand how the soldiers of North Vietnam saw themselves as fighting for their homeland rather than as invaders.

The importance of this imperative cannot be overemphasized. Even if it can be accomplished only to some very small degree, it remains essential. The feeling of confidence that one's actions do have effect is a prerequisite for action of any kind. The alternative is cynicism and apathy.

One way of instilling a sense of global efficacy might be by "adopting" a village in another country. The children in American classrooms would have their counterparts in classrooms around the world; they could exchange information about themselves, their schools, their families, their towns. If the children could in some way help their "adopted" counterparts, they might begin to feel globally efficacious, to feel that what they do matters in the world and is noticed and appreciated. Also, children can be helped to see that their own life-styles and consumer habits can have global consequences. Eating less meat, turning down the thermostat, driving smaller cars, having fewer children, hosting a foreign student, giving to a disaster relief fund, or not doing any of these things, will have an impact on others and can be seen as small actions that collectively help shape the world.

THE END AND THE BEGINNING

The search for imperatives for global education is a cyclical process, as indicated in Figure 1. The logical beginning of our search for imperatives for global education is our conception of world society. Though we cannot know what the world will be in the future, we know that two characteristics must obtain: order with progress and

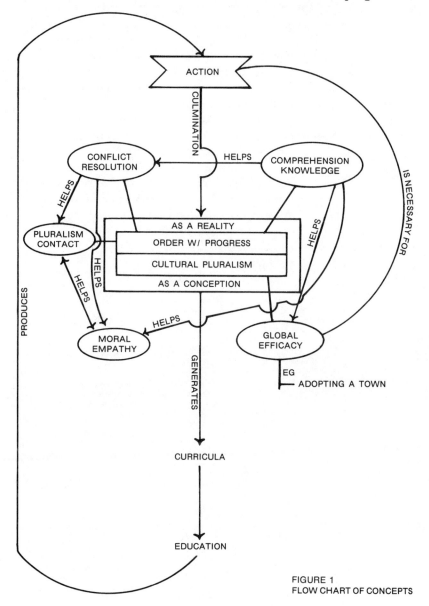

FIGURE 1
FLOW CHART OF CONCEPTS

cultural pluralism. Along with these, we want to promote global citizenship and foster political action and cross-cultural involvement.

From this conception we derive our imperatives. The first of these is to recognize our true interests and loyalties and to resolve any possible conflicts among them. Each person must learn to think of himself or herself—and of everyone else as well—as an individual, as a member of the human race, as an inhabitant of the planet Earth, and as a citizen of a global society. In order for this imperative to be accomplished, knowledge and understanding of the immensely complex global scene are necessary.

Resolution of conflicts of interest enables the development of a new pluralism, one not based on the divisive factors that have dominated in the past. Increased nondestructive cross-cultural contact helps and is helped by a capability for moral empathy on a global scale. A sense of global efficacy is the foundation for initiative and involvement, or global citizenship in action.

The five imperatives that we have outlined for global education should be viewed as the philosophical basis for the generation of new curricula to promote international citizenship. Following chapters attempt to give some picture of what these curricula might look like. Ideally, the education yielded by these curricula will ultimately induce the sorts of actions that will culminate in the realization of our original conception of global society.

NOTES

1. Marshall McLuhan, *Understanding Media: The Extensions of Man,* McGraw-Hill, New York, 1964.

CHAPTER FIVE

Elementary School Programs

Donald N. Morris
United States Committee for UNICEF

T he world-centered schools described in Chapter 1 offer a vision of what might be. However, there are programs and components of programs being carried out in schools throughout the United States that offer the exciting prospect that some of what "might be" actually is. The purpose of this chapter is to share with the reader some glimpses into a few selected global education programs at the elementary school level. This is not to propose that any single program meets all the objectives discussed by Becker, deals with all the obstacles described by Torney, or fulfills all Joyce and Nicholson's imperatives. Global education, that synthesizing dimension of education which gives both a sense of unity and a perspective in which the individual is viewed in relation to other human beings and to planet Earth, is still very much in its infancy.

Global education is not global in the sense of being *all-encompassing,* nor is it synonymous with international or foreign studies. Global education at the elementary school level might best be described as a focus of education that facilitates development of the child's sense of himself or herself as a personal and social being and member of the various human communities of which he or she is and is becoming a part—home and family, neighborhood, the school community, and the various dynamic communities of political, social and economic consequence that are in themselves globally interdependent.

Global education at the elementary level must draw as heavily on a curriculum of affect as on a curriculum of cognition. Without getting into the age-old controversy as to the relative importance of these two dimensions of curriculum—which should be seen more as complementary than competitive—it should be noted that it is the affective function which evokes *active* response based on feelings of joy, sadness, love, hate, fear, anger, sympathy, empathy, or any combination of a large variety of human emotions. Efforts to disregard or otherwise divorce the affective from the cognitive should be recognized as both futile and potentially damaging to the child's personal development. Weinstein and Fantini underscore this danger not only to the individual child but to all of human society:

> The pervasive emphasis on cognition and its separation from affect poses a threat to our society in that our educational institutions may produce cold, detached individuals, uncommitted to humanitarian goals. Certainly, a modern society cannot function without ever increasing orders of cognitive knowledge. Yet knowledge per se does not necessarily lead to desirable behavior. Knowledge can generate feeling, but it is

feeling that generates action. For example, we may know all about injustice to minorities in our society, but until we feel strongly about it we will take little action. A link to the affective, or emotional, world of the learner is therefore necessary. *Unless knowledge is related to an affective state in the learner, the likelihood that it will influence behavior is limited.*[1]

CHILDREN'S ATTITUDES TOWARD THE WORLD

A first step in designing programs for elementary school children is to discover their attitudes toward and knowledge about the world community and its members. Goodlad and others reported on an attempt to determine the extent to which children tend to think beyond their own self-interest with one small group of nine-to-twelve-year-olds in California.[2] We borrowed and adapted two of the questions Goodlad and his associates used to see how a representative sampling of fourth, fifth, and sixth graders around the country would respond. Teachers were asked not to name or discuss any specific world problems before this exercise. They simply said:

Most of us have things we would like to see changed. (1) What are some of the things you would like to see different in this world? (2) If you could give some message to all the people of the world, what would you tell them?[3]

Children were asked to respond without concern for number of answers, length, spelling, or grammar.

This open-ended approach is most valuable for elementary school children as it gives them a chance to explore and express their own values. Conversely, forced-choice multiple-response questions, although easier to tabulate, unnecessarily limit children's thinking. Data from inflexible forms are more likely to lead to inferences of questionable validity than are data more freely expressed in the child's own words. Note the openness and variety of ideas expressed in the following answers to the two questions.

A sixth-grade boy from Denver responded:

(1) I would give food to all the starving people, I would like to see all the lakes, oceans, and rivers cleaned up, I would start doing something about pollution and litter, and I would not let there be a World War III. (2) I would say to them to reduce their eating and spending habits, and to walk and ride bicycles instead of driving so much.

In contrast, his classmate writes:

(1) I would like to see our country start giving money to the U.S. instead of giving millions to other countries. The U.S. is in trouble and we our giving our money to others. (2) To stop all the fighting and have peace. If everyone in this world would have peace we wouldn't need all money spent for the army, navy, air force.

Both boys show evidence of some knowledge about global problems. Both are aware of shortages and, to some extent, both seem to have some idea of values as they consider where to place limited resources. However, the first boy seems to show empathy for others in need since, as far as we know, he does not differentiate between the "starving people" at home or those abroad. If global perspectives imply seeing all human beings as having common human needs and the right to the basic satisfaction of those needs, we might infer that the first boy has achieved a higher level of global consciousness than the second.

From the first boy's comments about pollution, followed by the message to reduce eating and spending habits and consume less fuel, he would appear to have some idea of interdependence, linking eating and spending habits and fuel consumption with a concern for starvation in some other areas and pollution in general. (Needless to say one cannot and should not try to read too much into such statements.)

Both boys seem to share a perspective on the undesirability of war, with the second boy concerned with the money spent on arms. It would be difficult to say whether his primary orientation here was humanitarianism or fiscal restraint, but he does seem to place a value priority on giving money to the United States (to meet constructive domestic needs?) rather than spending it on potentially destructive military armaments.

The following responses selected from a fifth-grade class in Scarsdale, New York, are interesting in that they show different levels of understanding of the interrelatedness and interdependence of the global resource system.

One boy seems to show an understanding that the earth's resources are finite.

(1) I would like to see pollution stop, I would like people to be more content with what they have. (2) Don't be greedy or stingy.

His classmate has the best of intentions toward all people, especially the poor, but he seems to evidence no sense of relationship between unlimited wants and limited resources.

(1) I would like to see all of our poor people in the world to be given help, and lots of it! If all of our prices went way down it would be nice. And also if there was better income and less taxes it would be great. But the best thing of all would be if there was no polution and the whole world was clean. That would be the nicest thing in my life. (2) I would say don't polute. It's your life that's going to waist.

Responses from fourth graders were generally shorter and reflected fewer organizing concepts. Fourth graders in one Greenwich, Connecticut, school did make several responses that seemed to show a sense of concern for human rights, sharing, and responsibility to other human beings. Answers included:

(1) Change the land so starving people would be able to grow more food. Change the world's attitude from being prejudiced. I would like to see places like Africa have more schools. Let people have the chance to get to know each other better! (2) Let's have peace on earth. Let's share with others. Love people of all colors.

(1) When pictures are taken of hungry children—don't just walk away—help the family. Those who can share should share. Everyone should have enough money to buy food. Better homes for people. Equal rights for people. People are all the same. All people are human and should be treated the same. Schools should collect money and give it to charity. Neglected or sick people should be helped. (2) Give everyone an equal chance. Reach out and share your love. Stop pollution. Tell people to pick up paper—stop pollution. Millionaires should donate money—and help buy things for poor people. Clean out homes and give clothes to poor people. People should be nice to one another and not hurt anyone's feelings. Teachers out of jobs should go help the poor people. Be friends.

These responses show some sense of the unity of all human beings, particularly such responses as "let people have the chance to get to know each other better" and "reach out and share your love."

Fourth graders in a Chicago inner-city school, which each year emphasizes a common global theme on a schoolwide basis, tended to extend the "reach out and share your love" concept. In the message-to-the-world response, three girls expressed their feeling of bond with other children by writing, "I would like to be on the other side of the world to be free with other children"; "I tell you this Message so that you can no that We love all the People In the World"; and "I would be glad to let everyone know I care for them and like them."

The spirit of caring and sharing in the Chicago school came through in most fourth-grade responses collected. A few showed some sense of limited resources, for example: "President to try to help people but when we can afford it," and, "Let's cooperate so we don't have anymore wars and let's help each other when we can afford to give."

One fifth-grade response from the same school shows greater understanding of the need for more than talking and good intentions. "I would like to change the poor people of the world and give them food, clothing and most of all love and care, but there are not enough people who care but I can't do it all by myself or with my classmates help."

READINESS FOR GLOBAL EDUCATION

Although children are clearly aware of and interested in other people and places throughout the world and research has found that they are much more aware of global problems than we have given them credit for, debate goes on as to the proper time to introduce a global perspective into the curriculum.

In the past it was believed that children's interests were primarily associated with their everyday experiences, the "here and now," and so the kindergarten and primary level curriculum was limited to the boundaries of the local community. Children were constantly reintroduced to the postman, the policeman, the fireman, and all the other community helpers. Seldom were they given opportunities to make simple cross-cultural comparisons of such helpers or to study the concept of community in other lands.

In a study which tested and interviewed 287 second-grade children, Lowry found that they already knew from 64 to 85 percent of the concepts they were about to be taught.[4] Research by Kaltsounis on third graders showed an average of 37 percent prior knowledge of cognitive social studies content to be studied, with "several children knowing nearly everything they were supposed to study during the following eight or nine months."[5] These and other studies support Torney's contention in Chapter 3 that children are handicapped because never-to-be repeated opportunities are crowded out of the curriculum by redundant and heavily provincial social studies content.

Bertrand Russell placed a higher priority on the early introduction of geography and history than of science and mathematics. Park writes of the importance Russell attached to freeing the imagination of the young mind from the limitations of the immediate "here and now" with which the child is surrounded.

> [Geography and history] can give food for the imagination when . . . properly taught with the use of pictures. It is "good" that the student knows that there are hot countries, dry countries, flat countries, mountainous countries, black people, brown people, white people, and red people. This kind of information will "diminish the tyranny of familiar surroundings over the imagination" (a point worthy of consideration), and will make possible the feeling that distant places really do exist. Geography would receive most attention in the teaching of very young children.[6]

As for the early introduction of history with a global and intercultural emphasis, Russell would teach the folly of divisions among races, nations, and creeds and emphasize historical characters who did the most to dispel darkness and bring about peace and the improvement of the human condition in this world.[7]

King agrees with Russell about the importance of introducing a global perspective early in the child's educational career:

> It seems redundant to continually state that early childhood educators have demonstrated the sensitivity and awareness of young children to their social scene. Therefore, the social education of the child in a world society and for a worldwide culture can begin in the early years.[8]

> We need to begin early in the education of the child to prepare him to live in a multicultural society and a world culture. Worldmindedness means a sense of global responsibility. . . . We are calling for beginning the teaching of world perspectives in early childhood education and not holding back until the later years of elementary school. . . .[9]

Although there is some controversy about the readiness issue among child development specialists, Preston points out that there is really no essential contradiction:

> A primary-grade teacher can assume, as would Bruner, that the geographical theme of man's use of the land can be taught at any age. In applying the principle of readiness in accordance with Piaget, the primary teacher emphasizes those applications which the child can observe and test at firsthand. The

central problem of readiness is a question of fitting instruction—whatever its content may be—to the mental horizons and thought pattern of children at each successive stage of growth, whatever the pace of that growth.[10]

He adds:

It well may be that the proper issue regarding readiness is not "here and now" versus "remote" but rather superficial study versus study which brings out underlying principles, relationships, and processes.[11]

One program that tries to free the child from the tyranny of the "here and now" and breaks with the traditional pattern of concentric circles which so often serve as walls between the young child and the real world is the Project Social Studies program of the University of Minnesota's Social Studies Curriculum Center.

Edith West, Professor of Education and Director of the Social Studies Curriculum Center at Minnesota, explains the principles around which this curriculum was designed:

First, the curriculum developers have followed the principle of moving from the simple to the complex in terms of the degree to which a topic can be made to seem concrete either because it is easy to relate to past meaningful experiences of children or because of the kinds of media which can be used to teach it. Some slides, films, and stories can make certain topics about far-away places just as concrete as other topics which pupils might study in their local community.

The principle of cross-cultural comparison has been added to the principle of moving from the simple to the complex. Information about families and communities in other cultures can be made meaningful through a process of comparison, of identifying both similarities and differences. The usefulness of this organization for curricular purposes parallels its usefulness among social scientists who are turning more and more to cross-cultural comparisons in their efforts to develop explanatory and predictive generalizations and theories which will not be culture bound. . . .

Finally, the part-whole principle of organizing content has been combined with the other two principles. This principle calls for the study of the parts of a broader whole first and then moves on to a study of that whole itself.[12]

Adaptations of this curriculum have been made and used in a variety of schools across the country, and evaluations and reports of progress achieved toward what we have identified as the broad goals of global education are encouraging.

It is sometimes charged by critics of cross-cultural approaches that young children lack the sophistication with which to identify and compare basic human needs and cultural universals. Therefore, they will instead focus on the exotic, the strange and different, thus further dividing human culture and reinforcing stereotypes. This is not a charge to dismiss lightly, and it is for this reason that teachers and curriculum workers must keep in mind at all times their goals and objectives as well as the principles and key concepts of the curriculum when working with children. For this same reason it is also important that the materials which are used to teach children about other cultures are of the best quality available.

One of the early evaluations of the quality and effects of using the Minnesota Project program with children in grades one through four was done by Marlowe Berg in several schools in the Minneapolis–St. Paul area from 1967 to 1969. In taped interviews, children using project materials showed a significantly larger number of responses noting similarities between peoples of different cultures, including their own, than did children in other classes in the same schools. Conversely, the study reported finding no significant differences in the number of responses noting differences between themselves and other peoples of the world. Additional findings of this study related to global education concerns include the following: (1) the experimental group made significantly more responses noting awareness of different environmental uses; (2) the experimental group made a significantly larger number of responses evidencing their awareness of the fact that different ways of living are learned; and (3) the experimental group made comments noting differences in skin color later in the course of the interviews than did the control group.[13]

Somewhat similar affective results as well as positive findings at the cognitive level were found in studies of the Minnesota Project by Sax and Kaltsounis in Bellevue, Washington (1968–69), by Charles Myers in rural south central Pennsylvania (1968–70), and by Ron Savage in Fairfax County, Virginia (1972–73). In these studies various forms of standardized tests were used.[14]

One of the most fully implemented programs adapted from the Minnesota Project can be found in the public schools of Chelmsford, Massachusetts. Charles Mitsakos, social studies coordinator at Chelmsford, describes the goals of the program as follows:

The basic responsibility of the social studies program is the development of informed citizens fully aware of the need for insuring the dignity and worth of the individual, for personal involvement in improving the society they have inherited, and for recognizing the interdependence of all peoples.[15]

The program is designed to help children learn how to be both nation-minded and world-minded. Children explore questions such as: How are we alike? How are we different? Do we understand why people do certain things the way they do? How do these ways compare with the ways of other peoples we have studied? What does this tell us about all people? Children hopefully develop the understanding implied in the words of Archibald MacLeish, "To see the earth as it truly is, small and blue and beautiful in that eternal silence where it floats, is to see ourselves as riders on the earth together, brothers on that bright loveliness in the eternal cold—brothers who now know they are truly brothers."[16]

The Chelmsford public schools introduced the Minnesota Project Social Studies program in September 1968. Prior to that time the social studies program at the primary level had been based on the more traditional "expanding horizons" approach which used a text and related materials.

In the transition period, Mitsakos worked closely with Edith West and a team of Chelmsford classroom teachers in adapting and implementing the Minnesota Project curriculum to the needs of Chelmsford classrooms. They started with the first grade in September 1968, and by the spring of 1972 fourth graders had experienced nearly four years of the program. At that time, using the same standardized achievement tests administered to fourth graders in 1968 and 1969, Chelmsford found "significant growth" in postimplementation scores. Reported in grade equivalent norms, the postimplementation group averaged 5.3 compared to 4.5 and 4.8 averages for the preimplementation groups. Chelmsford children at all grade levels scored significantly higher than the norm group on categories within the test such as organizing, interpreting, and evaluating information. Teachers and staff also reported increased interest in global cultures and broadening of perspectives.[17] Such reports seem to indicate that no aspect of the social studies program is being sacrificed to achieve better global education.

It should be noted that all the materials produced by Project Social Studies at Minnesota were placed in the public domain in 1968 and are available to any teacher or school system with no copyright restrictions. Inasmuch as there have been several descriptions of the curriculum and the various units suggested at each grade level, we shall not take space in this chapter to list the scope

and sequence. However, the reader who wants more specific information may review the evaluative report in the *Databook* available from the Social Science Education Consortium, Boulder, Colorado. The complete program is now available through the ERIC system (the ERIC Chess Center is also housed in Boulder). The revised materials for both teachers and students, now known as *The Family of Man,* are available from Selective Educational Equipment, Inc., Newton, Massachusetts.

A 1976 evaluation report on *The Family of Man* material conducted by Mitsakos in cooperation with the social education department of the School of Education at Boston University is now available.[18] This study concluded that a carefully designed primary-grade social studies program with a strong global education dimension can have a significant impact on the formation of attitudes and understandings that children develop toward foreign peoples. Subsequent treatment of the data in this study revealed that this more favorable view and more comprehensive understanding included the United States and its people as well as other nations and other peoples, a fact that negates the argument made by some skeptics that time spent on global education results in a lack of understanding of our own country.

OTHER USERS OF THE MINNESOTA PROJECT

In visiting and observing classrooms where the curriculum and objectives of the Minnesota Project have been adapted and implemented, I have been less interested in particular units or activities used than in seeing evidence of the development of sensitivities and perspectives that reflect global learnings. I include the following personal observations as well as information from correspondence with a variety of schools using the Minnesota curriculum for some very particular reasons. When people read about "experimental" programs, they get the feeling that they take place in "showcase" school districts in middle- and upper-class suburbs—and maybe too often this is true. Thus, there is often a lack of identification with these schools by small-town, rural, or inner-city educators. Unfortunately, they feel that it cannot be done in "our schools" and in "our situation." If by sharing some observations made in out-of-the-way small-town schools in rural areas and in inner-city schools in Chicago and New York I can dispel some of that feeling, this section of the chapter will have served its purpose.

In early January 1975, at the invitation of Everett Keach, a member of the team that developed the project at Minnesota and now a professor at the University of Georgia at Athens, I visited Follow-Through Centers in rural Georgia at Jasper and Tate in Pickens County. This red clay area where white and pink marble cliffs and rocky outcrops beam brightly in the sun from the sides of rolling hills rising into the southern end of the Appalachians is "Foxfire" country, an area rich in folklore and local pride, if not in worldly goods. Where else would one find a community in which more than 54 percent of the families have annual incomes of less than $5,000 and 70 percent of the males have not graduated from high school and yet the elementary school is covered with slabs of exquisite marble? And where else can one observe incongruities such as privies and other unpainted outbuildings set on foundations of marble?

But a child who has studied many cultures in a variety of different cultural and physical environments might not be surprised to learn that people in Pickens County, Georgia, like people around the globe, survey the resources in their immediate environment and make use of them to meet their needs wherever possible. Is it really incongruous to find a marble school at Tate, Georgia, when one of the largest centers of marble quarrying in this country is literally next door? What can children learn from this about economic concepts of relative scarcity and of relative costs of transportation of heavy building materials? Why are buildings in one place in the world built out of brick while in other places they are made of wood, sod, stone, or even ice? Focusing on such seemingly mundane matters can help fulfill Joyce and Nicholson's imperative to render the complex global scene comprehensible in terms children can understand.

By studying their local community along with communities around the globe, children can learn to use organizing concepts to help them see relationships, classify information, and guide their search for new learnings. Without the advantage of a curriculum which opens windows on a wide world of different environments, a child might consider it natural to have a marble school, marble steps, and pieces of marble to play with. After all, the material comes from the ground and seems to be lying around "everywhere."

I talked with nearly a dozen of the teachers and staff of the Pickens County Follow-Through Program at the Jasper center and later at Tate. They want the children they teach to have the opportunity to learn about the world beyond the pine-forested hills of north Georgia, and they perceive the Minnesota Project as a vehicle with which to accomplish their goal. Their primary purpose in helping these "disadvantaged" children learn about families and communities throughout the world is to help them learn about themselves as living, growing, important human beings.

Linda Pruitt, director of the Follow-Through Program, states:

> To work toward total development of the child, the need to involve many "significant others" in the educational process is evident. Provision of child needs for the "nutrients" of life—socially, physically and academically—will result in a positive self-concept in that child.[19]

(In Chapter 3, Torney pointed out that a positive self-concept may be prerequisite to the development of a global perspective.)

Pruitt further explains the emphasis on looking for things common to all human beings among different cultures and, in recognition of the developmental stages of young learners, how large photo prints and artifacts are used.

> In studying different cultures, children learn the customs and beliefs of many people. They come to know that, while there are many differences in the world's people, there are many more similarities than differences.
>
> To make social studies units come alive, pictures tell many details. Before they reach the stage of development in which symbols have a great deal of meaning, pictures and concrete objects are essential to understanding of children.[20]

To what degree do children in this program really understand the important ideas in these social studies units? I had the privilege of talking with and listening to a group of second graders in Mrs. Eubank's class following a lesson from the unit on a kibbutz family in Israel. I was particularly interested to learn what concepts stuck with them. Sitting on a rug, eyeball to eyeball, I asked how they felt about the boys and girls in Israel and the other countries they had studied. I asked what they thought were the most important things each child should have in order to live and grow up to be a happy, healthy human being.

The first responses, "food and clothing," were not too surprising. But the depth of feeling and understanding that seemed to come through in the subsequent responses almost made me think they had studied the United Nations Declaration of the Rights of the Child.[21] The next response was offered very quietly by a shy little girl: "We all need friends." This was followed by "house." A boy, in a spontaneous outburst that almost trailed off apologetically, said, "We all hafta have a name." Nodding agreement and reinforcement,

I asked why, and he seemed to respond with a feeling that it was important for each of us to have a sense of identity and to be able to call our friends by name. A little girl with glasses said, "We all need eyes to see with," and almost immediately another child added, "And we need to be able to walk and run." A short discussion followed about the importance of being healthy and how all children need some health and medical care at times.

With a shy little smile, one youngster sitting at the side of the group looked up and said simply, "Play and have fun," which struck me again as being very close to the wording of the Declaration of the Rights of the Child. Another boy said, "You hafta have English." Without responding I turned to one side of the group and spoke a few words in Spanish and then to the other side and asked a question in German. The boy who had mentioned English laughed and said, "That's not English." Again there was some thoughtful discussion of how we need to know English to talk to some people, but we need other languages, too, if we are going to learn to know and talk with our world neighbors. At this point it was nearly time to move on to another classroom, and one little girl who had not yet spoken said slowly but clearly, "We all need love and somebody to care about us." Obviously, these children had achieved the sense of moral empathy with other people that Joyce and Nicholson feel is imperative for development of a global perspective.

In that short discussion and in their own words, these Follow-Through children from rural Georgia had touched upon nearly every significant point in the Declaration of the Rights of the Child. I left copies of the full text of these rights for their class to examine, and the more I thought about it the more certain I was that every child should be challenged to think about these basic rights in one form or another.

As we drove away from the school and past the marble quarry, I remarked to Everett Keach that what I had seen was what global education is really all about. If we could just provide the kind of curriculum, committed and competent teachers, and warm human environment that I observed in the Follow-Through Program at Tate School, we would have the answer to part of our search for an exemplary program in global education.

Gulfport, Mississippi, the number-one banana port on the Gulf of Mexico, is also part of the Follow-Through system which uses the Minnesota Project curriculum through its cooperation with the Mathamagenic Activities Program of the University of Georgia. Other programs linked to this particular Follow-Through system are found primarily in the southeast, but some are as far away as

Pocatello, Idaho. The Gulfport program is representative of a school district in a small to medium-sized city in contrast to the relative isolation of Pickens County. Nearly 25,000 military personnel are concentrated around Gulfport. Alice Smith, director of the program there, told me that they make frequent use of parents and other military personnel to bring in a wide variety of artifacts from different parts of the world. At one point, they had scheduled resource persons just back from Asia, Africa, Europe, and the Middle East.

After using the Minnesota social studies curriculum for several years, Smith said that she was most impressed with the importance placed on different forms of music and the arts. She observed the development of new sensitivities in the children, teachers, and parents as a result of the richness of the cultures studied in each unit. Certainly the beautiful color pictures that were sent to me showed evidence of an abundance of activities and projects that children had experienced in studying the Hausa family, the Japanese family, the Soviet family, the kibbutz family of Israel, and the Quechua of Peru.

PROVIDING EXPERIENCES FOR ELEMENTARY SCHOOLCHILDREN

If we are to concern ourselves with the total experience of the child, we must make that experience come alive as much as possible. The large pictures and concrete objects used in the Follow-Through programs, stories, films, role playing, and other drama experiences help. But the ideal experience in learning about another culture is to live in that culture. Many elementary-age boys and girls have traveled to distant lands with parents who are in the military, government service, or in business with overseas branches, and many older students in secondary and college level programs have participated in international exchanges (see Chapter 7). Although uncommon at the elementary school level, there are a few such programs in particular which have been quite successful.

EXCHANGE PROGRAMS

Burke Elementary School (named for Admiral Arleigh H. Burke) in Boulder, Colorado, had an international exchange program which involved the whole school and its neighboring community, in spirit if not in actual exchange. The exchange was planned well in advance so that children of both Burke and Green Hills Elementary School in Mexico City could study each other's culture and language before actually boarding the plane. Phil Martinez, principal at Burke, explained the program as follows:

> The children are matched by sex and interests and assigned to a host child and exchange family. Eighteen children from Burke spent July 1–21 [1974] in Mexico living with the exchange family and participated in about six group social and cultural outings, besides the visits of the individual families. My wife and I acted as chaperones and stayed at the house of the English department chairman.
>
> The Mexican children visited the Burke families from July 25–August 15 with six functions. The Burke community, being a self-contained area, were aware of the children from Mexico, because they were visible playing with their children and their neighbors.[22]

In addition, a full-school-year exchange involved two students per year.

Pictures were taken of the Burke group's trip, and the participating children became resource persons throughout the school, sharing their experience with those who were not able to go. Two sixth-grade boys, Craig Perzan from Burke and his exchange mate, Ricardo Vasquez from Green Hills, presented in every classroom a slide program with a discussion about boys and girls and their culture in Mexico.

I asked Phil Martinez what the basic goals of this program were. Was it primarily a bicultural experience program or was it envisioned as something larger? He responded that it was part of the total educational experience at Burke, in which the goal is to develop broader perspectives and "to learn that people all over the world are very much alike, having the same human needs and problems."

The total cost for each child, paid by the family, was $130.00 including airfare, ground transportation, and administrative cost. Theoretically there was no room and board cost. Although the host family had to support a guest, their own child was absent for an equal amount of time. Martinez reported, "It was a voluntary program that received increasing support not only from the participating families but the community as a whole."

If this were only an interesting experiment in which a few children were able to travel and experience another culture, it might still be worthwhile as far as it went. But this program's planning of educational goals and total school programs to multiply the effects of the exchange on the lives of children in the two communities in two nations went beyond that. (More information on student exchange programs can be found in Chapter 7.)

Another program still in its initial steps involves children and their teachers in an exchange of ideas and articles through various forms of communication including letters, audiotapes, photographs, pictures, local lesson materials, cultural artifacts, magazines, newspapers, stamps, currency, TV guides, recipes, road maps, city maps, postcards, and a series of charts made by the children sharing ages, heights, weights, hair color, and other physical characteristics of each class. According to Carol Sarabun, social studies teacher in the fifth/sixth grade wing at Parkway Elementary School in Greenwich, Connecticut, the idea is to share as much information as possible between the Connecticut children and their counterparts in Manchester, England. Working through a sociologist and lecturer in education at the University of Birmingham in England, the teachers and children involved in this project hope to chart and compare sociological data on their families and to involve other schools in different nations in order to compare their initial findings. Though limited in scope at this time, the intent is to help children draw generalizations that can eventually be tested for validity in a global context.

Whether a school participates in an exchange of student representatives or letters, tapes, and other forms of communication along with a variety of cultural artifacts, a well-planned exchange program that offers young minds as many kinds of intercultural sharing as possible cannot help but provide children with a global perspective and add richness and beauty to their learnings.

THE MULTICULTURAL CENTER IDEA

Not all children will be able to experience other cultures directly. A multicultural experience center in Houston, Texas, offered children who might not otherwise participate in international exchanges or visits an opportunity to experience other cultures without leaving their city. The program fulfills another of Joyce and Nicholson's imperatives—to promote pluralism and allow individual cultures to flourish and enrich one another.

From the outside, People Place looked very much like any other school building in an inner-city area. But on the upper level of Anson Jones Elementary School were six most unusual classrooms, each devoted to a different country or culture. What made it most exciting was the "hands on" experience offered to each child who entered. Much more than a well-stocked museum of realia, pictures, and cultural motif and design, People Place allowed children to dress in the costumes and clothing of the culture, participate in a variety of games, play different musical instruments, taste some of the national foods and spices, and interact with a teacher/resource person native to the particular culture being visited.

The six classrooms—transformed into replicas of cultures from Africa, China, Germany, India, Mexico, and USA/Texas—were coordinated to allow for the development of comparative cultural relationships. The native resource teachers and the supervisory staff made every effort to provide a series of authentic multicultural experiences, choosing those least likely to suggest or reinforce cultural stereotyping. Each exhibit included carefully selected samples of currency, art, music, literature, games, food, clothing, and a replica of a typical household. Thus, children had a better chance to view cultural differences as varied responses to the same basic human needs, a concept critical to the development of global awareness.

The planners of People Place realized that not all Houston elementary children could be served directly by that one facility. Furthermore, to reach a significant number of children, no individual child could spend more than one morning or afternoon there. But teachers in the seventy-two Houston elementary schools involved in the 1975–76 school year (chosen on the basis of being "most racially isolated") were encouraged to extend multicultural learnings to their own schools and classrooms.

The actual visit may be only one exciting highlight of intercultural study for many of Houston's elementary-age children. Nearly 15,000 children per year visited People Place, but by sharing their experiences with other children in their own school, they affected a much larger number than could otherwise be accommodated.

By incorporating some features of exchange programs, the total program served to increase understanding among various ethnic groups in Houston as well as to help Houston residents understand people of different countries. By bringing in children from three different schools for each session, People Place provided a primarily tri-ethnic grouping in which children shared their multicultural experiences. The total group at each sesssion was divided into smaller tri-ethnic groups for visits to each culture. Then they were assembled again at a final session in the USA/Texas room to bring into focus the many contributions of each culture and their interrelationships within the United States and Texas.

The most important educational objectives of this program include developing respect for other peoples, developing a positive self-image, and teaching the interdependence of all peoples. With such objectives clearly in mind, a project of this nature, varied in size and scope according to local need and funding, could be a most important component in building a global education program.

SCHOOLS IN THE INNER CITY WHICH REACH OUT TO THE WORLD

It has been noted elsewhere in this book that global education is often thought of as "elitist" and that it is only relatively affluent suburban schools that have the inclination and resources to seek a global perspective for their programs. Throughout this book we have tried to offer examples to show that this assumption is incorrect. I have already described the Follow-Through programs in rural Georgia. I would like to discuss now some programs I observed in inner-city schools that attempt to promote a global perspective among their "less advantaged" students.

In visiting, observing, and talking with teachers and students at P.S. 173 in New York, literally in the shadow of the George Washington Bridge, I found a strong sense of what I would identify as a global perspective. This old, five-story brick building, with its steel-fenced stairways and bleak, battleship-gray corridors built on an island of concrete and asphalt, seemed an unlikely place to look in a search for global education programs. But in fact, the search led to the discovery of a kind of global village behind that harsh façade. Among the more than 1,000 students enrolled from kindergarten through sixth grade are children from over sixty different countries (either first or second generation), and the cycle of movement of old and new immigrants is continuing.

Irene "Kelly" Sonnenfeld, an art teacher with a master's degree in social studies education, explained how this movement of new students into P.S. 173 from all over the world brings firsthand communication at the children's own level. One boy who had recently come from Bangladesh told how he and his family had lived in large sewer drainpipes before emigrating. Felix, a tall, handsome boy from Ecuador, told how his father gathered the family together after the third disastrous earthquake hit their area. But the dimension of suffering and deprivation was not the only communication he brought to his classmates. Felix brought with him from Ecuador a richness of human spirit and cultural heritage which he exemplified in his person and in his art work. I happened to meet him again at the subway station following my visit, and as he said hello and beamed recognition from a warm and confident smile, the cold January chill seemed to fade away.

This is a school where children are making materials such as intercultural calendars and booklets with favorite recipes from around the world, which they exchange at school and share with the community. This is a school where different ethnic holidays are celebrated by songs and dances shared by children from all ethnic backgrounds, a school where Brotherhood Week is a major focus of curriculum and instruction and where the spirit of that week spills out into the weeks and months preceding and following.

This is a school in which upper-grade children are "producing" and "publishing" materials for the primary children. This is a school in which a bulletin board features "Our Most Recent Letter from Our New Foster Child, Jaime, from Ecuador." In Spanish and English, Jaime's letter tells of the way he celebrated Christmas, of the Nativity scenes, and about the "Ano Viejos" or rag dolls representing the old year which are burned on December 31 at midnight.

This is P.S. 173, a community of children with ties all around the world who worked for months making artworks and crafts, collected items from their homes and the neighborhood, and then held a bazaar in which they raised $1,000 for UNICEF's World Child Emergency Fund. Mrs. Sonnenfeld, who supervised the project, and Mrs. Milner, a sixth-grade teacher whose class arranged and managed the bazaar, explained that these children had no money of their own to give but wanted to take on this project to help other children less fortunate than themselves. Maybe Felix and his friends at P.S. 173 living on an island at the foot of the George Washington Bridge have learned something about no man being an island and about how to reach out and build bridges between cultures. They have certainly acquired a belief in their own ability to be efficacious in the improvement of the world, another of the imperatives for global education set out in Chapter 4.

In many ways Louisa May Alcott Elementary School on Chicago's North Side is very similar to P.S. 173. The school reflects a wider range of socioeconomic backgrounds in that it draws from the luxury apartment buildings and condominiums on or near the lakefront, an area sometimes referred to as the "Gold Coast," as well as from the inner city. Alcott has about half the enrollment of P.S. 173 and reflects a somewhat more stable population. As the principal, Mary McManus, said to me on my visit in November 1974, "Our student body looks like a group from the United Nations." Although for years they recognized the rich diversity of cultures represented in their school and drew from them for their social studies and related subjects, Alcott has developed a new program specifically with a global perspective that has added many new strengths to their total educational program.

One weakness so often overlooked by educators—even social studies teachers—is that by allowing too much separation of curriculum into social studies and other specific subjects at the elementary level, we limit and even subvert the very learnings we hope to develop through global education. To avoid this pitfall, McManus and her staff worked closely with the children to develop a theme or organizing concept that would infuse the total educational program with a global perspective. For the 1973–74 school year, they decided on global interdependence, which the children chose to express with the lines from the Walt Disney song, "There is so much that we share/That it's time we're aware./It's a small world after all."[23]

The global education program at Alcott included Head Start, kindergarten, and all the regular grades plus the EMH classes, the reading resource center, the library, the physical education program, the learning disability room, and the Teaching English as a Second Language program. Space does not begin to allow a description of the many varied units, activities, projects, and regular assembly programs through which the dynamic developments from this global education program were shared with the school as a whole and the parents and community. However, Alcott publishes a mimeographed 24-page booklet each year that gives many insights into what can be done with a full-year schoolwide commitment to global education.

Impressed with what he had heard about Alcott School, Rick Soll, a *Chicago Tribune* reporter, decided to go back to fifth grade to get a story on what was happening in the elementary classrooms of the seventies. He spent a full week at Alcott in 1973 and came back again in 1974 to spend another week with the same class as sixth graders. The following excerpts from a series of articles written by a reporter, not an educator, tend to confirm my observations based on a two-day visit.

Soll found the element of expanding perspectives on the world in the language arts program:

> Every day I spend in Miss Byrne's classroom makes me more and more aware of how wide the world has become for people who are 10. Their neighborhoods are only home bases—they grow up in the world. We traveled the globe yesterday during a

creative writing assignment that demanded a description of the street on which each of us would like to live.

He gives his reactions the following day:

> We read our creative writing assignments out loud, descriptions of the street on which each of us would like to live. The street locations varied, but they were all held together by the common cement of one word—peacefulness—and my classmates made it clear that they hope for a world where "peacefulness" is a state of mind and not just the opposite of war.

On his last day in the fifth grade, he describes an assembly program:

> Standing on the stage in the auditorium, they sang "Everything is Beautiful," and there was no doubt that everything was. The little Japanese girl stood next to the little Chinese boy who stood next to the little girl from the Philippines who stood next to the little black girl who stood next to the little white boy from Germany. And together, smiling their nervous smiles and rocking back and forth and into one another, they sang about a beautiful world filled with beautiful people.[24]

A year later, after spending a week in sixth grade at Alcott, Soll observed:

> Changes occurred which cannot be calculated by tabulating new test scores or by observing neater penpersonship. It takes more time than that to notice the subtle and remarkable ways in which a child's mind grows and begins to reach out for a larger chunk of the world.
> *It is in their relationship with the world as a whole that my friends in Alcott School registered their finest progress.* [Italics mine.]
> Times have changed. Nothing is fixed and the world is infinite for today's young people. And both the teacher and the pupils seem happy in this world of controlled doubt.[25]

During 1974–75, the schoolwide global education theme was "The Story Teller in Cultures around the World." Again from the youngest child in the school to the oldest, a wide world of wonder and excitement linked old and young of every ethnic and cultural background together in their love of storytelling. McManus reports that studies ranged from the simplest primary stories through fairy tales, myths, legends, and other folklore to the study of other forms of storytelling from ancient times through medieval periods and the building of the great cathedrals as upper-grade children studied the stories told in the stained glass windows of the cathedral at Chartres. All children enjoyed the stories told through pantomime and puppeteers. Alcott children learned how traveling storytellers borrowed and shared, spreading ideas from one culture to another and bringing people closer together long before instantaneous communication and more rapid transportation systems made it an increasingly "small world."

But global learnings were not limited to stories and storytelling even though they provided a focal point. In addition to studies relating to the main theme, children at Alcott put their global learning into action. They feel a part of their family is involved whenever a disaster strikes anywhere in the world. Following the reports of suffering and need in the wake of Hurricane Fifi in 1974, three fifth-grade girls organized an effort to help the victims in Honduras. Yolanda Fronteny, Waleska Concepcion, and Diana Meyers spoke to other classes, made posters, enlisted helpers, and in so doing contributed to the education of all the children of the school in terms of sensitivity to human needs and information on Central America. In my interview with Yolanda I found that they also learned much about organization and administration of such projects and the problems of storage and transportation.

In a mimeographed booklet Alcott published on its schoolwide theme for 1975–1976, McManus wrote:

> The selection of the Bicentennial as the Alcott School theme for 1975–76 was not only appropriate for our nation's two hundredth anniversary but also a natural outgrowth of our previous years' themes "It's a Small, Small World" and the "Storyteller and World Cultures."

And in a telephone interview she emphasized how the contributions of other nations and cultures were used to give a greater multicultural and global perspective to the bicentennial theme. But lest we give the impression that Alcott, in its efforts to provide a global perspective for children, is less concerned with competencies in the three R's, it should be noted that the 1976–77 global theme was "Reading for Global Understanding."

In my final interview with Miss McManus, she summed up the philosophy behind their global education program. "We believe in what we are doing, and we put much effort into trying to get our students from all the different ethnic, racial, and socioeconomic backgrounds to develop a feeling and a perspective of being a part of each other and caring for the welfare of each other. We do it because we *want* to—but we also do it because we *have* to, if we are to live together in our community." This statement seems to have a note of quiet urgency in it that may well need further emphasis in many of our schools today.

"AUTHORITATIVE" MATERIALS THAT SUBVERT RATHER THAN SUPPORT

Little has been said thus far about materials used in the elementary school that may help to develop global perspectives. Can we assume that curriculum materials, textbooks, and other school-approved supplementary materials are all positive or at least neutral in this area? Unfortunately, we cannot. We do not have to search too far to find textbooks, reference books, and even curriculum guides that work against the formation of global perspectives. For example, the *World Book Encyclopedia Dictionary,* generally considered to be of good quality and recommended for elementary schoolchildren, had the following entries under *global* and *globalism,* which we cite in their entirety:

global   1. of the earth as a whole; world-wide: global unrest. He became a freewheeling idea man on global affairs *(Time).* 2. shaped like a globe; spherical.

globalism   1. the principle of the interdependence of the entire world and its peoples. 2. concern for the rest of the world at the expense of national self-development and self-interest.[26]

We do not have to run a semantic differential study on *unrest* and *freewheeling* to discover the negative connotations initially introduced to the child here. Fortunately, the second meaning of *global* stays in the realm of geometrics. But what then of the error of omission of other important and valid meanings of the word *global?*

In defining *globalism* at least the principle of world interdependence is introduced first, but the writer of this entry either consciously or unconsciously has declared that globalism is in opposition to national self-development and self-interest. The "authority of print" is a weighty factor for children, especially something as precisely "correct" as a dictionary. Is this not the place children are taught to turn to if there is ever any doubt as to what a word means?

But what is most disheartening is to find curriculum materials with objectives purposefully planned (we must assume with every good intent) to develop global perspectives and to discover that the supporting material actually subverts the achievement of those objectives. The following example is the basis for a complete fourth-grade study, a nine-month period in the lives of children in their most formative years. It was sent to me a few years ago as an "exemplary" model of an elementary guide heavily concerned with global and international study.* The two paragraphs below are taken from an "Overview of Social Studies—Level Four."

The nine-year-old pupil continues to broaden his understandings of life around him. Through an in-depth study of our state of _____, the pupil should be able to make some generalizations about the economic development of the state and how its topography, climate and resources have affected this development. Through comparison and contrast with other areas of the world the understanding of our state is enhanced.

The study of Canada and Mexico, neighbors to the north and south of the United States, leads to a realization of the important contributions of these areas to our economic and cultural development. Man adapts to his environment as he meets his basic needs for food, clothing and shelter. People of all countries are interdependent in our present civilization.

The intent of these introductory statements is clearly to develop conceptual understanding of the commonality of all humankind, the basic needs shared by all, and the interdependence of all humankind. However, the frame of reference that is suggested by the subsequent questions asked of the nine-year-olds as they begin their study works against the development of such concepts.

For example, Unit I starts out, "Why Is Our State an Important State?" This may seem innocent enough, but what are the implications of such a question? Are certain states more important then others? If so, on what criteria are they to be judged? Is Rhode Island least important because it is the smallest, or is it Alaska because it is remote? These implications could have been avoided had the unit been introduced in an interdependent frame of reference. If the question were to read, "Why Is Our State Important to the Growth and Development of Our Country?," the concept of the part-whole relationship would have been stressed.

---

*These comments are not made with cynicism, as the guides that the examples are taken from for the most part reflect a thoughtful blending of goals and supporting topics and activities that were far more world-oriented than many guides.

Unit II has a similar problem—but in a wider context—when it asks, "What Makes Canada an Important Country?" Though the idea that there are important and unimportant countries may be valid on the basis of certain specific criteria, the unit headings which follow do not even focus on the importance of states or countries. Worst of all, it seems that the curriculum writers could not bring themselves to say in Unit III, "What Makes Mexico an Important Country?" Instead they broke the parallel pattern previously established and wrote, "How Do the People of Mexico Meet Their Needs?"

Why is it that Canadians are shown as important while Mexicans are shown to have needs? Are these "needy" people likely to evoke the image of important persons in the minds of nine-year-olds who have been led to associate "importance" with citizens of their state and of Canada but "needs" with the people of Mexico? While teaching the concept of the interdependence of all peoples is the intended educational objective, it would seem that by implication the frame of reference is set for the child to perceive one group of people as needy and thus dependent rather than interdependent. And as for affective learning and development of self-concept, how might a child of Mexican-American heritage feel about such references to our light-skinned Anglo neighbor to the north, who speaks "our" language, and our darker-skinned Hispanic neighbor to the south, who speaks an "unfamiliar" tongue?

Unit IV is introduced by the title, "How Do the People in South America Secure Their Needs and Wants?" If there was any doubt in the child's mind about who is needy and who is important, this heading would remove them. Certainly the people of South America and Mexico have the same basic needs as do the Canadians and the Americans. Would it not have been more consistent with the stated objectives to introduce all four units with questions about how each group of people is important to the others and how each group meets its common basic human needs?

Furthermore, by switching concepts in the introductory portion of the four successive units, there is a much greater risk that the perceptual centration phenomenon referred to by Torney in Chapter 3 might interfere with the child's ability to relate the importance of all human beings and the common needs of all human beings. This conceptual linkage is critical in the development of the child's concept of interdependence.

Items which are much less obvious and certainly far less damaging nevertheless can be invisible barriers to developing global perspectives. To illustrate this point briefly, consider the following sentences taken from a fine guide developed by some of the top educators in a state department of education.

> The student is in daily contact with media forms which continuously introduce him to happenings within as well as outside his community and nation. Via television and radio the average first grader is already exposed to national problems such as pollution, inflation, and crime; to international issues such as war, trade, and cultural misunderstandings; and to other topics dealing with his political, social, and economic well-being.[27]

By placing pollution and inflation (and even crime) in a context that categorizes them as "national" problems, we unnecessarily risk limiting our perception of these problems as global in scope. Certainly the biological and economic well-being of all the world's peoples depends upon treating pollution and inflation as global problems. To suggest that national inflation is not directly related to international trade in our increasingly interdependent world is to prepare a curriculum for an era long gone.

The following paragraph, commenting on curriculum guides and the lack of focus on international understanding found in them, should be read carefully before checking the end-of-chapter note to see the date of publication.

> Even very young children in the nursery school, kindergarten, and lower elementary grades are having contacts with the outside world. Curriculum guides for these age levels focus attention on such themes as "living together in the home," and "school and neighborhood" but rarely mention "international understanding." Yet, because the interests and needs of children help to determine the curriculum in most schools, relations with other peoples have become a vital part of the learning experiences. Today all peoples are within the enlarged "neighborhood" of American boys and girls.[28]

Our "today" is now well over two decades later and, as we have seen, there are many more curriculum guides which mention international understanding and global perspectives. The problem now is to evaluate carefully to see that ongoing programs and their supporting materials are of a quality consistent with the high goals we establish for global education.

The truth of the matter is that it is not an easy task to find high-quality materials for children that have as a primary focus the development of global perspectives. This tends to lead educators to the logical conclusion that we will have to make do with what is available. There is a substantial school of thought on that subject that draws another conclusion.

Ann Pellowski, Director-Librarian of the Information Center on Children's Cultures, warns:

> The popular adage "Every little bit helps" simply cannot apply when one is concerned about introducing children to other cultures. If the material is derogatory instead of objective, or vivid but totally inaccurate, chances are it will hinder rather than help. It would be better not to attempt an introduction to another people if it cannot be done with sensitivity and care.[29]

Pellowski is an authority on international and intercultural understanding in the field of children's books and has consulted and written widely on this topic. In a January 1975 memo commenting on intercultural and global dimensions in children's books in the seventies, she wrote:

> In the past five years, there has been a dramatic increase in both the number and quality of children's books dealing with ethnic or intercultural situations, but these are not generally global in perspective; rather, they tend to restrict themselves to one or two regions or countries, or, if they are global in terms of coverage, they limit their subject to one theme, such as the energy crisis or the food situation. All too frequently, the point-of-view is entirely American, discussing the global situation mostly as it affects us in the U.S., and only peripherally as it appears from the point of view of Asians or Africans or others.[30]

Although the picture is not yet bright in the quality dimension, there is evidence that it is improving.* Children's books, particularly textbooks, are being reviewed far more carefully than in the past by most publishers, if not out of a new awareness of their social and cultural responsibilities, at least out of the knowledge that organized groups are looking over their shoulders for inaccuracies and biases. Women's rights groups, children's rights groups, religious and secular groups, black, Chicano, native American, and various other ethnic groups are taking an ever more active part at the local, state, and national levels in determining what should be

---

*Sources listing books for elementary schoolchildren will be found in the Annotated Bibliography at the end of this volume.

taught about cultures, ethnic groups, races, religions, and sexes.[31] For the most part this has made a positive contribution to the area of global education. But problems do arise when one group gains the power through pressure group tactics to dictate their point of view to the detriment of all others.

One good example that demonstrates how textbook publishers are responding to the rapidly expanding need for high-quality globally oriented materials at the elementary school level can be found in a new social studies series called *Windows on our World.** In a fifth-level unit, "The United States in the Global Community," the authors use a case study to show how one community, Columbus, Ohio, is linked to the rest of the world. The following excerpts might well be studied from the perspective of one's own local community with thoughtful consideration given to incorporating a similar case study in any community that is searching for promising components with which to build an exemplar program of global education.

> Look at the map of the United States on page 464. Can you find Ohio? It is one of the North Central States, just below the Lakes. Columbus is near its center. How many miles is it from Columbus to Canada? To Mexico? To the Atlantic Ocean? To the Pacific Ocean? How can a city so far from other countries be linked to them? We shall soon see. [32]

In the pages that follow, the authors introduce families in the community who receive friends from abroad and who travel to other parts of the world. The children of the Martin family show their father two new toys, a whistle made in Germany and a racer made in Denmark. As father and mother put groceries away, they think of the bananas from Honduras, the cocoa from Africa, coffee from South America, and mandarin oranges from Asia, and they decide to make a family game of finding ways their household depends on other parts of the world.

> So that very evening all the Martins went on a "treasure hunt." They searched in drawers, closets, and cabinets for anything that had a label or stamp showing that it had come from some foreign land. It made quite a list.
> Then Helen and Tom Martin explained that there were

---

*Space does not permit a review of all the newer elementary social studies materials. We do not imply by the example cited any endorsement of a particular publisher's materials. Rather we have chosen to quote extensively from one section of one book of this series which develops an exemplary idea at the elementary school level.

dozens of other things in their home that had come from distant countries. Often these were made in America from something grown in another country or on another continent.[33]

The Martin family is shown later that evening gathered in the living room discussing the newspaper, which includes news about eleven countries. They find that their magazines and books include many other countries. In the background, a stereo album of a British rock group is playing. A television news broadcast brings more of the world to them.

Subsequent pages use Columbus as a case study to examine the many ways it is part of the global community. Lists of imports and exports, the different languages that are used to communicate with other countries, and the international language of music and art that are shared through museums and other cultural institutions in Columbus are examined with questions designed to stimulate young readers' minds about world links to their own communities. Relatives overseas, foreign students here, churches in Columbus with world contacts, banks with international departments, businesses that deal with other business concerns abroad, and local branches of multinational corporations are discussed.

One section of this unit helps simplify some of the more abstract links with the world, such as feelings and beliefs, by stating some beliefs and immediately associating them with examples of action that demonstrate the concrete forms which abstract ideas can take. Pointing out that with citizenship comes a responsibility to try to make the world a better place, the authors call attention to local involvement in the annual UNICEF Day activities in Columbus and how UNICEF helps needy children in over 100 different countries. They also link beliefs with action by noting how Columbus, led by the black community and a local radio personality, raised over fifty thousand dollars for the African Relief Drive following a severe drought in West Africa.

In our efforts to promote global awareness we must not forget the importance of the child's awareness of the local community. I have become increasingly convinced that to be effective any realistic program of global education for children must have much of its roots in their own daily lives and the relationships of their own communities to the rest of the world. Everyone lives in some local community on this globe, and as valuable as it most certainly is to see the world from space to gain new perspectives, we must not overlook the individual child and his/her experience base in a given part of that global whole.

Certainly this is recognized in the development of the frame of reference and varied supporting material used in the "Big Blue Marble," a half-hour program presented daily on many public television stations and one of the finest productions ever to appear in children's television programming.

The following words are sung by children in the opening scene of the program while a view of the earth from space is shown:

> The earth's a big blue marble when you see it from out there
> The sun and moon declare our beauty's very rare
> We sing pretty much alike
> Enjoy spring pretty much alike
> Peace and love we all understand
> And laughter we use the very same brand
> Our differences, our problems from out there there's not much
>   trace
> Our friendships they can place while looking at the face
> Of the big blue marble in space.[34]

Although the words link unfamiliar concepts such as the solar system and space with the common experience of friendship and laughter, the critical element of relating global perspectives to the direct experience and interest of the child is assured by having the camera zoom in on real children from every part of the globe actively participating in the daily life of their respective communities. The global frame of reference is continually reinforced by frequent shots of an animated character who becomes a globe on which the places to be visited are located in relation to the rest of the world. We would do well to observe and learn from this series. If by chance it is not scheduled in your viewing area, you might want to find out why.

An example of supplementary materials that recognize the need to relate the global frame of reference to ideas and institutions that directly affect the lives of children and their communities is an inexpensive elementary teacher's kit available from the U.S. Committee for UNICEF, *Teaching about Global Interdependence in a Peaceful World.*[35] It is a combination of resource and teaching material with a background and guide for primary and upper-grade teachers. It includes three distinct subunits incorporating simple simulation and role-playing exercises for children at all levels.

One part of the kit develops the idea of global interdependence through discussion and role playing about health and disease. It shows that in all parts of the world people must recognize that they are interdependent—dependent on each other—if they are to stop the spread of "killer diseases." Efforts by every nation to stamp out smallpox are related to the child's own experience of vaccination upon entrance to school or to shots or vaccinations for other diseases. Also, direct experiences with illnesses children in the class have had are used to illustrate the human suffering and loss of productivity that result from epidemics in any part of the world.

Another lesson linking language arts and social studies with interest in stamps and collecting starts with Benjamin Franklin as the first postmaster general and uses a simple five-nation simulation exercise in which groups of children devise rules and regulations for individual countries without regard to the postal regulations and procedures of the others. As they write letters and try to send international mail without first negotiating agreements with recipient countries and those through which the mail must pass, they discover how interdependent they really are.

In a later round of this exercise, the children participate in a simulated international conference similar to the one that created the Universal Postal Union one hundred years ago. They finally realize that no one nation could establish a worldwide mail system and that each nation depends on every other nation to carry its global mail—a fact of global interdependence that touches families and businesses in every community.

Other similar points are made in this kit and a new companion kit, *Teaching about the Child and World Environment*.[36] The three units in the latter relate worldwide environmental concerns for the earth, the oceans, and the atmosphere to the child's own experience and develop the idea that we all have a vital common interest in our environment. The two complete kits can be ordered from the U.S. Committee for UNICEF.

One way to get around the problem of scarce materials for global education is to produce them in the classroom with children. Care must be taken to ensure quality, and the same criteria and questions applied in evaluating commercial materials can be used as part of the production process. This is particularly appropriate for the elementary level, as we have noted before that global education material is relatively scarce here, and it is an ideal way to actively involve children in cross-age activity—that is upper grade children can prepare material and work with younger children as was noted in the world-centered schools of Middleston in Chapter 1.

In P.S. 173 in New York, described earlier, fifth and sixth grade children decided they wanted to produce something of their own that expressed how they felt about themselves and the people of the world. They put their messages into illustrated books and materials they made for themselves and for younger children in the school. One such book, *Trees Are Like People,* reads as follows:

> Trees are like people. They come in a variety of sizes, shapes and colors. Some are very old and some are young. A tree can be very fat or very thin. Some may be tall, but others are short. One tree will live all alone. Others will mingle in a large group. A tree may live in many different places, warm or cold. And nature endows them with an assortment of glorious colors.[37]

But there is no way words could ever convey the beauty and warmth of expression shown in the children's illustrations and their love and concern for all of humankind.

TEACHING GLOBAL REALITIES TO CHILDREN

This brings us to another dimension of reality and experience in global education for the child. Joyce and Nicholson charged us to teach global education in terms faithful to reality. While it is true that there is much that is rich and beautiful in this world, the child whom we may try to shield from awareness of the deprivation and suffering that also exist is deprived in another way. Global education, if it is to be a valid program, must deal with those aspects of the interdependence of all human beings that are not so rich and beautiful. In a special issue of *Social Education* on "Global Hunger and Poverty," I discussed the "doomsday approach" versus "oversimplification."

> Two additional problems that must be considered in teaching global interdependence at the elementary level are: (1) focusing on negative factors to the extent that children lose hope; and (2) oversimplifying highly complex problems. Either of these extremes is dangerous and irresponsible. Nevertheless, it would be equally irresponsible to fail to teach children about the real world or to help them face the problems of an increasingly complex, interdependent world.[38]

It would be irresponsible not because children will lack the information—they will find out from other sources—but because we did nothing to help them develop cognitive understandings of the causes of human deprivation and suffering, and because we did not help them develop empathic understandings that could motivate them to join with other human beings in efforts to alleviate such deprivation and suffering.

I believe that it is important to help children develop a realistic perception of the world, one which does not overlook or oversimplify the very real problems we must face together. This perception must enable us to view the world from a variety of perspectives and search for clues that help us discover new paths to positive humanistic goals.

I have not said much thus far about the phenomenon of perception in the development of a global perspective. People often confuse perception with perspective, and there are different meanings for each term used in different contexts. For my purposes, I define them as follows. *Perception* is the act of perceiving meaningful clues or parts with which to build mental images or wholes in the mind. *Perspective* is the frame of reference, point of view, or way of looking at a given object or event. To a large degree, perspective is the single most significant factor in determining perception. To complicate matters a bit more, there seems to be a relationship between the mental images we stockpile in our mind and our perspective or world view. The more mental images we have relating to a given idea or concept produced as a result of viewing the world from one kind of perspective, the more similar images we generate. These selective perceptions thus self-generated further act to reinforce that perspective and cause us to become more certain that ours is the only valid perspective, that is, the "right" way to view things.

Seymour Fersh writes of the various "right" ways people had of viewing the world in times past and present. Fersh shows how difficult it can be for people to change their perspectives, but he ends on a positive note by writing:

> It is now essential that new assessments of our situation be made in advance of experiencing them. Just as physical scientists are trying to devise ways of detecting evidence of approaching earthquakes, we must try to anticipate the implications of new human conditions.
>
> To change our perspectives is not as difficult as it may first seem. The ways in which we view the world, other people and ourselves is, after all, the result of education, formal and informal.[39]

With this in mind, programs in global education at the elementary level might be purposefully designed to include a series of perception exercises gradually progressing from the simple to the more complex. In such exercises, the learner would be challenged to view seemingly obvious facts or perceptions from a variety of different perspectives or viewpoints in order to discover alternative ways of explaining less obvious phenomena or problem situations.

Most of us have seen simple line drawings or visual illusions involving figures or pictures which are quite different when viewed from different perspectives or with different contexts in mind or when partly covered. We have laughed at our distorted reflections when seen in the curved mirrors of the carnival or amusement park arcades. Such common experiences can be drawn upon to make the point that we cannot always trust our eyes to make accurate reports to the brain.

For example, a penny may be dropped into a large glass bowl filled with water and children asked to gather in a circle around the bowl. Ask each one to look closely and to determine exactly where the penny is located in the bowl. Then ask three or four volunteers from opposite sides of the bowl to take a pointer or other straight stick and insert it into the water at a predetermined angle. The stick will seldom touch the penny and will instead appear to be bent or broken at the surface of the water. For younger children this simple experience can help them learn that things are not always as they appear to be.

As they begin to learn more about the phenomenon of refraction, they learn to make adjustments for what their eyes report. This idea can be most useful in introducing a discussion about some of the "obvious" things our limited perceptions tell us about the world around us. For example, the world appears to be flat. People of different colors and from different parts of the world may appear to be quite different from ourselves, despite the fact that we are all one species and are more alike than different.

By directly involving the child in simple classroom exercises in perception, we can facilitate the development of a most important global understanding—that all human beings have the same basic needs, but that it is the variety of responses to these common needs learned from their respective cultures which make them appear to be so different. That process of learning to see the overriding interdependence and basic commonalities in the varied environments and cultures in our world is what global education is all about. It is learning to test our initial perceptions against new sets of perceptions gained when we try to imagine how different things might appear from another point on this globe, from another culture, and from a variety of other perspectives.

"BOTTOM LINE"–THE CHILD'S SENSE OF INTERDEPENDENT RESPONSIBILITY

How might we sum up the glimpses we have shared of various components of global education at the elementary school level? What most significant desired outcome could we identify for one who insists on a simple "bottom line" output against which we might be held accountable?

Any good global education program must first be designed on sound goals and objectives and based upon sound curriculum and instructional practices as well as principles of child growth and development just as any other dimension of the elementary curriculum should be. But as a reflection of the rapidly changing world in which we live, the global dimension must be conceived as a dynamic one, flexible enough to move with the individual interests and imagination of the child, yet structured enough to provide a common base of experiences and learnings built around the dual themes that all humankind is a single species and our planet Earth is a single system.

On the other hand, we must guard against static curriculum design which tends to serve the learner a neatly packaged, fresh-frozen world. We must also beware of well-meaning curriculum designers who would lead us to accept a vast collection of interesting international facts and content as global education, just as we must beware of others who would have us accept exhaustive and intensive study of too few cultures.

We must not introduce younger children to complex cultural patterns too quickly, nor must we let advocacy of the widening horizons/expanding environments theory deprive them of appropriate opportunities to develop global perspectives from simple cross-cultural comparisons. True, we must observe the principle of moving from the simple to the complex. But on that simple level we must move across a wide enough sample of cultures, comparing and contrasting similar institutions and elements within those cultures to enable the child to form her own generalizations at her own level of understanding.

We must provide and produce high-quality materials which will not subvert or render less effective the other elements of the total program. We must listen to our children, hear what they are asking, and learn what they know and what they feel. In order to develop positive perspectives on the world of people "out there," the child must feel positive about the person "in there."

Once the child begins to perceive the global society of humankind as a part of self and self as a responsible part of that society, no matter at what level of simplicity, perspectives on global interdependence and global resource systems as well as other more complex organizing concepts are likely to follow. If, however, early development of wider perspectives on humankind and the self in relation to the total environment are not forthcoming, the chances of developing global perspectives will be significantly diminished. As responsible educators we must understand this and act accordingly as we plan our curriculum and instruction for the elementary child. To do less would be to abdicate our own responsibilities.

Today, more than ever before, it is our responsibility to teach children to be cognizant of the way in which their own individual actions, multiplied by hundreds, thousands, and millions, affect themselves and all other humanity. As we begin to recognize our increasing interdependence, we must also begin to assume increasing responsibility for the interdependent effects of our actions. It is this developing sense of interdependence—the feeling of being linked with all humanity in one huge global system with many sets of subsystems—which can help the child begin to view himself or herself as one very important part of the whole planetary system. And without the capability to generate some form of this sense of *interdependent responsibility* in the learner, no educational program—regardless of how excellent it may appear to be—can begin to qualify as an example of what global education should be.

NOTES

1. Gerald Weinstein and Mario Fantini (eds.), *Toward Humanistic Education: A Curriculum of Affect*, Praeger, New York, 1970, pp. 27–28.

2. John I. Goodlad, M. Frances Klein, Jerrold M. Novotney, Kenneth A. Tye, and Associates, *Toward a Mankind School: An Adventure in Humanistic Education*, McGraw-Hill, New York, 1974, p. 91.

3. Ibid.

4. Betty C. Lowry, "A Survey of the Knowledge of Social Studies Concepts Possessed by Second-Grade Children Previous to the Time These Concepts Are Taught in the Social Studies Lessons," unpublished doctoral dissertation, State University of Iowa, 1963. *Dissertation Abstracts*, vol. 24, 1963, pp. 2324–2325.

5. Theodore Kaltsounis, "A Study concerning Third Graders' Knowledge of Social Studies Content Prior to Instruction," *The Journal of Educational Research*, vol. 57, March 1964, pp. 345–349.

6. Joe Park, *Bertrand Russell on Education*, Ohio State University Press, Columbus, 1963, p. 123.

7. Ibid., pp. 123–124.

8. Edith W. King, *Educating Young Children . . . Sociological Interpretations*, Wm. C. Brown Company, Dubuque, Iowa, 1973, p. 96.

9. Ibid., p. 127.

10. Ralph C. Preston, *Teaching Social Studies in the Elementary School*, 3d ed., Holt, New York, 1968, p. 65.

11. Ibid., p. 66.

12. Edith West, *The Family of Man: A Social Studies Program*, Selective Education Equipment, Newton, Mass., 1971, pp. 34–35.

13. Charles L. Mitsakos, "Evaluation of the Family of Man/Minnesota Project Social Studies," presented at the Social Studies Orientation Conference, sponsored by the National Science Foundation, Indiana University, Bloomington, June 19, 1974, p. 2.

14. Ibid., pp. 3–5.

15. Charles L. Mitsakos, "A Report on the Social Studies Program to the School Committee," unpublished report, Oct. 2, 1973.

16. Charles L. Mitsakos, "Social Studies in the Chelmsford Elementary Schools," unpublished paper, 1975.

17. Ibid., pp. 2–3.

18. Charles L. Mitsakos, "FAMES Project: Final Report," Chelmsford, Mass., 1976, pp. 10–11.

19. Linda H. Pruitt, from Introduction to "Children Learn What They

Experience," Pickens County Follow-Through Program, Jasper, Georgia, April 1974, p. 3.

20. Ibid., p. 14–15.

21. The full text of the Declaration and a free booklet on the rights of the child can be obtained from School Services, U.S. Committee for UNICEF, 331 East 38th Street, New York, N.Y. 10016. During 1978 and 1979, additional free material on the rights of the child will be available in preparation for and in celebration of the International Year of the Child, scheduled to coincide with the twentieth anniversary of the Declaration of the Rights of the Child.

22. Phil Martinez, personal communication, January 1975.

23. "It's a Small World After All," ©1963, Wonderland Music Co., Inc., Burbank, Cal., Words and music by Richard M. Sherman and Robert B. Sherman.

24. Rick Soll, from a series of articles for the *Chicago Tribune,* April 16–23, 1973.

25. Rick Soll, "Pupils Become Wordly in Year," *Chicago Tribune,* April 14, 1974.

26. *World Book Encyclopedia Dictionary,* A–K, vol. 1, Field Enterprises Educational Corp., Chicago, 1973.

27. The guide used in this example is not referenced here, as we presume this state department of education would not wish to be cited directly in this context.

28. Howard R. Anderson (ed.), *Approaches to an Understanding of World Affairs,* 25th Yearbook of the National Council for the Social Studies, Banta Publishing Co., Menasha, Wis., 1954, p. 316.

29. Anne Pellowski, "Internationalism in Children's Literature," in Mary Hill Arbuthnot and Zena Sutherland, *Children and Books,* 4th ed., Scott, Foresman, Glenview, Ill., 1972, p. 757.

30. Anne Pellowski, personal communication, January 1975.

31. For guidelines for evaluating global education materials, see Pellowski, "Internationalism," in Arbuthnot and Sutherland, op. cit., p. 616.

32. David C. King and Charlotte C. Anderson, *Windows on Our World: United States,* Houghton Mifflin, Boston, 1976, p. 145.

33. Ibid., pp. 150, 153.

34. "Big Blue Marble," © 1973 by Alphaventure Music Publishing Corp., New York, words and music by Skip Redwine.

35. Donald N. Morris, *Teaching about Interdependence in a Peaceful World,* Elementary Teacher's Kit, School Services Department, U.S. Committee for UNICEF, New York, 1975.

36. Donald N. Morris, *Teaching about the Child and World Environment,* School Services Department, U.S. Committee for UNICEF, New York, 1976.

37. *Trees Are Like People,* a book published by the children of the fifth and

sixth grades of P.S. 173, Manhattan, under the supervision of Mrs. Irene Sonnenfeld, February 1965.

38. Donald N. Morris, "Teaching Global Interdependence in Elementary Social Studies: Old Concept—New Crisis," *Social Education,* vol. 38, no. 7, November/December 1974, p. 673.

39. Seymour Fersh (ed.), *Learning about Peoples and Cultures,* McDougal, Littell, Evanston, Ill., 1974, p. 118.

CHAPTER SIX

Secondary School Programs

David C. King
Center for Global Perspectives

A global perspective is not a quantum, something you either have or don't have. It's a blend of many things and any individual may be rich in certain elements and relatively lacking in others.

(Robert G. Hanvey, *An Attainable Global Perspective,* Center for Global Perspectives, New York, 1975)

If we apply Hanvey's partial definition of a global perspective to schools, we can say that every school adds to a student's world-awareness. Some schools clearly do a better job of it than others. In researching this chapter, I knew I would not find the 21st Century High School described by the Andersons. The goal, instead, was to find programs that were particularly "rich" in some elements of global education and schools that addressed themselves to some of the barriers to a global perspective discussed in Chapter 3.

The results of my search were heartening. I repeatedly encountered signs indicating that over the past ten years there has emerged a wide variety of programs that are moving secondary schools in the direction of world-centered education. These programs are alternatives rather than interrelated portions of an overall reform movement. Team-teaching, learning by doing, multidisciplinary approaches, improved curriculum materials, community involvement, international exchange—these are among the mix of opportunities now available. People are choosing among them according to local needs and constraints. Of course, not every school in the country has chosen to follow one of these pathways. But the alternatives are there, and an increasing number of people—from individual teachers to entire school districts—are taking advantage of them.

To begin describing this range of options, let me describe one of the more ambitious programs in some detail.

TOWARD WORLD-CENTERED SCHOOLS: A MODEL

The location is Jefferson High School in Daly City, California (the community that was once immortalized in song for its "ticky-tacky" houses). More precisely, the location is a single-story building on the edge of the campus—one of those "temporary" classrooms put up some twenty years ago that has now assumed a sort of bleak permanence. My first impression did not give me the feeling that I was about to enter a world-centered school.

Inside, I found myself in a room crowded with about thirty students—black, white, Chicano, Asian-American—and a single teacher, a man endowed with boundless energy and patience. There were no desks in the room and no chalkboard. It looked more like the field office of a construction company than a classroom.

The students were engaged in an array of activities that bore little resemblance to "normal" classroom procedure. Two were talking on telephones. Two more were painfully composing letters on rickety typewriters, while another group was checking backpacks and boxes lined against one wall. A cluster in one corner was debating about the feeding of farm animals. And the remainder were gathered in front of a large wall chart, where a girl was changing name tags under headings that included Public Relations, Food, Finances, and Transportation. And the teacher, Reno Taini, was everywhere—reminding students of special assignments, collecting reports, answering questions.

Then Taini asked for their attention. Instantly there was silence, but there was also an air of suppressed excitement. "We're ready," he announced. "For the next two weeks, we'll learn to survive in the wilderness."

What I had witnessed were the final preparations for the first part of a course called the Community Environmental Education Program. This is actually a one-semester school-within-a-school, a period when sixty juniors and seniors devote themselves exclusively to the program, with no other courses or commitments.

The program has been in operation since 1967, beginning with some small federal grants but now operating on a semester budget of $300. The program relies on donations for other resources and facilities. In most school districts, it would be difficult to institute such a marked change in school procedure, with students actually being pulled out of the classroom for half the year. Taini and his associates had long, persistent struggles with the administration, other faculty members, the school board, the state, and parents. Once an experimental year had been approved and turned out to be a great success, opposition to the program melted. It must be remembered, though, that any program representing a marked departure from traditional school procedure encounters a maze of obstacles.

The course begins with a two-week orientation session called the Wilderness School. Following the planning sessions I had witnessed, the students head for a wilderness area in northern California. The sixty students are divided into groups of seven or eight, each with its own instructor. For practically all the participants this is their first exposure to outdoor living; for some, it is the first excursion beyond the surroundings of Daly City. In describing the Wilderness School, Taini considers it "the foundation for decision making, exploration of personal and community resources, group sharing, trust, and the development of personal initiative. This trip sets the pace for the semester's work."

One of the first and most important lessons that emerges is a sense of responsibility for one's group. Everyone suffers if firewood isn't gathered, or drinking water isn't stored, or a meal is poorly prepared. When a problem arises, the students learn to deal with it immediately and directly. In the middle of a hike, they might stop, peel off their backpacks, and work out whatever obstacle has emerged. One instructor pointed out that his most difficult task was to avoid taking responsibility in these situations.

Learning to work together in this survival setting thus becomes a living exercise in one of the goals described by the Andersons. As one of the Middleston principals said: "We believe it is very important for children to develop a sense of responsibility for the welfare of groups in which they are citizens."

The students also begin to develop new ideas of their relationship to the immediate environment and to total world systems. "They come here," Taini says, "worried about a date they're missing or the fight they just had with a boy friend or girl friend. Suddenly they find themselves facing a new set of needs—some very basic ones like food, water, shelter, and group cooperation. In the classroom, I can develop little concern for the need to protect, say, the planet's water system. Once they've been on this trip, that need takes on a new significance. The learning is reinforced later in the semester when they explore the Daly City water supply—where it comes from, what unhealthy elements it contains, what the future prospects are. They can then make vivid connections between Daly City and here and begin to see how the two relate to something larger."

The Wilderness School also involves study and activities, some of which the students help arrange. Much of this has to do with outdoor living—identifying edible plants, basic survival and first-aid techniques, and soil studies. The program also includes creative writing, math in nature, painting, poetry readings, mapping, selected reading, and group discussion of school and home problems. Such learning activities, in the wilderness setting, are probably more suitable to this age group than any other. The teachers involved are convinced that younger students would not be capable of the self-discipline needed to plan and carry out a learning program while on a camping trip.

I asked one of the instructors how the experiment in group living affected race relationships. He seemed a little surprised by the question. Then he said, "I guess I've been involved in this for so long that I haven't thought about that lately. By the second or third day, the students think of each other more in terms of group membership than racial origins. That feeling of belonging persists through the semester—and I hope and trust it extends beyond that."

Student response to the training period seems to support the optimism of the instructors. Here are a few samples of what participants wrote about their experience:

> ... It's unbelievable how everyone trusts one another and are honest with one another, it's great.

> I felt we were all one family because we all worked together. I learned more up there in five days than I would learn here in a month. It was a far-out trip. I saw animals up there I never saw before. When we went on hikes the teachers didn't act like teachers but like friends because they had time to explain things and they would help us in any possible way they could. I felt everyone was my brother and sister. I know a lot more about people and especially myself.

> We have finally reached the outer limits of civilization. We have been removed from the hum-drum life of the "city" people and have been transformed into the country bumpkin of yesterday. It is truly a beautiful, wonderful thing . . . to strip the smog, the fog, the outer covers of the "City." I have never enjoyed myself so much in a long time. I'm ALIVE and WELL.

The strong group feeling may be what Torney described as an "unplanned outcome"—an outcome that in this case helped to overcome one of the major barriers to a global perspective. In discussing attitudinal and motivational barriers, Torney pointed out that self-esteem may be an important prerequisite "to fruitful experiences in an intercultural context," but noted the danger of achieving a "defensively high level of self-esteem." The students in the Wilderness School appear to emerge with (1) a strong sense of feeling that "I can do it," and (2) a special comradeship with group participants of diverse racial and ethnic backgrounds. Interactions with teachers and other students on the trip provide the differing perspectives which help students "reconcile the various conflicting interests of individuals who share the same earth," the first of Joyce and Nicholson's imperatives.

Particularly in view of the inner-city background of the Jefferson students, the Wilderness School offers important beginnings in expanding areas of awareness. For the rest of the semester, this training provides a background for exploring the local community and for learning about the world beyond Daly City.

The program has three project phases, with groups of ten working for a four-week period on each. One project, called the Farm Phase, centers around a donated plot of land. Here students take part in a 4-H Club project. They gain experience in gardening, horticulture, and the management of small farm animals.

The Urban Phase involves students with the community. As much as possible, they arrange their own programs—job internships, field trips, community service work, and intensive job exploration. Student responsibility for designing programs was stressed in the Anderson's scenario; it is also emphasized in many of the designs for reforming secondary education.[1] In the Community Environmental Education Program, students' responsibilities also include organizational tasks, keeping records, managing finances, and helping to gain the support of individuals and businesses in the community.

The third phase of the program, Environmental Research, engages each student "in a specific and self-selected research project." The base of operations for this project is a research station constructed by the students on the seacoast. Marine biologists, ecologists, and other scientists from local universities participate in the program as resource advisors.

Of course, this Jefferson High School program does not contain all the elements needed for students to gain an adequate world view. In fact, the course could be criticized for being "experience rich" and "information poor." One could argue, for example, that there is too much concentration on the immediate environment, without a concerted effort to relate local concerns to global issues. And yet, the program is "rich" in key elements of global education, particularly in providing a transition experience for students from a racially mixed inner-city school. Student initiative and responsibility, group cooperation, experiential learning, community involvement, and environmental awareness—all are important ingredients in making schools more world-centered.

If the Community Environmental Education Program at Jefferson High School were an isolated phenomenon or the product of an alternative school, then it could not be said to indicate a significant change in the nation's secondary schools. But if we return to the idea that this program is just one of many viable alternatives, its relevance to improving global education becomes more clear. To explore some of these other alternatives, I will take a twofold approach. First, I will give some idea of the range of activities taking place in close geographical proximity to Jefferson High. Second, the concluding portions of the chapter will survey some important trends in other parts of the country.

THE MICRO LENS: ACTIVITIES IN THE BAY AREA

To gain some idea of how prevalent innovative programs like Taini's are, I decided to survey activities in the same region of the country—the San Francisco Bay Area. The choice of location was not only convenient, it was also useful in providing a wide range of school climates, from racially mixed urban schools to predominantly white, middle-class suburban schools to a variety of rural districts. To narrow the focus further, I chose a limited slice of time—a few days in the fall of 1975. Here is what I discovered going on simultaneously—and I'm sure that there was a good deal more that I simply didn't find out about.

There were some schools using the community as a classroom, which recalls the Andersons' world-centered schools' philosophy, "We strive to create an educational commonwealth in which the community is part of the schools and the schools are part of the community." In Contra Costa County, for example, two dozen students were studying water quality in the Sacramento Delta. They were not doing so in a school laboratory but in a boat leased by the school district for regular scientific excursions. At designated spots, students learned about the Delta ecosystem, then took their water samples, analyzed them, and tried to determine the sources of contaminants as well as reasons for variation in pollution levels. For some of the group, the river study was part of a combined science–social studies course which ranges from a study of local conditions to a simulated Law of the Sea conference. Such "hands-on" experiences can aid in another of Joyce and Nicholson's imperatives, to "render the immensely complex global scene comprehensible in terms faithful to reality."

A few miles inland, students in the San Ramon School District (a rural, upper-middle-class region) were preparing for a field trip to study facilities and activities at the Port of Oakland. This group of juniors and seniors are part of an experimental program called "Offcampus Education," which bears some resemblance to the Jefferson High project.

For a full school year, the group's classroom is the entire Bay Area, with daily trips to offices, factories, museums, government agencies, and areas for nature studies. The course is full-credit and combines English, social studies, and science. The participants have found the program exciting and rewarding, and teachers report that students who have participated in their junior year show a marked increase in maturity and interest when they return to traditional courses as seniors. Some program teachers are currently taking part in workshops conducted by the Center for Global Perspectives,* with the goal of finding more ways to relate the activities to global concerns.

San Ramon schools also have a program in Outdoor Education that is similar to activities now underway in a number of schools throughout California. Fourteen percent of the district's young people have been involved in the project, which is carried on both during the year and over the summer. For children in the lower grades, Outdoor Education involves on-the-spot science studies. The program for high school students includes back-packing trips in the Sierra Nevada, combining physical education, biology, and history, plus the experience of gaining new insights into the interdependence involved in group membership.

Berkeley has a somewhat different approach to outdoor education and community involvement. There, I learned about a program that was largely the work of one man. When Dr. Herbert Wong became principal of a Berkeley school, he was dismayed by the sterile appearance of the rooms and the barren stretches of asphalt that surrounded the building. He launched a campaign to improve the physical appearance of the school and to involve the community in the effort. His approach was to conduct a series of weekend "courses" called "It's a Small World: Structures and Processes of Environmental Education." The participants were parents, students, teachers, business people, and members of organizations concerned with ecology and conservation. The program gained momentum and support, including the backing of local utility companies and the Chevron Chemical Company.

In the process of transforming the school, the course provided the participants with new ways of looking at the world around them. They discovered that they could do something about their "built" environment, and they began to appreciate how much natural beauty was to be enjoyed in an urban setting. As one participant said, "It brought back to me that special thrill of discovery that had meant so much when we were children."

Dr. Wong's program was establishing a new relationship between community members and the school. The institution ceased to be a place that intruded on people's awareness only when their children had problems or when a bond issue was to be voted on. Now it was becoming a functioning part of their environment for which they felt a special responsibility. Plans are now underway to gain the cooperation of the city government in blocking traffic from one street

---

*Formerly the Center for War/Peace Studies.

adjoining the school and creating more park area in a nearby vacant lot.

Others in the Bay Area were involved in bringing personal views of other cultures into the classroom. Betty McAfee, Media Coordinator for the Berkeley Public Schools, had used part of a sabbatical year for a trip to the People's Republic of China. Out of this adventure came a series of short films and filmstrips on life and educational practices in China. They received wide exposure in classrooms and in workshops conducted by the Bay Area China Education Project (BACEP).

Yvette Lehman had taken a sabbatical trip to Israel to acquire data for her education course at Hayward State University. While there, she received word that she and three other Bay Area women had been granted visas for a tour of China. She flew back to Oakland, repacked her luggage, and headed for the People's Republic. The four women used the trip to produce filmstrips on the changing role of women in China. The first showing of these materials was in a church hall, with a large audience composed primarily of Berkeley teachers. Other programs were planned for church groups, women's organizations, business associations, and local schools.

Two visitors to the Bay Area during my brief survey period added to the impression that global education increasingly involves cross-cultural communication. One of the visitors was Lord Montbatten, a gentleman who had made the somewhat unlikely transition from Supreme Commander of Allied Forces in Southeast Asia in World War II to director of a truly international school. The school has campuses in Wales, Singapore, and Vancouver and is called the International Council of World Colleges. The combined student enrollment is 340, aged sixteen to eighteen, representing forty-one countries, including the People's Republic of China. Lord Montbatten said he had become convinced that this approach to school organization is "incomparably better than national education." An international school, he insisted, takes us "a giant step away from education that fosters a philosophy of 'my country, right or wrong,' and it is that philosophy which creates wars."

The second visitor was Michael J. Aucken, Research Officer for the Tasmanian Environmental Centre in Hobart, Tasmania, Australia. He planned to spend two months in the United States studying environmental education programs. He also hoped to establish a data bank of environmental education materials to be shared by groups in Australia and the United States, an idea not far removed from the student exchange of ideas with their counterparts in other countries described by the Andersons. One innovation Aucken mentioned was an Australian program called "Garbage Truck in

Reverse." Schools or classrooms pay an annual fee to a group of young people who supply recycled materials for school use, the materials ranging from yarn to automobile parts.

Of course, there were dozens of other visitors to the region during this brief period. Many of these became classroom visitors through such organizations as the Council on World Affairs and the United Nations Association. In addition, there were many Bay Area students involved in overseas travel or exchange programs.

One school was taking its entire student body (twenty-four) for an extended stay in another culture. This traveling classroom is an alternative school called the San Francisco School on Wheels. It was about to launch its second learning-through-travel program, which would carry its students across the United States and then into Mexico. Advance preparation included acquiring background information for student-designed projects to be completed in Mexico. These programs designed to acquaint students with other cultures help fulfill Chapter 4's imperative to "promote the kind of pluralism that will allow individual cultures to flourish and enrich one another and people everywhere."

Many teachers in the area were involved in far less exotic efforts to help their students gain a global perspective. There are dozens of programs which give considerable attention to teaching about contemporary global concerns, considering future alternatives, and developing an understanding of the interdependent nature of life on our planet. Some of these programs are particularly important for their cross-disciplinary approach, usually combining social studies with either science or literature.

As a model, though, I would like to describe one that is perhaps not as glossy as other examples might have been. I've chosen this particular school because it addresses itself to one of the major barriers to creating world-centered schools. The barrier is that global education often appears to be a product of white, middle-class schools; little is done to develop a global perspective in poor or racially mixed neighborhoods. The Report of the National Commission on the Reform of Secondary Education expresses the concern in these terms:

Few students from inner-city schools or school districts with low-income families are given even an introduction to [global issues]. Research makes it clear that international education as now taught in the nation's high schools is an elitist subject.[2]

Unfortunately, the commission's findings are valid and signs of progress in this area are slim. However, there are a number of dedicated teachers who are striving to remedy the situation. The work of a team of teachers at a high school in El Cerrito, California, offers a good illustration.

The program at El Cerrito is limited to social studies but encompasses all high school grades. While far from being in a ghetto area, the El Cerrito school shares many of the problems of inner-city districts. Most of the families that provide the school population have low incomes. Roughly half are nonwhite, including blacks, Chicanos, and Orientals. Classrooms are overcrowded; teachers and administrators appear harrassed and overworked. Few of the students are college-bound; many are labeled as "low-achievers," which frequently means that the individual sees little relationship between school and his or her world outside.

Within this setting, a group of eight social studies teachers are in the second year of a program designed to add a global perspective to the curriculum. They coordinate their activities to develop a four-year sequence in which the student's learning will build on experiences from the previous year. They try to develop teaching strategies that will increase learner motivation and provide a variety of learning experiences. In the eleventh-grade American history course, for example, students work on a contract system. Each student selects from a list of projects and with the teacher works out a calendar for completion of each phase of the program. At the time of my visit, the class as a whole was meeting as a Congressional International Relations Committee, preparing a variety of foreign aid bills which would be put in the hopper for later study and debate.

I also visited a ninth-grade class in a course built around a series of simulations. The themes for the year included decision making, revolution, war/peace issues, and population-food equations.

I watched part of a simulation on the subject of revolution, this one focusing on the causes of the French Revolution. What I witnessed did not have the appearance of a model program. The students were restless, moving about with apparent lack of purpose, talking, passing notes, sneaking bits of a forbidden candy bar, losing things, and offering various excuses for lack of preparation. It is precisely this lack of order that leads many teachers to shy away from simulations, simulation games, and role playing. The teacher's role as authority figure becomes submerged in the currents of physical movement.

But through this apparent lack of order, I could see that something positive was happening; a thread of meaning involving every individual created a certain unity. Each person was aware of the inequalities that had been established in the room. Even though taxes were being paid in play money, those who saw their envelopes being emptied felt a real sense of loss—just as the gains and set-backs in a session of Monopoly are very meaningful to the participants.

At the close of the period the royal family was allowed to leave first, followed by the nobility, and then the rest. Even this simple symbol of privilege rankled with those who had to wait and then rush to their next class. Similarly, an announcement that at their next meeting the king and queen and nobility and clergy would be allowed to bring food to class—an almost unheard of treat—created considerable consternation.

After the last "woman peasant" had left, the exhausted teacher apologized for the lack of decorum. "But," she explained, "if we keep the kids in straight rows, with perfect order except for those who are rehashing the text assignment, we don't gain much but boredom and resistance. At least with this, they're active and involved. They still might not do much better with the reading assignments I give, but they do begin to gain a feeling for some of the concepts we're trying to deal with."

Simulations, incidentally, seem to work well with students of all ages, from kindergarten through college, and can be an important means of making comprehensible the immensely complex global scene, an imperative for global education programs set forth by Joyce and Nicholson. Among other advantages, simulations or "games" are successful because they involve activity rather than rote learning and they make good use of an almost universal enjoy-ment of games. In a sense, this is applying to learning situations the principles that make Parker Brothers' Monopoly such a success. And many of these devices are directed toward cross-cultural under-standing and awareness of global concerns. Bafá Bafá, for example, is a cross-cultural simulation developed by Garry Shirts, director of Simile II. It was originally designed under contract with the United States Navy Department as a training device to help officers over-come such barriers to acceptance of others as misperception, stereo-typing, and language differences. The game has proved highly suc-cessful with Navy personnel. It has also been widely used in schools and is adaptable to junior-high grades as well as high school.

In terms of numbers involved and potential for change, one of the most impressive programs then taking place in the Bay Area was the newly formed California Task Force for Global Education. Initi-ated by members of the State Department of Education, the Task Force is also sponsored by the Center for Global Perspectives, the

Bay Area China Education Project, San Francisco State University, and the United Nations Association, with financial support from local foundations.

Under the Task Force's auspices, about 100 teachers were taking part in an intensive three-day program on the campus of Mills College. They came in small teams from schools, districts, county offices of education, and professional organizations. Following this orientation session, each team was committed to starting an in-service training program at its home site. The three-day meeting included workshops in such topics as problem solving, global multimedia, processes for achieving curriculum change, and examples of "curriculum materials with a global perspective."

In regard to the program, Wilson Riles, California's Superintendent of Public Instruction, wrote:

> The efforts of the California Task Force for Global Perspectives in Education seem to be the only major organized thrust in California today to address these issues [of global interdependency in the curriculum]. . . . I am delighted to support this thrust which evidences that committed educators can make a difference in their profession without major financial commitments. I look upon this workshop as a beginning. The resulting changes in a small number of school districts should demonstrate to the rest of the State what can be done. Hopefully, this will result in a broadening of commitment and ever increasing inclusion of this priority in the curriculum of the schools of California.[3]

An important aspect of Riles' assessment is that the reform of education in the direction of creating world-centered schools must be approached with little expectation of financial assistance—at least for the present. Foundation funds are scarce, and the budgets of state education departments and school districts are stretched thin. Although such events as the energy crisis and environmental deterioration have helped create a new awareness of the problems and pressures of global interdependence, the impact of these events has not yet been comparable to the launching of Sputnik in creating a national consensus for reforming public education. Unless such a crusading zeal does emerge, efforts to change the curriculum will usually have to be low-budget programs.

One response to these budgetary constraints has been to create in-service programs in global education that will offer college credits to teacher participants, thus providing incentives and cost-sharing.

For example, while the Global Task Force was in session, the East Bay Council for the Social Studies and the Atlantic Council were conducting a seminar titled, "Passengers in the Same Boat: The United States, the Third World and the Common Market . . . Teaching About World Crises." Teachers could obtain one semester of college credit for attending.

At the same time, forty other teachers in the Bay Area were taking part in a five-week program conducted by the Center for Global Perspectives. The purpose of this college-credit project was to explore ways of using elements of the existing curriculum to help students gain a better understanding of the dynamics of interdependence in local as well as global affairs.

Other Bay Area organizations were also engaged in preparing low-cost teaching materials and strategies. The Bay Area China Education Project provides a variety of services to schools, including film rentals, training programs, and curriculum materials. The World Without War Council has long been involved in such activities. In addition, Helen Garvey, SNJM, has directed the preparation of a curriculum on peace education for schools in the Oakland diocese. The program, Education for International Peace, is now being used by a number of Catholic secondary schools throughout the country.

A number of groups publish and disseminate materials developed by and for teachers using a newsletter or mimeograph format. Not Man Apart, a San Francisco organization, issues a monthly publication on such concerns as worldwide environmental problems. The issue that came out during my survey period included an article entitled "Schools for Planetary Education" by a professor at Teachers College, Columbia. There was also a special pull-out supplement for classroom use containing a tenth-grade unit on energy, written by Mark Terry, a teacher and author of *Teaching for Survival.*

A fairly close look at one area of the country, then, reveals that an encouraging number of individuals and groups are demonstrating a growing commitment to global education. With the possible exception of the California Task Force for Global Perspectives in Education, there was little or no coordination among these efforts. Rather, people were selecting those options which fitted best with their particular needs. Unfortunately, there are no data on the qualitative or quantitative effects of these diverse efforts. One suspects that an evaluation would reveal that only a fraction of students was acquiring anything approaching an adequate global perspective.

The fact remains, however, that these programs and innovations not only persist but tend to proliferate as more people learn of new opportunities. Perhaps this kind of gradualism is the only realistic course we can follow in working toward world-centered schools.

THE MACRO LENS: SIGNPOSTS THROUGHOUT THE NATION

Let me switch now to a larger view and consider some of the things that are happening elsewhere in the country. The signposts of change toward a global perspective in secondary schools can be divided into four categories: (1) improved texts and teaching materials; (2) agencies promoting change—outreach programs by organizations concerned with global education and by some state departments of education; (3) examples of specific programs in individual schools or districts; (4) programs aimed at overcoming some key barriers to a global perspective.

TEXTS AND TEACHING MATERIALS

The development of global education cannot be separated from the quality of curriculum materials. If textbooks and supplementary materials do not help develop a global perspective, then the effort to do so will be limited to the small minority of teachers who are willing to go beyond standard classroom materials. John Goodlad has made an observation that can be applied to the crucial role played by curriculum materials:

> More and more we realize, even if we do not act on the realization, that principals and teachers have a remarkable facility for taking what is thrust upon them by would-be reformers and wrapping it up in the culture of the school so as to render it benign or impotent. The literature on change offers the straight-faced conclusion that the most successful innovations are those demanding little or no change on the part of the teacher![4]

For many teachers—perhaps the vast majority—the basic hard-cover text remains the principal tool of teaching. In this area, too, we find an opening up of new alternatives, particularly in materials published since 1970. Commercial publishers have shown an increased awareness of the need to add a global viewpoint to texts in many subject areas. Occasionally, the result is little more than window-dressing—a chapter in a United States history text called

"America in the World," which may be merely a survey of the nation's role in world affairs since 1945. (One publisher in a blazing advertising headline asks: "Is the Global Perspective Missing from Your Curriculum?" The ad then proceeds to list traditional texts in such areas as western civilization.)

However, many publishers have vigorously pursued a more world-centered curriculum. For example, in Chapter 1, a student described her work in a course called the Program for Studies in Global Society. Her class first studied characteristics of human history prior to the emergence of the nation-state and then explored the worldwide impact of nation-state development. Teachers today can approach world history in precisely this manner. For example, *Patterns in Human History* (produced by the Anthropology Curriculum Study Project and published by Macmillan, 1971) provides inquiry materials which challenge students to analyze the transition from traditional to modern societies, using an anthropological approach which relies heavily on case studies. A broader survey, with heavier concentration on political and economic factors, can be obtained from the pioneering text by Leften Stavrianos, *A Global History of Man* (Allyn and Bacon, 1970), or a more recent text, William H. McNeil's *The Ecumene: The Story of Humanity* (Harper & Row, 1974). An alternative approach is provided by the material in the Indiana University World History Project (Ginn, 1977), which develops broad historical themes such as "Nationalism and Imperialism" and "Social and Political Order in the Modern World." In describing the rationale for the program, project director John M. Thompson states, "Knowing the common past of all peoples is crucial to understanding ourselves and the future, and we must find exciting ways for students to become interested in and learn about our total experience on 'spaceship earth.'"[5]

Thus, teachers of world history can continue to teach the traditional course with its heavy emphasis on the achievements and implied superiority of western civilization. Or, they can choose among the growing list of titles which strive to offer a truly global history.

Similarly, courses in area studies no longer have to be those dry culture surveys of the past which achieved little beyond the reinforcement of ethnocentrism and negative stereotypes. Many of the more recent texts place special emphasis on materials written by members of the culture being studied. Others, like the new McDougal, Littell series, provide materials designed to promote cross-cultural empathy and understanding. One title in the series,

Learning about Peoples and Cultures (1974), helps the student directly confront such barriers to understanding as stereotyping, perception, communications, and ethnocentrism.

A world-centered approach need not be limited to texts in the social studies. Many collections for high school literature courses now present readings which emphasize human commonalities. A good example is a collection called *Mix* in the Harcourt Brace Jovanovich New World Issues series (1971). Through poetry, drama, and short stories from a wide variety of societies (only two selections represent the United States), students discover various points of view on human beings' relationship to nature, to one another, to work, prejudice, poverty, and war. *Worlds in the Making: Probes for Students of the Future* (Prentice-Hall, 1970), while relying heavily on American and English authors, contains such unit titles as "Coping with Change" and "Exploring Spaceship Earth."

In science materials, too, especially those dealing with environmental issues, there is a new emphasis on developing an understanding of the planetary nature of our life-support systems. Scholastic Book Service, for example, offers a multimedia course called *Human Issues in Science*. The four study units are titled "Ourselves," "Energy," "Our Changing Earth," and "Hunger." Even companies that lean heavily toward traditional text materials are likely to offer optional titles like the Globe Book Company's *Oceanography and Our Future*.

In the past, creative teachers managed to piece together their own courses, using paperback books and often relying heavily on the school's Xerox machine and a relaxed attitude toward copyright laws. Another trend of the past decade has been the development of attractive supplementary materials, including books and multimedia packages, tailored for high school use. These enable teachers to broaden text coverage or to structure their own courses, with expense differing little from the purchase of hardcover texts. University film libraries and school district media centers help provide a wide range of low-cost materials.

Many of these materials deal with contemporary global issues— population pressures, food and other resources, the oceans, the spread of nuclear weapons, the causes of international conflicts, and the variety of dangers threatening the environment. Simulation games, collections of readings, films, filmstrips, cassettes, and multimedia units offer a variety of learning activities.

At the Harwood Union School in Moretown, Vermont, Jonathan Weil teaches a ninth-grade course in economics that he has constructed entirely from supplementary materials. The central theme is one of the concerns expressed by a principal in Chapter 1: "Many of us anticipate that scarcity rather than expanding affluence will be a hallmark of the future our students will inherit." Weil challenges his students to confront the hard choices and conflicts which emerge in a world of limited resources and expanding population.

The course is introduced with a multimedia unit titled *Patterns of Human Conflict,* developed by the Center for Global Perspectives and produced by Warren Schloat Productions (now Prentice-Hall Media). The unit consists of a series of three filmstrips combined with readings (poetry, short story, drama, journalism). Using an inquiry approach, the students begin by developing their own definitions of conflict; as they work through the materials, they broaden and modify these beginning statements. They discover that conflict is a natural and normal part of life and analyze such factors as why some conflicts are dysfunctional, how conflicts are resolved, what conditions will intensify a dispute, and so on.

The unit enables the learner to analyze conflict situations on all levels of social organization: a youth facing a crisis over drugs; a community and eventually the nation confronting racial issues in the march on Selma, Alabama; the world community encountering complex issues in trying to establish rules for the use and protection of ocean resources.

The concluding filmstrip leads the class into a simulation. The students learn about a mythical community in Maine facing the dilemma of choosing between preserving their environment while stagnating economically or allowing a lumber mill to establish a large growth-oriented operation. The students are assigned roles based on individuals and groups they encountered in the filmstrip; they debate the issues in town-meeting fashion and arrive at their own decision for the community. The material stresses the idea that the aggregate of such dilemmas and decisions has far-reaching consequences in an interdependent world.

With this as a beginning, Weil builds the rest of his course on readings, field trips, role-playing situations, educational television videotapes, a simulation called the "Land-Use Game," and a filmstrip titled "Man and Hunger." The concluding portions of the course focus on alternatives for increasing food production, improving distribution, and slowing population growth.

This mix of various supplementary materials is becoming increasingly common. One reason for the trend is that the courses become more activity-oriented, involving the students in role playing, decision making, and inquiry learning. At the same time, most of the teachers I've talked with about multimedia programs mention their value in waking up their students to the urgency of pressing global issues. Jack Linden, of the Cherry Creek Schools in Englewood, Colorado, expresses a common view. "Even with students who are middle-class and college-bound, there is very little awareness of the fact that we live in a really interdependent world." Simulations and audiovisual materials, he feels, are an important way of creating interest and awareness. Only then can the teacher "move the students into discussion, reading and research on the international implications" of course materials. Art Thesenvich, at Burnseville High School in Minnesota, illustrated this approach by developing a teaching unit on understanding China which relies almost exclusively on films, a technique which also enables the class to analyze the stereotyped images presented by commercially produced feature films.

While curriculum materials have improved, they are only one building block in constructing world-centered schools. Textbooks, by themselves, are not adequate to the task of developing a global perspective. A range of supplementary materials can provide the basis for world-centered courses, but only if the teacher is convinced of the need. This last point has two important implications. First, a massive campaign is needed to convince teachers that a global perspective is essential for today's students. Second, for education to develop such a perspective, world-centered learning must involve most subject areas and all grade levels.

The tasks of persuasion, developing materials, and providing in-service training programs have largely been assumed by organizations concerned with global education and a few state departments of education.

AGENCIES PROMOTING CHANGE

State education departments are in a unique position to expand global education beyond those innovative programs which now involve only limited numbers of schools or districts. State curriculum frameworks, for example, do have an impact on schools; if these documents were to stress the central role of world-centered education, schools would begin searching for ways to implement the stated objectives. State departments can also promote global education through their functions of establishing training requirements for teachers, promoting (or adopting) textbooks, and setting up in-service programs to provide experienced teachers with the best materials and teaching strategies.

So far, few states have evidenced a willingness to assume these obligations. It is significant, for example, that fewer than 5 percent of the nation's teachers have ever taken a course with any "international content or perspective."[6]

In contrast to this pattern, some states play a leading role in promoting global education. Indiana, New York, North Carolina, and one or two others are the leaders in this regard.

A survey of recent activities in New York State demonstrates the potential for bringing about change represented by state education departments. In 1970, the regents of the University of the State of New York issued a position paper on proposals for strengthening the International Dimensions of Education.[7] A plan of action was proposed that would be developed around seven themes: conflict resolution and international cooperation; demography and the problem of population growth; intercultural relations; comparative urbanization; science, technology, and society; humanities and the arts; and language.

To implement this broad plan, the State Department of Education developed a series of programs which included the following:

1. A special project on studies in international conflict and conflict resolution (initially supported by a grant from the Institute for World Order) developed six simulations, teacher's guides, and other materials for secondary school teachers. A series of workshops, involving an estimated 750 teachers, was designed to strengthen the teaching of international conflict. By 1975, over 20,000 copies of the program materials had been distributed to teachers and schools.

2. With the cooperation of the Metropolitan Studies Program at Syracuse University, two self-study guides on comparative education were prepared. The state supported the establishment of a Center for Comparative Urban Studies at the City University of New York. One outgrowth of this program has been the production of eleven documentary films on cities in India that are used in both high school and college courses.

3. A study group, drawing on faculty members from such institutions as Cornell, Columbia, Rochester, and the State University, was organized to stimulate interest in the role of science and technology in shaping global society. This group has played an active role in planning the agenda for a major world conference on science and technology to be held in 1979 under United Nations auspices. For high school use, a study unit on India's natural resources was prepared for the ninth grade earth sciences curriculum. Other instructional materials have been developed, such as a filmstrip on the Green Revolution.

4. Over an eight-year period, a series of grants was secured from foundation and government sources to support an innovative approach to self-learning major languages. The program has become nation-wide, with formation of the National Association for Self-Instructional Language Programs. Some forty-five colleges and universities are involved, about half of them in New York State, offering instruction in twenty languages to an estimated 1,000 students each year.

5. A study guide for Latin America was published in 1972. A special feature of this effort was that curriculum consultants from Mexico and Peru spent a year working with the department and with schools and communities to improve teaching about their countries.

6. About 125 secondary school and college teachers have been involved in study programs in Eastern Europe, the Middle East, India, and China.

A special role in New York State's efforts has been played by the Center for International Programs and Comparative Studies. The Center has been in operation for more than a decade now, persisting through periods of funding uncertainties and lack of bureaucratic and public interest. There is a full-time staff of about thirty people, with offices in New Delhi, India, as well as Albany and New York City.

The Center's work has included exchange programs with educators in India and the establishment of a Foreign Areas Material Center, which has proved a valuable resource for teachers throughout the country. A major Center effort is conducting workshops and seminars on various aspects of global education. In efforts to improve area studies programs, for example, nearly 200 workshops had been held by 1970, involving more than 3,500 individuals.

In assessing the impact of these efforts, Ward Morehouse, Director of the Center, admits that "aside from scattered pieces of evidence . . . there is nothing systematically developed to demonstrate how student knowledge and understanding of the rest of the world have been changed during this period." However, plans for such evaluation are now underway. In addition, Morehouse points out that "there is very substantial qualitative evidence which has been accumulated by the Center throughout the years to indicate improvement in courses, materials being used in classrooms, and the curriculum in individual schools and colleges."[8]

From a purely subjective point of view, I can attest to a changing climate within New York State schools. My daughter, while a student at Grand Island Central School, took an exciting and innovative humanities course, which replaced traditional English and social studies. The students developed an increased understanding of the societies which have produced the art, drama, music, and literature that make up the course. In addition, she joined in a two-day trip to Albany for a conference on China called "China Today." It was clear from her enthusiastic comments that this was one of those special educational experiences that would not be forgotten. Few such opportunities were available when I was teaching in New York a decade ago.

Indiana offers another example of a statewide effort to provide a global perspective in secondary education. The Department of Public Instruction has changed course descriptions and added new components to emphasize cross-cultural learning and, where possible, cross-disciplinary approaches. The traditional World History course has been changed to World Civilizations to stress non-Western historical trends. New courses have been added in such areas as ethnic heritage, urban development, and African, Asian, and Latin American studies.

A sixty-minute videotape on global education was developed for in-service training and was initially shown to students in education courses throughout the state via the Indiana Higher Education TV network. A revised version of the tape is now available for rental. In-service workshop programs have been pursued for some time to train teams who can work intensively in their home areas.

John Harrold, of the Department of Public Instruction, has emphasized that it is still too early to measure the impact of these programs on what happens in the classroom. However, he points out that there has been a marked increase in workshop participation. A few years ago it would have been difficult to attract interest in a conference on "teaching about interdependence." Now, attendance is consistently higher than anticipated.

As in many states, Indiana benefits from close cooperation with the university system. The Social Studies Development Center at Indiana University has been a major force in curriculum development and dissemination programs. Recently, the Center established a new project, the Mid-America Center for Global Perspectives in Education. Directed by James Becker, this Bloomington-based program is designed to improve communication and cooperation among agencies involved in global education. Activities cover a five-state area—Illinois, Indiana, Kentucky, Michigan, and Ohio.

Another illustration of cooperation between universities and secondary schools is provided by the University of Kentucky. It sponsored a conference in the spring of 1975, Teaching Perspectives for Global Studies, with participants including teachers, curriculum supervisors, and administrators. The goal of the conference was "to demonstrate a number of global studies materials and teaching strategies which are flexible enough to blend with local curriculum expectations while maintaining the global perspective necessary in today's world of shrinking distances, rapid communications, and global problems."

The Center for Teaching International Relations (CTIR) at the University of Denver has long been engaged in conducting in-service training programs for secondary school teachers and preparing academic courses in global education. More recently, CTIR has relied on the work of local teachers to develop a wide variety of teaching materials, including ethnic heritage studies and comparative studies on such topics as modernization, the role of women, communication, and work and leisure.

Private organizations engaged in "outreach" programs also play a major role in alerting teachers to new materials and techniques, developing and testing world-centered curriculum units, and conducting in-service programs and conferences. Some of these organizations, like the Overseas Development Council and the Population Reference Bureau, have recently developed programs designed to reach an audience of high school teachers. Other groups, including the United Nations Association, UNESCO, World Affairs Councils, American Universities Fieldstaff, and organizations concerned with specific areas (such as the Japan Society) continue their efforts to provide information and resources. Professional organizations, too, have demonstrated a growing concern for making schools more world-centered. The National Education Association, for instance, chose as its bicentennial theme "Education for Global Community."

The Center for Global Perspectives, in addition to outreach programs, has taken on the task of working with scholars and teachers in a long-range program to define more precisely what elements of learning are needed to attain a global perspective. This task is concerned with the fact that there remains a great deal about global education that we do not know. We cannot say precisely what information ought to be taught, or how, or at what stage of the school career. We have not yet developed a K–12 sequence that would indicate what skills, knowledge, and attitudes provide most promise in developing "international literacy."

One approach devised by the Center is to develop a sequence for the learning of certain key concepts—like "conflict" or "interdependence"—which involves all the social science disciplines and frequently the humanities and sciences as well. The frameworks being developed are oriented toward existing courses in social studies, science, and literature, rather than toward the creation of new courses. The assumption is that we can begin teaching about such concepts in the early grades, building on the child's daily experiences and familiar surroundings. Later, as more is learned about the concept and applied to experience and course material, it will become natural for the student to use one or another concept for organizing a wide variety of phenomena. Thus, a young person who understands something of the nature of interdependence is better equipped to analyze the complex pressures and tensions that emerge from increased interdependence on a global scale.

This conceptual approach offers only one of many avenues to be explored in developing a clearer definition of global education. Other individuals and groups are engaged in such explorations. The Aspen Institute for International Studies is preparing a series of position papers for the National Commission on Coping with Interdependence; Ward Morehouse has written a number of monographs on the problems schools face in coping with interdependence; Robert Hanvey, in his position paper for the Center for Global Perspectives, tentatively identifies five dimensions of "an attainable global perspective"; and the Social Studies Development Center at Indiana University is developing a framework for teaching strategies called "Guidelines for World Studies."

This definitional work promises to be a lengthy process. In the meantime, programs of dissemination and in-service training cannot wait. We are forced, in effect, to go with what we have—to develop more and better materials and to include far greater numbers of teachers in the effort to provide what we do know to as large a segment of this generation as possible.

SPECIAL PROGRAMS IN INDIVIDUAL SCHOOLS

In individual schools and districts throughout the country, innovative programs have been established which illustrate the increasing variety of alternatives now available. While none of these programs offers a comprehensive design for a world-centered school, each contains at least some of the elements needed to move us in the right direction.

The range of activities varies widely in scope and direction. Donald Thompson, a social studies supervisor in Racine, Wisconsin, is arranging exchange programs with schools in Poland. Joseph Schneider, at West Leyden Township High School in Illinois, creates awareness of connections with other parts of the world by taking his classes on tours of Chicago's temples, churches, import businesses, and the port. A Connecticut teacher at the Parkway School, Carol Sarabun, has arranged an imaginative information exchange with a school in Birmingham, England. Working on the premise that as a student's "awareness of increasing global interdependence expands, he must develop simultaneously a heightened sense of individuality *and* a broadened global perspective," the students deal with such questions as how they learn about their surroundings, their past, their future. The information they compile is then exchanged with students in Birmingham, providing a glimpse of how contemporaries in another society deal with the same questions. In Cambridge, Massachusetts, Lawrence Kohlberg and others have established a school-within-a-school called the Just Community School. The philosophy, as explained by Kohlberg, states, "As a minimal goal of civic education, we would aim to raise the level of moral thinking in all children to the stage that will enable them to understand the principles behind the Declaration of Independence." Getting high school students to that point "will be no easy task. . . . To reach this goal, family, community, and school must work together to establish societies based on principles of justice."[9] To work toward this goal, staff and students draw up a constitution and make decisions on a town-meeting basis. The hope is that "processing real life moral dilemmas in community meetings should lead to change" in the ability to grapple with such problems.

Probably the most common approach to change involves remodeling the curriculum to provide a global perspective in existing courses or in the design of new courses. Often this change involves a single school and relies on the creativity of only a few people. Al Bell, a teacher in Findlay, Ohio, changed the title of his Modern World History course for seniors to a global-awareness course called World Affairs. The year's program is focused on such concepts as interdependence, conflict and war, power, food/hunger, and energy.

Bell, in common with many teachers, finds that his students have little idea of the interdependent nature of world society or the implications of that interdependence. To overcome their initial lack of concern, he relies on simulations, film, and television documentaries. In the unit on power, for instance, the class begins with the simulation game Starpower. The game creates a three-tiered society in which the lower levels encounter increasing frustration in trying to make gains in a game which allows the most powerful group to make or change rules. Starpower has long been an effective device for creating a visceral sense of what it means to be a have or a have-not. Films like *Failsafe* and documentaries such as ABC's "Missiles of October" help to develop the awareness Bell is after.

Some efforts at redesigning courses and teaching strategies involve entire schools and occasionally entire school districts. The Howard County Schools in Columbia, Maryland, used a summer workshop to restructure high school social studies. Fred Czarra, Supervisor of Social Studies, and twenty-five teachers designed a course for ninth graders called Global Perspectives. Course activities include (1) exercises designed to help students develop guidelines for the "clear discussion of public issues"; (2) "independent research into cultural and geographical regions using the tools of the economist, geographer, political scientist, historian, and sociologist"; and (3) a series of units on the "global environment," past, present, and future. Student work is carried out through three types of activities—required, alternative, and optional. Throughout the course, there is a mix of text, outside readings, simulations, and audiovisual materials.[10]

Another important approach in globalizing the curriculum in individual schools is the attempt to combine disciplines. At the Lansdowne Senior High School near Baltimore, Thomas Fort (social studies) and Benjamin Poscover (science) developed a course titled Society-Environment-Science. They relied heavily on student suggestions for modification of the program. In addition to learning about environmental issues, each student takes part in a committee project to explore a local situation. Resource persons in the community are also frequent visitors to the course. Visitors have included a U.S. Senator, a Zero Population Growth spokesperson, and representatives of the Atomic Energy Commission, conservation organizations, and local action groups.

A similar course has been developed at the Cherry Creek Schools in Englewood, Colorado, by John Christianson, a biology teacher, and Mark Hampshire, in social studies. The multimedia unit "Patterns of Human Conflict" is used to introduce the course and leads to a study of the worldwide nature of environmental concerns. The students explore the relationship of their own community to global issues, studying such topics as resources, land use, future planning, and the activities of multinational corporations.

The Cherry Creek unit, which shows the local community's ties to the world, illustrates one of the most exciting new developments in global education—and one that was emphasized by the Andersons in their depiction of world-centered schools. This approach has important advantages. It encourages students (and adults) to gain a better sense of their community, and it enables people to see how individuals and the groups to which they belong are linked to the webs that unite the world into a single system. Or, as the Andersons phrased it, this becomes "a study of the international relations of everyday life." At the same time, community-world explorations serve the goal of creating a closer involvement between school and community.

The pioneering work in providing a framework for studying the community and the world was provided by Chadwick Alger and his associates in the Program in Transnational Intellectual Cooperation at the Mershon Center, Ohio State University. In a publication titled *Columbus and the World*,[11] the program showed how to make an inventory of a community's ties to global networks, exploring business activities, foreign travel, international organizations, religious affiliations, relatives living abroad, and so on.

Building on Alger's work, Charlotte Anderson and Barbara Winston have developed a series of classroom strategies, for both elementary and high school use, called "Your Community in the World: The World in Your Community." Activities include making inventories in the home, the classroom, and the community of goods made in other countries and plotting the nation of origin on a large wall map; using the local telephone directory to list and map such entries as restaurants specializing in non-American foods, translators, steamship companies, electronic equipment, and so on; analyzing events described in daily newspapers; and listing local organizations with overseas connections. Students are encouraged to enlist the involvement of parents, local newspapers, and businesses.

The results of these activities are exciting and eye-opening, not only for the students but for the adult members of the community who become involved. The program helps teachers, in Charlotte Anderson's words, "develop children's perceptual awareness so [students] can see in their everyday lives involvement in transnational or global processes. We can help them look with a new eye at their local community, at the people and activity immediately around them."[12]

A number of other programs have had the same goal of involving the school with the community and both with world networks. The Kettering Foundation tried a controlled experiment in Findlay, Ohio, to see if a variety of programs—conducted by the news media, local colleges, and community organizations—would increase global awareness. The findings of the test suggest that increased exposure to global concerns will result in increased community awareness.

Another program, called the Illinois Southern Project, is designed to provide ways to help citizens of the region understand "the range of impacts associated with their land-use decisions." The project is preparing a set of materials for use by community groups titled "An Illinois Reader on Agriculture, Energy, Environment and the Global Food Crisis."

At the Stamford Catholic High School in Connecticut, Mary Caplice, CND, works with the diocese of Bridgeport in a variety of global education programs involving both schools and church groups. One ongoing project is called "Perspectives: The Parish, the Community, the World." Topics include studying the local scene in terms of power/powerlessness and examining issues involving world resources and citizen responsibility.

OVERCOMING BARRIERS TO A GLOBAL PERSPECTIVE

In Chapter 3, Torney outlined a number of key obstacles to creating a world-centered perspective in students. Many of the programs described or mentioned in the present chapter deal with some of those barriers. However, there are some major barriers to a global perspective which require special consideration.

First, Torney presented strong evidence to support the idea that by age fourteen young people tend to lose their "plasticity" in attitudes. Opinions become more rigid, and there are indications that stereotyping of others actually increases between grades 7 and 12. As Torney points out, these findings do not mean that it is impossible to encourage understanding and acceptance of others. Instead, the lesson to be drawn is that great care must be taken in developing curriculum materials and teaching strategies that can contribute to positive attitude change.

There are some recent efforts that address this need. I mentioned earlier the McDougal, Littell book, *Learning about People and Cultures,* edited by Seymour Fersh. In having students deal directly with such barriers to understanding as prejudice, stereotyping, and miscommunication, it seems likely that they can then approach the study of other peoples in a more open-minded manner, rather than merely repeat thought patterns that produce negative results.

Al Bell and his associates at the Findlay High School use a similar approach to their World Affairs course. Bell writes that their materials and strategies deal with "objectives in cultural perception, developmental processes, cultural empathy, and cross-cultural conflict." In one unit, each student is given a data sheet for an unnamed country and tries to work out a strategy for improving the standard of living "without sacrificing key cultural values." Students do the exercise twice—first individually and then in small groups where ideas must be defended or modified. The class then judges each group's proposal. Bell concludes, "Students seldom leave this unit without some feeling for the complexity and difficulty in the decisions that the leaders of developing countries must make."[13]

Patterns of Human Conflict, also described earlier, has as one of its goals the development of more positive attitudes toward conflict. Research has shown that young people tend to regard conflict as harmful, often associating it with violence, and feel that it is to be avoided if at all possible. An objective of the multimedia unit was to encourage students to see conflict as natural and normal, to observe that it is frequently functional and can be dealt with constructively. The program was tested by Glenn Newkirk of the University of Denver. The results indicated that students in the experimental groups revealed not only a better understanding of conflict but also a "significant" change in attitudes.

Another troubling barrier to a global perspective was described in Torney's discussion of the UNESCO recommendations. She points out that self-esteem is important as a prerequisite to successful international experience as well as an end in itself. The assumption is that before an individual can profit from training designed to improve intercultural communication, he or she would need to have a moderately high level of self-esteem and group esteem. Those concerned with global education must confront this issue for two reasons. First, a global perspective has little value if it is limited to a privileged segment of society. Second, the problem and solution are circular; that is, world-centered schools will help foster self- and group esteem for all groups, which, in turn, will make global education more effective.

I wish I could report marked success in this area. I can't. Efforts to improve the self-image of minority group members have been uneven, inconsistently financed, and without clear-cut objectives and approaches. Global education in inner-city schools remains limited to a few creative programs such as those described earlier in this chapter.

Despite this lack of progress, there are indications that this issue can be dealt with more effectively. Edith King's work in the education department of the University of Denver has stressed the importance of self-concept in the socialization process. In an in-service training program on the "intercultural dimensions of the classroom," she encourages teachers to use song to study multiethnic backgrounds, use resources to develop the intercultural dimensions of the classroom, use management of social conflicts to teach world-mindedness, and foster positive attitudes toward racial awareness.

Through the Ethnic Heritage Curriculum Materials Project of the Social Science Education Consortium, King and her associates conduct workshops which allow participants "to examine curriculum materials, curriculum strategies and methods for teaching about the multi-cultural nature of American society and the role of ethnic heritages in the programs of elementary and secondary schools." Another product of the project has been the careful evaluation of practically all ethnic heritage curriculum materials produced in the past five years. More than 1,000 curriculum items have been analyzed and an annotated bibliography is being prepared. This will enable teachers at all grade levels to locate materials most suitable for their local needs.

Schools that are undergoing the rigors of integration would seem unlikely markets for programs in global education. In these situations, however, it may be that the renewed interest in "magnet" schools offers an important opportunity. In the Dallas suburb of Richardson, a magnet school was recently established at a formerly nonwhite school. It offered an attractive and diversified curriculum, stimulating activities, and a low teacher-student ratio. White parents began to send their children to the school, suggesting that quality education was a more important factor than race. The school is now fully integrated, with no reports of tension and with many families on a waiting list.

The magnet-school concept was first started in Philadelphia in the 1960s, with little success. More recent experiments in Richardson and Minneapolis have been received much more favorably, perhaps indicating that this is an idea whose time has arrived. If this should prove to be the case and more schools are transformed into magnets, it seems important that a world-centered curriculum be one of the alternatives offered.

Despite my emphasis on the wide range of alternatives available for creating more world-centered schools, I do not mean to imply that the problem is well in hand. There is a gap between national need and the uneven progress of global education in secondary schools. On particularly gloomy days, one suspects the gap is widening. A review of the positive efforts undertaken by so many counterbalances the pessimism with a measure of hope. It is this guarded optimism that we must build on, expanding opportunities and persuading all teachers to choose among the options that exist.

NOTES

1. See, for example, Jerrold M. Novotney, "Human Relations in a Mankind School," in John I. Goodlad, M. Frances Klein, Jerrold M. Novotney, and Associates, *Toward a Mankind School,* McGraw-Hill, New York, 1974; also, *The Rise Report,* Report of the California Commission for Reform of Intermediate and Secondary Education, California State Department of Education, 1973, pp. 16–17.

2. The National Commission on the Reform of Secondary Education, *The Reform of Secondary Education: A Report to the Public and the Profession,* McGraw-Hill, New York, 1973, pp. 14–15.

3. Letter to Task Force participants from Wilson Riles, Superintendent of Public Instruction, California Department of Education, October 1975.

4. John I. Goodlad, "A Perspective on Accountability," *Phi Delta Kappan,* vol. 57, no. 2, October 1975, p. 110.

5. Marvin Pasch and John M. Thompson, "The Indiana University World History Project," *Social Education,* vol. 39, no. 6, October 1975, p. 370.

6. From a 1973 survey by the American Association of Colleges of Teacher Education, reported in a personal communication.

7. *International Dimensions of Education,* a Statement of Policy and Proposed Action by the Regents of the University of the State of New York, State Education Department, Albany, 1970.

8. Unpublished conference version of a paper by Ward Morehouse, "Strengthening the International Dimensions of Education in New York State: A Case History," 1975. Quoted by permission of Dr. Morehouse.

9. Lawrence Kohlberg, preliminary draft of "Moral Education: The Research Findings," 1975.

10. Quotations are from a course description, "Global Perspectives Social Studies Curriculum," Howard County Public Schools, Columbia, Md., 1975.

11. Chadwick Alger and the Staff of the Mershon Center, *Columbus and the World,* Mershon Center, Ohio State University, Columbus, 1975.

12. Variations on the Columbus-in-the-World theme are available in David C. King and Charlotte Anderson, *Windows on Our World: The United States* (Houghton Mifflin, 1976, elementary social studies program) and, in a high school version, in Intercom, no. 78, *Teaching toward Global Perspectives,* Center for Global Perspectives, 218 E. 18th St., New York, N.Y. 10003, 1975.

13. A more complete description of the course is contained in *News and Notes in the Social Studies,* Spring 1975.

CHAPTER SEVEN

Other Agencies Promoting a World-Centered View: The World Outside the School

Stephen H. Rhinesmith

AFS International/Intercultural Programs

NOTE: This chapter was prepared with the assistance of Peter White, University of California, Los Angeles.

P revious chapters have concentrated on school programs designed to promote a world-centered view in students. It must be remembered, though, that students spend a great deal of time outside the school and come into contact with people other than teachers and administrators. Even in the ideal world of Middleston, where many people from the outside come into the school, students leave the school for varying periods of time and outside agencies offer programs in which students and other members of the community can participate. A world-centered perspective will never emerge in more than a superficial way if schools are the only agency of society that promote it. Fortunately, many other groups, agencies, and programs are heavily involved in sharing the burden.

EXCHANGE PROGRAMS

A primary means to achieve a world-centered view has been domestic and international student exchanges. These programs offer an opportunity for "personalized contact" with people from another culture. Through participating in such programs by being an exchange student or by hosting students from another culture, American young people, their families, and their communities begin to expand their perspectives on American cultural assumptions and values and are exposed to the "relativity" of these values vis-à-vis other world views. Exchange programs fulfill Joyce and Nicholson's imperatives to promote pluralism and to encourage international citizenship through empathy with other cultures.

In the early twentieth century, American proponents of exchange programs assumed that greater international contact would increase prospects for peace in the world. Because of the expenses involved and the difficulties of travel, however, exchange opportunities were primarily available to the wealthy and became more of a way to "broaden" the individual participant's "horizons" than to offer meaningful intercultural experiences or to enrich programs in the schools and communities left behind.

As early as 1932, exchange programs began to emphasize bringing foreign students to this country. It was hoped these visits would demonstrate the better standard of living achieved in the United States, show the results of a free-market system based on a democratic government, and further the principles of personal freedom in speech and behavior. Since the focus was on what the foreign students would take back with them, few systematic attempts were made to extend the benefits of the programs to the American schools and communities involved.

It was not until the Mutual Exchange Agreement Act of 1962 that the United States officially acknowledged that Americans also had something to learn from people in other countries. Americans were encouraged to travel abroad to learn about other societies and to gain a greater understanding of American society by viewing it from different perspectives. It was in this context that exchanges began to be viewed as more than simply an individual-to-individual contact and became a resource for all those in the school and community who were unable to participate directly.

In the late 1960s, in the context of domestic racial and political strife, many private exchange programs came under increasing attack for their lack of diversity in selection of candidates and in placement opportunities. In response, many programs raised scholarship funds to support students from a variety of ethnic, racial, and socioeconomic backgrounds. At the same time, a second, and perhaps more significant, development occurred. As people became conscious of the diversity of candidates who should be involved in international experiences, a new realization emerged that the significant differences existing in the United States in themselves held a rich opportunity for the development of new perspectives on American society. Those who promoted student exchanges as a way of bringing about peace between countries began to realize that exchanges within the United States could help various groups better understand the differing values and viewpoints they held about the future of American society. While there has been no extensive research on domestic or intranation exchange programs, experiences of educators involved in these programs suggest that domestic intercultural experiences contribute to a student's ability to perceive and accept the cultural variability which exists both on a global basis and within his or her own nation or community.

BENEFITS OF EXCHANGE PROGRAMS
Unfortunately, most discussions of student exchange programs focus on the benefits to the individual student involved. The consequences of well-conceived and well-planned programs are far more widespread.

In programs involving a family-living experience for an exchange student, the host family receives an in-depth exposure to someone from another culture and gains new perspectives on life in another society or different region of this country. When a family makes a commitment to take in a student from abroad or from another ethnic or racial group in the United States, its members commit themselves to a "family learning project" which can be related to the formal educational experience of the children in school. More schools should think about the possibility of helping American host families carry out independent study projects. They should be helped to analyze the cognitive and affective changes which they experience during a year of confronting on a very personal level their specific values, attitudes, and beliefs.

Since most educational exchange programs, whether international or domestic, require the support of a local community group, they can provide an opportunity for various segments of the community to work together and share responsibility for the program. One can find throughout the United States today communities in which a domestic or foreign exchange student has become the focal point for people to work together who otherwise would never have met. These programs make great contributions to a unified community perspective as well as give people the experience of working with diverse cultural groups from their own community.

In addition to community support groups, some exchange programs require the participation of a school-based student club to work in conjunction with the adult organization on fund-raising and other support services. Thus, not only are the working groups culturally diverse, but both young and old are represented. Students are also given the opportunity to take an active role in school and community affairs.

Individual schools can benefit from participation in exchange programs in a variety of ways by using as resources students who are visitors to their schools and their own students who have participated in exchanges. Exchange students can often become resources for curriculum development in social studies, world area studies, foreign languages, or the fine arts. In some communities, exchange students from the high school have served as teachers' aides in elementary and middle school classes to "personalize" the life styles of other nations for youngsters who may have difficulty on a conceptual level. The presence of someone from another culture provides an excellent way of dealing with some of the cognitive barriers Torney discusses in Chapter 3.

An exchange student often becomes the focus for a high school international relations club or ethnic heritage study club which considers the life, customs, traditions, and beliefs of the student's culture. These clubs usually sponsor programs, exhibits, or other activities which make the information they have gathered and the insights gained available to others in the school and the community.

Some schools use their domestic or international exchange student as a focus for an "international week" or a "heritage week" during which many different school activities are developed centering around the culture of the visiting student. Various clubs in the school give musical or drama presentations representing the cultural group; home economics classes study ethnic or national cooking; student government simulates the student's home government structure; and the school may present an evening or Saturday program for the community during which various school groups present their interpretation of life in the student's home country or home region of the United States. The possibilities are limited only by the creativity of the people involved in the program.

The preceding examples of the "ripple" effects of exchange programs are gleaned from actual experiences of students, families, or volunteers who are involved with AFS International/Intercultural Program (formerly the American Field Service). From its origin as a private ambulance service in World War I, AFS has, since 1947, provided family-living and school experiences in the United States for over 55,000 teen-aged students from eighty-four countries of Europe, Asia, Africa, the Middle East, and Latin America and similar experiences abroad for over 35,000 American teen-agers. Currently, approximately 6,000 students from sixty countries participate annually and thousands of volunteers around the world work on the selection, placement, and support of the students and families who take part in the programs each year.

Although most well-known student exchange programs deal with students at the high school level, the International School-to-School Experience (ISSE) arranges exchanges for students as young as eleven years old. ISSE grew out of the Children's International Summer Villages program when it was felt that the summer program was not reaching enough children; school-to-school exchanges were developed to reach a much larger audience. Students chosen to be part of the exchange represent their whole school and carry their experience back to the others who could not participate directly. James Cass commented on this program as follows:

> Person-to-person contacts across cultural barriers are by no means a sure bridge to international respect and understanding. The difficulties of achieving One World are far more complex than we believed a generation ago—or have even accepted fully today. But without an increasing number of person-to-person contacts, we are unlikely ever to achieve a peaceful world. Learning a foreign language grows more difficult with age—and so does full acceptance of an alien culture. The evidence suggests, however, that 11-year-olds have far fewer problems with either—that significant changes in atti-

tude do occur and that in a high proportion of cases they are lasting. Perhaps one of the secrets of a peaceful future is to catch them while they're young.[1]

Thus far schools in Guatemala, India, Iran, Liberia, Mexico, and the United States have actually participated in the exchange of children. Global educators from Ghana, Hong Kong, and Pakistan have become actively associated with ISSE, and responses from Canada, Finland, Germany, Japan, Puerto Rico, and Sweden have been reported recently at the ISSE International Office.[2]

OTHER TYPES OF EXCHANGE PROGRAMS

A common way that people make contact is through visitors' bureaus. Staffed by part-time volunteers and often affiliated with universities, these groups are called upon when individuals or delegations from outside the country or region are in the area. Members of the bureau organize visits to places of interest, put on luncheons, and, most popularly, invite the visitors to their homes for dinner and conversation. These exchanges are widely agreed to be mutually valuable. Americans obtain a personal perspective on other countries, while foreign guests can break through the movies-and-television stereotypes to see how "real" Americans live. The National Council for Services to International Visitors (COSERV) was established in 1961 to coordinate these local visitors councils. Similar services are performed on a less regular basis by church clubs, labor union auxiliaries, the YMCA, senior citizen groups, and others.

Other opportunities exist for teachers to travel abroad for a summer or semester or for a school year. Many teachers serve as tour leaders on group study tours for students. These programs usually are scheduled for from three to ten weeks during the summer, and the tour leader's role involves supervision of a small group of students. Often the program focuses on a special interest such as art or a foreign language, and the tour leader either acts as teacher or works in collaboration with other teachers from the country being visited. In other programs, teachers can go abroad to live with a family and can either teach or study in the foreign school system. Many foundation or government-supported fellowship programs offer stipends for such travel.

Other types of student exchange programs also exist. In many cities, voluntary phases of school integration have involved busing inner-city students to all-white or suburban schools. In order to help alleviate some of the tensions and adjustment problems involved in participating in another culture, schools have developed exchange programs so that students could experience living in the culture for short periods of time. For example, during the late 1960s, Palms Junior High School was one of those designated a host school in an experimental enrichment program in Los Angeles. Participating families from the inner city first visited the predominantly white school during the summer for a picnic to get acquainted with the school and its community. Later, some of the students who would be bused to the school the following fall lived with families from Palms School for a weekend.

One very popular activity which has evolved during recent years is a short-term exchange in which an entire school club, usually one devoted to foreign relations or ethnic heritage study, may develop an exchange with students from a nearby or distant community who are racially, ethnically, or socioeconomically different. In Rochester, Minnesota, the John Marshall High School AFS Club arranges exchanges for from 35 to 50 of its members who spend a week living with families in another AFS community in some other state, attending school and becoming involved in community affairs. The next week they play host in similar fashion in their own community to students from the other school. After such short-term exchanges are completed, the two clubs may develop a program in which they get together once again during the year to discuss their experiences.

The latter is a typical activity of the more than 800 high school student clubs sponsored by AFS. Other programs providing similar activities with different groups are "big brother" or "big sister" efforts which provide cross-cultural or intercultural experiences for young people interested in being a friend to a disadvantaged boy or girl.

SPONSORING ORGANIZATIONS

Basically three types of organizations sponsor intercultural educational opportunities at the precollegiate level: nonprofit, profit-making, and governmental. The private nonprofit organizations are the oldest and most experienced in the field. Since World War II, a number of private profit-making organizations have developed as the demand for international educational opportunities could not be met by the nonprofit field alone. The basic difference between the nonprofit and profit-making organization is that the former is normally supported by a large volunteer network and is operated as a community service. For the most part, profit-making organizations deal only with American students wishing to go abroad and have little experience in sponsoring foreign students in the United States.

Government-sponsored opportunities for educational exchange are generally limited to college and postgraduate levels or reserved for elementary and secondary teachers and administrators. Agencies offering opportunities for teachers include the United States Office of Education, the Peace Corps, and UNESCO. While the United States government does not provide programs for student exchanges, the Bureau of International Educational and Cultural Affairs of the newly formed International Communications Agency provides funds to assist private nonprofit organizations engaged in these activities.

A list of agencies sponsoring international and intercultural exchanges is provided in the Annotated Bibliography at the end of this volume. Several sources provide background information and guidelines for evaluating programs.[3]

OTHER OUTSIDE-OF-SCHOOL PROGRAMS

Exchange programs have been only one activity among numerous and widely varied efforts to bring a greater global perspective to American schools and their communities. However, the strengths of the exchange format—intimacy, individuality, direct experience— have at the same time imposed limitations on its impact. Not every student, much less every community member, can participate in an exchange or come in contact with exchange students during their stay, nor are the more important personal lessons of the exchange experience readily transferrable to others. How, then, to give a more world-centered experience to the great majority of American students who do not travel abroad and to the community members for whom television or a glance at the daily newspaper may be the only contact with the world outside the United States?

The heterogeneous response of universities, governmental agencies, civic and professional organizations, and private foundations to this question can be grouped into three broad types: school-based, community-based, and media-based. The roots of all three modes can be tracked back to many of the same impulses that gave rise to the student exchanges of the post-World War II years.

The founding of the United Nations, for example, was accompanied by the determination that future generations be spared the horrors of war by building defenses for peace in the minds of individuals everywhere. In the United States, that task was to be largely the responsibility of the schools and other educational agencies. Much like the "Americanization" of immigrants a half a century before, schools were expected to help "internationalize" young people through curricular programs that stressed knowledge of other countries and other peoples.

Parallel to the emphasis on education for a peaceful future, there was the pressing need for immediate training of the thousands of Americans who found themselves involved in the country's astoundingly expanded role in world trade and business, economic development and reconstruction, international military alliances, and diplomatic activity. There was a feeling, too, that all Americans were caught up in this new world posture and that a higher level of general knowledge among the public at large was as valuable as specific preparation for overseas posts. Hence, the proliferation of organized short-term or episodic contacts with a world perspective— occasional seminars and conferences on international topics sponsored by service organizations, the spread of university extension courses and adult evening classes in world affairs, public library displays on foreign countries, community folk and ethnic festivals, and innumerable other activities. One facet of this type of response was the appearance of totally new organizations, such as the nationwide United Nations Association of the United States, and the strengthening of existing groups, such as the World Affairs Councils, that function in major United States cities. More important numerically, though, were the many traditional community groups—churches, business and professional groups, youth clubs— that began to incorporate an international component into their regular functions.[4]

Finally, the postwar years saw a tremendous leap in the technology that enabled societies to communicate with one another. The spread of radio and television, combined with the worldwide trend toward urbanization, literally brought home to millions an awareness of events and problems throughout the world. In the United States, as elsewhere, impressions thus formed were often unintended—a side effect of news broadcasts or brief glimpses on television. But there were also daily barrages of highly sophisticated efforts to affect the ways in which people perceived the nature of the emerging world community. This political and cultural propaganda was not issued only by governments; large corporations, political organizations, and communications networks in nearly every country used the airwaves and printing presses to shape public consciousness on international topics. Indeed, many American ideas about evolving world issues such as economic relationships, the end of colonialism, and hunger have been influenced by such a combination of casual contact with news media and exposure to interest-group indoctrination.

In the following sections, we will discuss the school-based, community-based, and media-based responses as they evolved up to the 1970s. A number of contemporary examples from each category will be used to illustrate the diversity of efforts to increase the world-awareness of American citizens.

SCHOOL-BASED PROGRAMS

Other chapters have discussed in detail attempts to bring about changes in the school curriculum in order to promote global perspectives. Often groups outside the school have contributed to these efforts, such as the Social Studies Curriculum Center at the University of Minnesota described by Morris or the Bay Area China Education Project that King discusses. Several other brief examples will be offered here to describe further how agencies outside the school can contribute to programs to enrich the world-centered perspective of students.

The Diablo Valley (California) Education Project, in conjunction with the Rosenberg Foundation and the West Coast War/Peace Center, held a series of areawide teacher workshops in 1974 to draw up a new set of social studies curricula. The organizing topic was "U.S. History and World Civilization through the Lenses of Concepts: Conflict, Interdependence, Self-Identity," and the response was overwhelmingly favorable. Soon the East Bay Council for the Social Studies and St. Mary's College were brought in as part of a widening network of cooperating school and community organizations. The new materials were field-tested in ten other districts in the region, and the staffs in some of these went on to introduce original programs of their own. The Diablo Valley team then turned to resource services, acting as a test-and-evaluation center for world affairs materials drawn up anywhere in the East Bay group of school districts. Additionally, the project was given a contract to apply its conflict resolution strategies, developed in the classroom programs, to administrative problem solving in the district at large.

A major strength of the Diablo Valley project as a whole has been its search for ways to expand community activities outside the school setting. With a number of other groups, it sponsored a districtwide Model United Nations program that brought together close to 400 secondary students for a two-day conference. The project's Community Advisory Board, originally intended to certify the project's content "as a force for social change," disbanded after only one year because the program had already solidly established itself with area educators and with the community. Therefore the project staff has taken on the task of identifying existing parental groups and bringing them together to work on appropriate issues. Through its multifaceted network of cooperating groups, the Diablo Valley Education Project attempts to deal with what Ward Morehouse calls the greatest need of world-centered learning: the raising of "civic literacy on key interdependence issues."[5]

The notion of bringing the world into the classroom has also been a concern of one of public education's major support systems, the universities. Because they are physically and temperamentally removed from the elementary and secondary school classroom, universities concentrate their efforts on the preparation of personnel and materials rather than on direct application. This role is not new. What has changed in the past decade is the much broader interpretation that universities have given to their traditional tasks, and this is nowhere more evident than in the area of education for world perspectives.

Probably the strongest impetus for this new role has been the federal government. Under the National Defense Education Act (NDEA) area studies centers for Latin America, Africa, and Asia were funded at major universities across the country. Their fundamental objective continues to be training graduate-level students in the cultures, languages, and social systems of the developing world. But recently the NDEA efforts have begun to diffuse the enormous quantity of basic research carried out at the centers. "Outreach" plans have become an important aspect of efforts by centers to disseminate their research in usable form to junior colleges, state education departments, community organizations, and schools. This represents a valuable potential resource available to groups working directly in world affairs education. The Division of International Education at the U.S. Office of Education has compiled a description of the outreach activities of forty-five centers for international and language and area studies. It is available to the public on request.

Three NDEA-sponsored Latin American centers have done much of the pioneering work in the "outreach" field. Where their activities overlap, such as in curriculum development and dissemination, the three have set up informal coordinating and information exchange committees. At the same time, each has put the larger part of its efforts into servicing educational groups outside of the university.

The University of Florida (Gainesville) built its outreach program around nontraditional materials for elementary and secondary social studies units. Central to the materials is the concept of value clarification. The classroom exercises (there are no formalized texts to follow) are situational contexts or "short, incomplete case studies, in which the student is forced to project himself into a decision-making situation, and then, through the value clarification questions that follow, to justify her decision."[6] The contexts are Latin American—a tourist, a student, the child of a landowner or a peasant, social settings that require a shift in behavior—and each section is followed by a series of increasingly probing questions for students about obvious relationships and their more subtle meanings. The "personalization strategy" employed by the University of Florida's NDEA center attempts to have North American students "perceive and experience events in the manner in which Latin Americans perceive and experience them."[7]

The Latin American Center at the University of California, Los Angeles (UCLA), is also working on a culture-based approach to international studies for public school courses. But its most innovative contribution to the "outreach" format has been its growing involvement with junior (community) colleges. In the summer of 1976, a team of fifteen selected junior college instructors, under UCLA supervision, spent six weeks in classroom and cultural studies in Mexico and then designed curricular materials in different fields—anthropology, history, music, art, political science—for the postsecondary level of instruction. It was the first time that such a program in a Latin American country had been funded by the federal government. The fifteen instructors now function as an informally coordinated network for area studies information at their campuses throughout southern California. The University's Latin American Center, in turn, acts as a depository of materials and a resource center for junior colleges.

The Institute for Latin American Studies at the University of Texas (Austin), in contrast, has drawn up an ambitious Latin American Culture Studies Project that proposes bringing together a spectrum of public agencies that deal with education. The project's broad-based focus on intercultural learning is reflected in the composition of its advisory board: officials from the Texas Education Agency, professors from the university, a high school teacher, a Mexican-American priest, and a community activist.

An institute study confirmed the belief that the university's greatest impact on the state's bilingual/bicultural effort could be made through familiarizing elementary and secondary teachers with Latin American culture, concepts, and history. Therefore, several miniresource centers will be set up around the state in cooperation with the Texas Bilingual/Bicultural Center. They will offer short-term training seminars and access to the courses and materials held at the university and will provide updated classroom materials that are sensitive to the state's large Latin American population. Participation in the centers is open to all community groups as well as teachers and administrators.

A second concern of the Texas plan is the quality of services offered by public libraries. In addition to sending out reviews of available publications on Latin America, the university committed itself to upgrade the libraries' ability to obtain, organize, and present area studies materials in local communities. Conferences for librarians have been held, and these will eventually lead to a trilateral support relationship among the university, the libraries, and the bilingual/bicultural resource centers.

The Asia Society (112 East 64th Street, New York) maintains liaison with many of the university outreach programs on Asian Studies. Among the better known of these programs are the University of Michigan's Project in Asian Studies Education (PASE) and the Berkeley-Stanford Joint Center, the Bay Area China Education Project (BACEP). Both PASE and BACEP provide a variety of materials and services to teachers. The Committee on Secondary Education of the Association of Asian Studies and the Service Center for Teachers of Asian Studies, located at Ohio State University, can also be useful resources.

Although it is evident that recent programs to "bring the world into the classroom" involve much more than just the school setting, a great deal of effort still concentrates on curricular design and material development. However, even these areas are characterized by their sharp departure from the traditional emphases on facts-and-figures learning and ethnocentric comparisons with other cultures. As other chapters pointed out, simulations, value questioning, and "other-centered" materials are slowly supplanting the standard textbook for international studies in American schools. Even more remarkable is the extent of the trend to greater community or nonschool involvement in world social studies. Often disparate organizations—universities, community-action groups, political organizations, public agencies—are cooperating in a variety of ways that promise a more even continuum between what is taught in the classroom about world cultures and what is available in the community to build on that learning.

Nevertheless, a word of caution is in order. The difficulty of introducing and then supporting truly world-centered learning in the vast American educational system cannot be underestimated. There are many areas of the country—if not the major part of the United States—where little has been done in the past twenty years to alter traditional social studies content. Looking at just one segment of the field, the Carnegie Commission on Higher Education strikes a sobering note: "When one considers the total range of international programs in United States colleges and universities, those relating to high schools and other community groups are few indeed."[8]

COMMUNITY-BASED PROGRAMS: LOCAL GROUPS AND INTERNATIONAL PERSPECTIVES

Schoolchildren are not the only Americans who come in contact with organized programs that try to increase world awareness. The myriad of internationally focused activities carried out by groups in towns and cities everywhere often goes virtually unnoticed by the public precisely because the activities take place as parts of other ongoing programs with which the groups are more readily identified. A community group may sponsor a bake sale to aid UNICEF; a Boy Scout troop attends a worldwide scouting jamboree; the Junior Chamber of Commerce hears a guest speaker on the topic of international food shortages. The unifying factor in these encounters with the world outside the United States is that they are planned and sponsored by groups in the community and intended to reach the rest of the community, not just children in schools. However, these programs are not usually thought of when efforts at promoting global perspectives are described since, for the most part, international understanding is not the issue around which the participating group is organized and continues to function.

Typical of community group involvement is the occasional sponsorship of individual functions with a specific international focus; these may be money-raising events such as fairs or community drives, but luncheons with guest speakers seem to be standard. The Kiwanis, Optimist, Lions, and Junior Chamber of Commerce groups are all well known for this format. In the case of several community service organizations, the international involvement is more permanent. The Lions, Kiwanis, and Rotary are international organizations that have member clubs in many countries composed, like chapters in the United States, of businesspeople and other local leaders. Exchange visits between clubs, cooperation on community projects (such as an American club's support for a health or schooling program sponsored by an overseas club), organizationwide newsletters, and international conferences all act to maintain the sense of common purpose across national frontiers. The impact of these activities on the community-at-large is usually felt through the individual members of the service organizations and through financial contributions that the groups make to international activities, such as high school exchange programs. The Rotary, in addition, finances its own nationwide student exchange scholarships. Recent college graduates are sent abroad for between six months and one year on independent research projects. The sponsoring Rotary clubs place no restrictions on the students, other than that they keep in touch with Rotary clubs in the country they visit and that they report back to the sponsoring clubs when they return.

The World Affairs Councils, which operate in most urban centers in the United States, aim at a broader and more deliberately educational impact on the community. Although the sole focus of the councils is international relations, their involvement in the field resembles that of other community organizations in that they do not identify with one particular issue or cause. The format of the councils' most apparent activities—luncheons, guest speakers, occasional seminars—are episodic in nature; but the councils' full-time staffs and year-round programs make these groups a permanent part of community-based international efforts.

Begun in the Middle West immediately after World War I, the councils were based on the concept that well-presented, balanced information would lead to the people's ability to make the best foreign policy decisions. After World War II, the councils spread nationwide. Today, they still sponsor talks by renowned world figures. But some councils have also expanded into a kind of interorganizational body to coordinate related activities in the community.

> Such Councils publish newsletters telling what other community groups are doing in the field, and the community groups check with the Council in order to establish dates that do not conflict with other organizations. The Council also serves the other groups by providing them with speakers, program ideas, and co-sponsorship.[9]

The first World Affairs Council, in Cleveland, has also been especially active in promoting international perspectives among local youth. Affiliated clubs at high schools, church youth groups, Scouts, and others carry out their regular activities independently, with the Council providing a coordinator to offer the same kind of support assistance it provides to other community groups.[10] The Philadelphia Council works closely with public and private schools in the area. For example, the Council has prepared eight global study units for secondary teachers entitled "Interdependence Curriculum Aid." Councils in Los Angeles, Cincinnati, and other cities provide similar services.

The Northern California World Affairs Council worked with the UN Association of San Francisco and the Bar Association of San Francisco in sponsoring an Oceans Conference for Bay Area high school students in 1974. The focus of the conference was on jurisdiction over the biological and mineral resources of the seas and the prospects for an international treaty to regulate their use.

Outside of the country's large urban centers, the most familiar form of community-based involvement with other nations is the "sister city" program. Local organizations in American cities and in foreign cities agree to coordinate an ongoing community-to-community relationship in order to further international understanding and goodwill. Most such pairings are facilitated by the National League of Cities, the U.S. Information Service, and Sister Cities International. Responsibility for the program's activities, however, remains with each town's Sister City committee.

Typically, contacts between the sister cities is at the personal and the semiofficial levels: mutual visits by municipal officials, teacher delegations, students, service clubs, and so on. The town's newspapers and other news media cover events in the associated town, national holidays are marked, and cultural events featuring the sister city's heritage are highlighted. The bond between these cities is often very real, and it is one with which individual citizens can identify personally. In 1970 and 1971, when Seattle was in the depths of an economic recession, its Japanese sister city sent boxes of food and other relief aid. After the 1976 Guatemala earthquake, American towns affiliated with Guatemalan towns spearheaded the collection of emergency shipments of food, medicine, and money for reconstruction.

Bringing the world to American communities, as we have seen, is a process as varied as the hundreds of local and regional organizations involved. The goal is broadly the same: to increase knowledge and understanding of peoples outside the United States. The scope of that undertaking may range from a single club in one town to a nationwide system of organizations, and it may extend anywhere from a single luncheon speaker to a years-long transnational relationship between whole communities. What ultimately unifies these grass-roots efforts is their dependence on the continued interest and enthusiasm of individuals.

THE WORLD IN THE HOME: MEDIA-BASED PROGRAMS
In this electronic age, our perceptions of the world are increasingly influenced by the biases of the large information-gathering networks. Government agencies, newspaper chains, and television

compete—and, too often, cooperate—to present a particular viewpoint about another country or international relations in general. Challenging the dominance of such networks in this primary field, where the building blocks of later understanding are formed, is a difficult task. Universities, citizens groups, and individuals who can shape textbooks and community programs simply lack the resources to gather and then disseminate fast-changing contemporary news items. Their efforts are in many respects secondary or *post hoc*. While the views of most Americans are being subtly formed through a daily barrage of "authoritative" and "objective" information, community groups have relied on weekly meetings, a film or a speaker, or a school program to create alternative, well-rounded world perspectives.

Within the past ten years or so, there have been numerous attempts by world affairs interest groups to enter the field of basic information gathering and dissemination. The high cost of publishing large-circulation newspapers or magazines or of staffing an independent system of foreign correspondents has necessarily kept these efforts to a small scale.

An excellent example of a community-centered information system is the Columbus in the World, the World in Columbus project. With the financial support of the Kettering Foundation and Ohio State University, the Program in Transnational Intellectual Cooperation has prepared a series of reports on Columbus's involvement with the world. Each report is a profile of the international contacts of a different segment of the city such as blacks, businesses, church groups, or the university.

> The goal [of the project] is to stimulate more interest in international activity in Columbus by making people more aware of this activity. . . . Hopefully, the citizens of Columbus will make more informed judgments about the ways in which their own community and job are interdependent with the world.[11]

The reports present information in a neutral, statistical form without offering an analysis. The flow of manufactured goods in and out of Columbus is documented, as is the number of Columbus tourists and their destinations and the number of foreign visitors to the central Ohio city. The university's overseas programs are listed, and the city's ethnic makeup is traced historically. The Columbus program acts as a resource center for any community group that needs this kind of information. Its actual ties to other groups are minimal, and it sponsors no international activities of its own. Reflecting this, the program circulates its pamphlet-style Brief

Reports throughout the community free of charge and invites citizens in to review the full reports or to contribute to future studies.

One result of the Columbus project has been the preparation of a resource handbook containing numerous sample activities and ideas for identifying links and relationships between individuals, groups, and agencies in a community and in the world. Entitled "Your State and the World," it was developed by the Mid-America Program at Indiana University for the Council of Chief State School Officers and has been distributed to all fifty states.

The Columbus project has sparked a number of similar information networks in such widely separated places as Richmond, Virginia; Oshkosh, Wisconsin; and San Diego, California.

In contrast to the Columbus program, which emphasizes gathering primary information, is the University of Texas's "Latin American Review." The "Review" is a half-hour radio show broadcast weekly as part of the university's Latin American Institute's "outreach" project. The first fifteen minutes of each program offer an English-language review of the coverage given to international events by the Latin American press. An alternative perspective to the one given in media in the United States is thus made available to the public. The second half of the program is varied; it may be a round-table discussion of Latin American political and economic trends, a discussion of a particular artist or writer, or a presentation of indigenous Latin American music. The Texas project, then, focuses on the analysis and dissemination of essentially secondary information in such a way as to promote the same kind of broadened community perspectives aimed at by the Columbus in the World series. Further, both approaches seek to reach the vast American public, including those who no longer attend school and who do not participate in community organizations. Thus, although the media-based approach to world-centered perspectives is the smallest and least well-known of the three discussed here, its potential, in the size of the audience it can reach, is by far the greatest.

The use of news media for elementary and secondary school students has also attracted greater attention in recent years and has moved significantly beyond the rote "current events" format. In Peoria, Illinois, the city's daily paper, the *Journal-Star,* has created a joint community-business advisory committee for its "Newspaper in Education" program. Working with Indiana University's Mid-America Program for Global Perspectives in Education, three teachers on the advisory committee drew up a guide for helping students learn about the world through the pages of the local newspaper. "Peoria and the World" first combs the paper for news items that demonstrate the many links—personal, financial, cultural—

between central Illinois and the rest of the world; the guide then shows how to organize the items around themes (sports, industry, food, exports and imports) and learning activities that can draw on the themes (spelling, geography, and so forth). The *Indianapolis Star* and *Indianapolis News* use the same approach in their program, "Indy and the World." These more innovative, reflective applications of media-based information provide what James Becker of the Mid-America Program terms the "critical links" (that is, data, conceptual frameworks, and theories on international relations) between the United States population and that population's understanding of how it relates to the world around it.[12]

Not surprisingly, efforts are also being made to use television more effectively for the promotion of international and intercultural concepts among school-age children. "Villa Alegre" (Happy Village), a half-hour Spanish-English bilingual program for four-to-eight-year-olds, is among the most prominent of such efforts. Essentially an attempt to heighten the appreciation of cultural pluralism in the United States, "Villa Alegre" uses stories, games, dances, and community life in an imaginary village to illustrate five major themes: human relations, the natural environment, nutrition, energy, and man-made objects. The basic concept that "Villa Alegre" hopes to impart is that different world cultures are "complementary rather than contradictory ways of organizing the social world."

The work of Prime Time School Television, a Chicago-based group, in encouraging in-school use of selected television programs children view at home is an imaginative and important development in this field. Other efforts of the Public Broadcasting System (PBS) in making available such programs as the "Big Blue Marble" and "World" indicate an increasing awareness of the importance of television as an educational tool.

In short, the shrinking and increasingly interdependent nature of the world has spurred efforts to help people better understand our changing reality. In the United States, those efforts evolved slowly from an American-centered approach based on factual material alone to the current accent on world-centered perspectives and world-centered solutions to common human problems. Although the bulk of the work continues to revolve around schools and students, there is a growing trend to involve the community as a whole through local organizations, the media, and programs that require the cooperation of schools, organizations, and individuals. The task, obviously, is enormous. But in promoting a better understanding of other peoples, all the various approaches are contributing to an equally important goal: a greater understanding of ourselves.

NOTES

1. James Cass, "Catch Them While They're Young," *Saturday Review,* Jan. 11, 1975, p. 53.

2. For further information on the program, write to the ISSE International Office, 826 Carpenter Lane, Philadelphia, Pa. 19119.

3. See, for example, National Council of State Supervisors of Foreign Languages, *Criteria for Evaluating Foreign Study Programs for High School Students,* MLA/ACTFL Materials Center, 62 Fifth Avenue, New York, N.Y. 10011, 1966; Michigan Foreign Language Curriculum Committee, *Criteria for Evaluating Foreign Study Programs for High School Students* and *Guidelines for Evaluating Foreign Study Programs,* Michigan Department of Education, Lansing, 1967; *Guidelines for the Appraisal of Travel-Study Tours for Secondary School Students,* endorsed by the Council of Regional Secondary School Accrediting Commissions and by the Administrative Committee, Commission of Secondary Schools, North Central Association, 5454 South Shore Drive, Chicago, Ill., 60615, 1968; *ERIC Focus Reports on the Teaching of Foreign Languages, Number 5, Foreign Study for High School Students: What's Going On?* available from the MLA/ACTFL Materials Center, New York, 1970; *A Guide to Institutional Self-Study and Evaluation of Educational Programs Abroad,* available from the Council on International Educational Exchange, 777 United Nations Plaza, New York N.Y. 10017; and U.S. State Department, *A Word of Caution: Private Work, Study on Travel Abroad Organizations,* Director of Public Information and Reports Staff, Bureau of Education and Cultural Affairs, Department of State, Washington, D.C., 1974.

4. The variety of such activities in the early 1950s can be seen in Samuel Everett and Christian Arndt (eds.), *Teaching World Affairs in American Schools: A Casebook,* New York, 1956, chap. 2.

5. Ward Morehouse, "American Education and Global Interdependence: Scaling the Shoulders of Atlas," unpublished background paper for the National Commission on Coping with Interdependence, July 1975.

6. *Cross-Cultural Inquiry: Value Clarification Exercises,* Center for Latin American Studies, University of Florida, Gainesville, 1974.

7. Ibid.

8. Irwin Sanders and Jennifer Ward, *Bridges to Understanding,* Carnegie Commission on Higher Education, New York, 1970; and Maurice Harari, "Trends and Issues in Globalizing Higher Education," American Association of State Colleges and Universities, Suite 700, One DuPont Circle, Washington, D.C., 1977.

9. William Rogers, *Global Dimensions in U.S. Education: The Community,* Education Commission of the International Studies Association, New York, 1972, p. 27.

10. Everett and Arndt (eds.), op. cit., p. 115.

11. "Columbus in the World, the World in Columbus," Brief Report No. 1, Mershon Center, Ohio State University, April 1974, p. 4.

12. Sallie Whelan, "'Peoria and the World' and '[Your Town] and the World'," *Social Education*, vol. 41, no. 1, pp. 20–26, January 1977.

CHAPTER EIGHT

Curriculum Planning for World-Centered Schools

M. Frances Klein

Pepperdine University and Institute for Development of Educational Activities, Inc. (|I|D|E|A|)
and

Kenneth A. Tye

Institute for the Development of Educational Activities, Inc. (|I|D|E|A|)

T he concern for global education is growing not only in the United States but in many other countries throughout the world. The need for children and youth to develop a global perspective has been well established in the preceding chapters of this book, and promising practices in schools in the United States have been described. When a trend such as this gains impetus, there is a tendency for educators to "get on the bandwagon" quickly without adequate thought and planning. The result is often discouragement or outright failure, and too frequently the idea or innovation, not the lack of thought or planning, is blamed for the disappointment. As a general message for this book, perhaps we should caution, "Protect us from the advocates of global education who do not plan carefully for its implementation in the schools."

Even though we believe the case has been established in this book and elsewhere regarding the critical necessity for education to help students develop global perspectives, it also is apparent that attempts to introduce global education into the curriculum have met with limited success. The lack of success can be understood more clearly when the complex problems encountered are made explicit. Developing curricula is a difficult task at best, and global education poses some particularly troublesome dilemmas. Our belief in the importance of what we are doing must be strong enough to provide the persistence needed to resolve the problems.

Curriculum development involves answering a number of difficult questions during intensive planning sessions and then monitoring the success of the curriculum during implementation. But before a specific curriculum can be planned, careful deliberations must take place to set educational priorities and to develop a rationale to guide subsequent work.

Schools cannot teach everything that is available to be taught. Students spend only part of their day in schools, and resources for schooling are limited. Time, money, and personnel are always in short supply in relation to the tasks to be done. Consequently, priorities have to be set. We face at least two problems when we think of setting curriculum priorities. First, the task itself takes time because the array of all possibilities must be considered in relation to the needs of the students, the needs of the local and national communities, and the needs of the global community. Second, setting priorities may involve not only the addition of new objectives and content but also an examination of what already exists in order to delete, clarify, augment, or cut back. It is this latter task which is often overlooked or not undertaken because of tradition, comfort with routines, or a reluctance to give up time-honored practices.

A new goal calling for developing global understanding cannot be simply tacked on to an existing program. If it has high priority—and we think it should—then the entire curriculum must be examined, and it may be found that global education will have to replace or require modifications in established curricula. This will require careful and perhaps even painful deliberations. It may also require taking difficult actions based on the agreed-upon priorities. But when priorities have been set after consultation with all those concerned about and involved in the process of schooling, the direction of future planning and action for curriculum workers becomes much clearer.

After priorities have been set, a critical step which is often overlooked by curriculum planners is developing and explicitly stating a rationale for their decisions and actions. If curriculum planning is viewed as a formative process, never ending, always open to new information, new needs, and new priorities, then we can see the usefulness of explicit statements about why decisions are made or why actions are taken. We believe the analysis offered by Becker in Chapter 2 and the imperatives discussed by Joyce and Nicholson in Chapter 4 are representative of the kinds of statements which might become significant parts of an explicit rationale designed to guide curriculum development.

By being explicit in the rationale for why and how decisions are to be made, tradition may come under question and action may be taken to change it. It is possible, for example, that if a school district looked at its social studies program, it would discover that United States history is taught to every student in the fifth, eighth, and eleventh grades and, in one form or another, at several other levels. A careful examination of the rationale would probably reveal that United States history became such a prominent part of schooling because (1) it was a vehicle for the Americanization of countless immigrants or children of immigrants and (2) it took on added importance in a time when contact with the world outside the United States was an improbability for most Americans. It can then be seen that these conditions no longer apply. An era of international interdependence and instant communication when many Americans will travel overseas at least once provides a rationale for traditional social studies offerings to be expanded to include a more global set of studies.

The preceding chapters define in many ways some of the desired results, the complex problems, and the available resources for developing global education programs. This chapter attempts to bring these together and add some additional considerations which we feel are important as a result of our experiences as curriculum specialists and from being involved in a global education project for the past decade.[1] We have divided the chapter into two major sections. The first section poses some basic curricular questions which must be answered in the process of planning and implementing global education curricula. It also pulls together some of the possible answers suggested in this book and in other sources. The second section discusses other problems which must be confronted so that schools can become more effective in helping students develop global perspectives.

CURRICULAR QUESTIONS

There are ten basic curricular questions which we believe ought to be answered during the process of planning global education programs. Some of these questions have been answered in previous chapters; for others we suggest some possible answers. The curricular questions center on the following topics: goals and objectives, learning activities, resources, methodology, content, organization, evaluation, grouping, time, and space. Beyond these, there are still further questions to be resolved about decision making, satisfaction, appropriateness, and comprehensiveness.

WHAT ARE THE GOALS AND OBJECTIVES?
One of the most pervasive questions in curriculum planning is, "What are the goals and objectives?" Goals are usually defined as broad purposes or directions which the curriculum should take, while objectives include the more precisely defined student behaviors which are the desired outcomes of the curriculum. We are very aware that whether or not objectives should be stated is a very controversial curricular topic. We believe, however, that goals and objectives must be determined if the curriculum is to have maximum impact upon the students.

Usually it is possible to identify some of the goals and objectives early in the process of planning, while others become clear as work progresses. Decisions about goals and objectives should never be considered as final but should be viewed as subject to modification as the curriculum evolves.

A school which hopes to develop a global education program must begin by involving community members, parents, administrators, teachers, and students in a discussion of goals. Statements of possible goals for global education are scattered throughout Chapter 1 and are suggested in most of the other chapters. In Chapter 1, two broad goals are identified for world-centered schools: students will understand their identities in relation to themselves as individuals, as humans, as inhabitants of planet Earth, and as members of a global society; and students will develop the competencies needed to cope with the problems, tensions, and tasks inherent in the above identities and in the conflicts stemming from them. Goals mentioned in other chapters include ability to appreciate diversity, communication with others, management of conflict, tolerance of ambiguity, ability to take on the role or viewpoint of another, trust of other cultural groups, ability to interpret customs and nonverbal behavior in differing cultural styles, respect for others, development of a positive self-image, and understanding of the interdependence of all people.

Prior chapters emphasized that goals must promote affective as well as cognitive learnings. Value clarification is mentioned as an important component, as is development of trust, personal initiative, and risk taking. Torney cites the importance of recognizing the interplay of the cognitive and affective dimensions of human growth. Cognitive skills and abilities such as comprehension of other peoples and cultures, knowledge about their environments, and an understanding of global problems are not by themselves enough to develop the kinds of outcomes desired. Young people must also value diversity in the human community, have positive attitudes toward others, and take a continuing interest in social problems.

Another goal of the curriculum should be to examine the role conflict plays in the interaction of individuals and groups. Students who are to become effective members of a global society must do more than understand how conflict can occur and be resolved: they must not be afraid of conflict but must be willing to recognize it openly and able to confront it in a positive manner. Torney suggests that denial of the existence of conflict in the social studies curriculum may carry the latent message that something must be wrong with the political system since only "safe" facts are taught. She also states that unwillingness to deal with conflict-producing problems such as war and overpopulation may be an obstacle to the development of a global perspective. She believes that one function of the curriculum ought to be to help students understand and not be afraid of the diverse pressures which produce conflict but which also lead to social progress.

Few who believe in the importance of global education would argue with the goals discussed above. They are terribly important, and yet they are also elusive and vague when one tries to use them to plan a program. The problem is to operationalize these goals into meaningful directions or objectives for guiding daily classroom activity. Objectives are needed which explicitly state the intended learnings of students—cognitive, affective, and psychomotor.

The goal of understanding and appreciating other people and other countries, for example, is broad and difficult to use in directing daily classroom procedures. It needs to be further refined as more specific and rigorous objectives. This goal might take the form of several objectives; for example, students should:

1. Have knowledge of how other people on the globe live and cope with their environment

2. Respond to people of other races, cultures, and religions in a positive manner

3. Be able to analyze the effects of the use and misuse of natural resources upon the peoples and regions of the world

4. Be able to comprehend varying points of view about issues

5. Be able to evaluate the effects of their behavior on other people[2]

These more specific behaviors begin to suggest how the curriculum can be shaped to achieve them. Resources such as books, films, and people must be made available in order for students to gain knowledge of other people and their ways of coping. The Annotated Bibliography at the end of this book lists sources that may be useful in making a selection. Personal contact under positive circumstances must be provided with people of other races and cultures. Various ways of doing so are suggested by Rhinesmith. Opportunities to analyze how the world's resources are being used and misused must be offered through a variety of media. The project to analyze the Sacramento Delta that King described is one way of beginning close to home. An array of viewpoints must always be presented and discussed so that students will comprehend a variety of positions on social issues and problems. Here simulations such as those described by Morris and King can be useful. Opportunities to comprehend and then evaluate the effects of one's behavior upon others must be presented in the daily operations of the classroom.

When goals are further refined into more specific behaviors which suggest classroom activities, their importance becomes much clearer. Goals affect all other curricular decisions.

WHAT LEARNING ACTIVITIES SHOULD BE PROVIDED?

A second question to be confronted in curriculum planning focuses upon how to provide quality learning activities for students. Learning activities are the opportunities or tasks provided to students to help them learn. The curricular question is, "What activities can be planned and developed for or with the students so that the desired goals and objectives will be achieved?"

A number of resources exist which can help teachers choose wisely from all the possible activities which a fertile imagination might generate. Tyler, Goodlad, and Raths, for example, have each carefully formulated a set of criteria intended to guide the selection of worthwhile learning activities.[3]

Both Tyler and Goodlad discuss one criterion which we consider to be essential and which seems to be particularly neglected in practice: the learning activity must provide the students with the opportunity to practice what we expect them to learn.

If the goals and objectives are directed toward a better understanding of humankind and toward the development of a global perspective, in order to provide practice, teachers and students might select activities such as role playing, interacting with a variety of people, writing an essay from the perspective of someone in another place, exchanging tapes, listening to music from another land, and reading foreign newspapers. Many other examples of activities which would help students practice behaviors specified in this objective can be found in the previous chapters of this book. The students in Middleston's schools were engaged in many types of activities, not just the traditional reading, writing, and listening. Students were learning in many other ways: interviewing, constructing, interacting, and using a variety of resources in the school and community. Such activities help assure that students will learn both vicariously and in direct ways, another criterion useful in selecting worthwhile learning opportunities. The programs described in Chapters 5, 6, and 7 also reflect many types of activities for learning which will involve students in firsthand and vicarious experiences.

WHAT RESOURCES ARE NEEDED?
The planning and development of learning activities is closely related to a third curricular task: the selection or development of resources to be used in the activities. A major task in this area is the selection of the learning materials (books, films, and other objects) or people to be used to promote learning.

This task is not simple because learning materials often undermine the goals and objectives of a global education program. Morris points out that even subtle differences between chapter headings, such as "Why Is America an Important Country?" and "What Do the People of Mexico Need?," can create an unintended impression in students. Torney refers to the fact that commonly used map projections carry a nationalistic message and that we lack symbols for global entities. The problem is not that materials for global education programs are unavailable; rather it is one of identifying learning materials that promote a global perspective and do not contain contrary hidden messages. In their descriptions of programs, Morris, King, and Rhinesmith often refer to specific materials. Other sources for materials can be found in the Annotated Bibliography at the end of this volume.

Learning materials such as books, filmstrips, cassettes, films, and realia are usually found in the classroom and represent an invaluable resource for learning. They must be augmented, however, with many other resources commonly overlooked by schools. The people in the school can be an extremely valuable learning resource. Using foreign students as a resource for global education was mentioned in several chapters. Staff and faculty members and parents who have traveled extensively or are from another country or culture can be resources for learning. The unique cultural heritage and personal qualities of each adult and student in the school and community can contribute to development of global perspectives.

Learning resources also exist outside the school. Many examples have been given of how the community can be used as a resource for learning. Businesses, industries, stores, churches, civic organizations, government agencies at all levels, community people, celebrations, the media, museums, wilderness areas, and parents as well as the artifacts which surround us in our daily lives are as valuable as the learning materials used in classrooms. An effective global education program must take advantage of these resources as well as the ones traditionally used in school.

WHAT METHODOLOGY SHOULD BE USED?

Closely related to decisions about providing quality learning activities and resources is another curricular question centered upon what teaching methodology is to be used. Methodology refers to the techniques that a professional teacher has in his or her repertoire which can be utilized in the process of instruction. Lecture, discussion, question-answer, problem solving, discovery, inquiry, role playing, modeling, and the like are all terms which describe teaching methods. When the array of goals, objectives, activities, and resources for global education programs is examined, it becomes apparent that a variety of teaching techniques is required.

The conceptualization of teaching models by Joyce and Weil[4] is a valuable resource for those involved in planning and implementing curricula. They group different approaches to teaching and related methodologies into three broad categories: information processing, personal, and social models of teaching. All are needed in global education programs. In an effective curriculum, students need to be helped in gaining and using information about their world—its people, resources, problems, organizations for governance, and patterns of social interaction. Students also need to grow in personal ways to develop their own system of values and understand how those values help direct their behavior. A positive view of self and others is needed along with skills such as goal setting and risk taking, the ability to be introspective, and a continuing desire for learning and growth throughout all of life's stages.

Equally as important as the preceding two areas of development is growth in social interaction. To gain a global perspective, students must learn how to interact with many types of people in positive ways, how to resolve conflict, how to function constructively as a member of a group, how to view social conflicts from a variety of perspectives, how to operate effectively in a pluralistic democracy, and how to grapple with complex social problems. For each of these areas, Weil and Joyce suggest alternative teaching methodologies.[5]

It should be noted that in most of the programs described by Morris and King, the teachers were not standing at the front of the class lecturing. They were participating in discussions, monitoring, observing, and, in some cases, completely out of the picture. The Andersons' description of the Middleston program created new categories of teaching personnel and called for them to perform new functions. It appears that if global education is to become a reality in our schools, teachers will have to augment their traditional roles and the methodologies they use in working with students.

WHAT CONTENT SHOULD BE TAUGHT?

Another major curricular question to be answered is that of what content will be taught. Content is defined as being the concepts and processes which students are expected to learn as they interact with the planned curriculum. Typically, these are taken from the disciplines: anthropology, psychology, physics, chemistry, art, music, mathematics, and so on.

The content selected must help achieve the goals and objectives of global education as well as being of such significance that it is worthwhile engaging students in the learning process with it. Morris has said that much of what is offered in the social studies is already known by the students. Also, much of what is usually taught consists of facts which are easily forgotten and subject to revision in our rapidly expanding fund of knowledge. This does not represent significant content. Perhaps more significant content could be drawn from topics such as how humans meet basic needs, the conservation and use of limited resources, peaceful resolution of conflict, skills in social interaction, and understanding human behavior. As the Andersons point out, one area students should study is their fellow humans—their processes, their needs, their values, their emotions, their thoughts. Other content such as global problems of war and overpopulation, human culture, and ecology is also mentioned.

A major problem in planning a curriculum in any subject field is to select content appropriate to the specific developmental level of the students and to build from one level to the next without becoming repetitious. The problem exists perhaps to a greater degree in social studies-history-global studies because we have not always examined the assumptions upon which our decisions are based— such as the great emphasis on American history in order to "Americanize" an immigrant population—or realized how much of the content merely repeats earlier learnings. Obviously, this is an area that requires close and hard scrutiny. We recommend that the summary of research on the development of cognitive abilities provided by Torney in Chapter 3 be reviewed and used as one basis for the selection of content.

HOW SHOULD THE CURRICULUM BE ORGANIZED?

King suggests yet another curricular question when he states that there is much we do not know about organizing curricula for global education. Since so many of the disciplines contribute to developing global perspectives, it follows that the curriculum should be multidisciplinary. No single area of study is broad enough to be the only basis for global education. The other chapters of this book provide a number of ideas about organizing the curriculum. Morris suggests that the curriculum should be organized around concepts—those which will serve to indicate relationships, organize knowledge, and guide further inquiry. Organizing social studies and science instruction around inquiry into social and scientific issues and problems is one option. Another possibility is to select key concepts from a content area to be the organizing elements: justice, resolution of conflict, and interdependence are examples from social studies. Morris further suggests that the roots of the curriculum must be in the daily lives of children and the relationships of their communities to the rest of the world.

Some kind of integration of learning is a characteristic of most of the programs described in previous chapters, especially the interdisciplinary programs in the middle school and high school described by the Andersons. When literature is studied, it is carefully and explicitly related to other learnings from art, music, science, and history. Learning is not seen as having neat compartments but rather is viewed holistically. Efforts are deliberately made to help students develop an integrated set of important learnings which will help them function as global citizens. In order for this to occur, the curriculum in school and experiences out of school must work together effectively. The messages which students receive about the interrelationships among the peoples of the world at school ideally should not conflict with what they hear discussed at home, read about, and hear over the radio and television. Where discrepancies in messages do exist from different educational sources, the student should be helped to examine each message carefully for the value positions being expressed, basic assumptions, accuracy, the extent to which vested interests are being served, and other such criteria. By such efforts, students will be helped to integrate their learnings into a meaningful, consistent, holistic view of our world.

However, the authors of this chapter are concerned with what appears to be a growing movement among curriculum workers to "integrate" global education into other curricula. We are concerned for two reasons. First, we suspect that this "integration" is politically motivated in that it is seen as a way to ease global education into the curriculum without having to face potentially difficult value confrontations. We know enough about value clarification and conflict resolution, however, to know that avoidance usually leads to later and more traumatic misunderstanding and conflict. We believe the value positions of all those concerned with the curriculum of the school ought to be openly discussed and potential areas of conflict identified as the curriculum is being planned. When such discussions are held in the initial stages of planning, objections can be dealt with in an open forum before a crisis situation develops.

Second, we have been "around the barn" with integration of curriculum before. The defenders of the disciplines (geography, history, music, visual arts) have a good deal of merit in their argument that efforts to integrate curricula, as have occurred in the social studies, often have resulted in the loss of significant content and processes of inquiry. Further, studies of learning tell us that integrative behavior is a phenomenon developed *in the learner*. We know that curriculum planners can do much to facilitate such behavior. We also know that the arbitrary bringing together of separate subjects does not necessarily develop such behavior.[6] To integrate the curriculum so that all the subject areas contribute to the development of global perspectives is a worthwhile goal. However, curriculum planners must not underestimate the difficulty of the task and must be willing to devote time and effort to working through the problems involved. In the end, the integration of global education into other subject areas may be more complex than developing new courses in global studies, but the opportunities for student learning will be greater than if single courses are developed and the ideas in them are not related to other subject areas. In short, we may be better off if we attempt to bring a global perspective into existing curricula rather than attempting to integrate curricula "with a global perspective."

WHAT KIND OF EVALUATION IS NEEDED?
Evaluation is a major focus of debate about schooling, particularly in these days of accountability. By evaluation we mean the procedures used for gathering, utilizing, and disseminating data about student characteristics and growth in cognitive, affective, and psychomotor behaviors. We do not refer to program evaluation, although that, too, is an important form of evaluation.

In considering student growth with reference to global education, one must consider the goals and objectives of the program. Since goals are usually broadly stated, they present problems in evaluation. For example, most programs have a goal to promote student understanding of people of other races, cultures, and religions. The problem is that the term "understanding" is not very explicit. It is made up of such component behaviors as interpreting, evaluating, empathizing, and valuing. In order to assess student growth, curriculum planners must spend time reflecting upon and defining such behaviors. Certainly, they cannot rely on measures of knowledge attainment as the sole measure of student growth in understanding other people, important as knowledge is. If goals are translated into more precise objectives, as we suggested earlier, the problems of evaluation are likely to become more manageable. When behaviors to be developed by global education are carefully defined, we are more likely to be able to evaluate student progress toward achieving them.

We already have adequate ways of evaluating student progress toward many objectives. For example, we would have little difficulty in evaluating knowledge of how other people on the globe live and cope with their environment or in measuring comprehension of varying viewpoints on social problems. Books by Bloom et al., Furst, and Gronlund are only some of the resources that may be helpful in this task.[7]

However, much of global education is directed at attitude development, which is difficult though not impossible to assess. Numerous global attitude scales exist and can be used at least as a basis for further work.[8] They could be helpful in assessing growth toward objectives such as responding to people of other races, cultures, and religions in a positive manner. Also, observation of student behavior can be helpful. Working harmoniously in a multicultural or multiracial group can be considered an indicator of student willingness to respond positively to others. Similarly, an increased willingness to consider the points-of-view or arguments of others would be another indicator. Morris shows how student statements can be gathered and analyzed to reveal attitudes.

Evaluation of student growth toward goals and objectives is not an easy task, but it is an essential one. It is difficult to improve upon a program unless one can assess its effects. Information about student growth can be invaluable feedback to help improve and strengthen any program. Such evidence, when reported to the public, can also help significantly in making educators more accountable and responsible in the eyes of both supporters and critics.

HOW SHOULD STUDENTS BE GROUPED?

Grouping is another factor which curriculum planners must consider. Education is generally a social enterprise, and usually students are taught and learn in group situations. Decisions as to how these groups are to be formed must be as carefully made as any other curricular decision. The grouping of students can facilitate or inhibit a global education curriculum. For example, the segregation of students by ability is counterproductive to the development of global perspectives by students because it creates a hierarchy of values relative to what is important for people to know, do, or become. It is better to have students of various abilities and aptitudes working together and learning, firsthand, of the unique contributions different people can make to problem solving, work, and group life.

An essential ingredient of a global perspective is appreciation of human differences. It seems to follow logically that student grouping on the basis of differences rather than similarities in abilities, aptitudes, beliefs, age, and even needs is an important structural consideration for curriculum planners. This is not a statement to be taken lightly, for it runs counter to most current thinking about how schooling should be structured. It also poses a particular problem for global education, which is often criticized as an elitist subject in that there may be considerable homogeneity in the students now exposed to global education content. A great amount of diversity is sometimes considered a handicap to curriculum planners and teachers because it increases the challenge to meet the varying needs and abilities of students. Although we recognize this as a significant challenge, at the same time we believe that diversity among pupils will add a valuable resource to global education programs.

TIME AND SPACE
There are two important curricular decisions which are often overlooked because the answers are taken for granted: the use of time and the use of space in curriculum planning and implementation.

The manner in which time and space are utilized in a school is often an indicator of the values of those who plan and carry out the curriculum. In our judgment, to restrict learning primarily to the time spent in school severely limits what students might learn from global studies. Students can learn much from their daily encounters with people before and after school hours, and they should be encouraged to notice how global events touch their everyday lives outside of school. As Becker pointed out, grocery store products come into our communities from all over the world, and the prices we pay for items like coffee, cocoa, and oil are determined by what takes place in many nations. It is often possible to capitalize much more than we do on learning time outside of school hours.

Similarly, to confine learning to the space defined by the walls of the classroom and by the school campus is to overlook other significant resources. The schools of Middleston use the community as an inherent part of the space for learning in a variety of ways. They also use time for learning in ways not confined to the time schedule of classes. Other chapters have described programs that move out of the traditional model of the school day defined and punctuated by ringing bells. From the People Place that Morris describes, to the Wilderness School King visited, to the exchange and community programs discussed by Rhinesmith, concerned educators can find many examples of ways to make global learning an exciting part of students' lives both in and out of schools.

FURTHER CURRICULUM CONSIDERATIONS

We believe that the answers given to the preceding basic curricular questions will determine the kind of curriculum which is planned. They are difficult questions to deal with, but there are resources to help. It would be simpler if we could end our chapter here by saying that when these ten questions are answered, an effective global education curriculum would be available. Unfortunately, this is unlikely to be the case. There still remain some very essential considerations that must receive attention in planning curricula.

DECISION MAKING

One such important consideration is the curricular issue regarding the degree of influence or consultation various groups should have in making decisions about the curricular questions. We believe that the people in and connected with the school must be involved in decisions about each of the curricular elements discussed above. But questions remain. Do parents select learning materials? Do teachers determine the use of time and space? Do students select objectives?

A major group often left out of decision-making processes is the students themselves. The programs described in all the chapters of this book call for the active involvement of students in all phases of their learning. Such programs do not present predigested ideas and facts from a lecturer; rather, students plan and implement their own curriculum. They determine their own objectives, design activities, search out materials and resources for learning, and seek help when needed. Present curriculum planning typically does not allow for the kinds of learnings which students gain when they make at least some of their own decisions about what they want to know, how they will learn it, and how to assess their progress.

As far as specific curricular elements are concerned, we feel it is appropriate that all interested parties be involved in both the discussion and setting of goals and in the determination of evaluation procedures. Teachers, along with district consultants, other knowledgeable professionals, and students should make decisions about all other elements of the curriculum.

SATISFACTION

Three further considerations require continuing attention during the planning process: satisfaction, appropriateness, and comprehensiveness. Satisfaction is a very complex concept consisting of such things as seeing value, purpose, or contentment in what one does, knows, or builds. We suggest that curriculum developers need to concern themselves with the question of satisfaction on the part of several significant groups. Questions such as "Will teachers be satisfied with the teaching materials?" and "Will students be satisfied with goals and objectives?" should be raised. Research on social studies teaching is not reassuring about the degree of satisfaction which students express with the subject.[9] More teacher and student involvement in decision making as well as more effective curricula might enhance satisfaction with programs.

We believe that the degree of satisfaction the student and teacher experience with the curriculum is important for a number of reasons. Higher satisfaction with global education courses will attract more students. Satisfaction will help to keep students and teachers involved and committed to their pursuit of global education studies. Satisfaction should also increase the chances of students retaining and acting upon their learnings after formal schooling in global education has ended. For these reasons, we believe that the amount of satisfaction students and teachers will experience with the global education curriculum ought to receive close attention.

APPROPRIATENESS

Appropriateness is defined as the degree to which the various elements of the curriculum are suitable for their intended purposes and students. For example, many efforts to contrast cultures have resulted in students stereotyping some peoples or thinking of them as "less civilized" or even inferior, instead of helping students to appreciate and respect diversity. If the curriculum is intended to teach global understanding, we must be sure that materials of instruction, learning activities, teaching methodologies, evaluation procedures, and the like are appropriate to this purpose.

Appropriateness also has to do with the developmental level of the students. While it may be appropriate for elementary-age children to learn about and experience various forms of human interdependence, it may be inappropriate to expect them to understand the workings of complex interdependent international economic or political systems. Torney's review of research on cognitive development will be useful here. She presents some evidence that middle childhood is a critical period in attitude development—a very basic component of a global education curriculum. Attitudes in this stage of development seem to be more flexible and less negative than at other stages.

Although a global education curriculum needs to be a K–12 sequence, it appears that there are phases of emphasis which ought to vary depending upon the maturity level of students. This leads to curriculum planning based on stages of development. Elsewhere, Tye outlined six phases of schooling, which vary in their emphasis, but all of which contribute to building global perspectives.[10] He suggests emphasizing relations with peers, adults, and things in the environment along with command of oral communication skills at the early childhood phase. The lower elementary phase would emphasize skills in reading, writing, and expression, and upper elementary students would primarily work on independent learning and inquiry strategies. In middle school, exploration and awareness become the major thrust along with extending the development of cognitive abilities, self-understanding, and self-awareness. These would be expanded at the high school level along with exploring relationships, planning and implementing courses of action, analyzing cultural, social, economic, and political systems, and studying humanities, arts, and philosophy. Each task would be continued until the student has accomplished it to such a degree that future learning dependent upon or related to it would not be impeded. Building the various emphases of a global education curriculum in at critical phases of development would significantly increase the appropriateness of the curriculum and, one hopes, the impact upon student learning.

Appropriateness also refers to other characteristics of students such as socioeconomic status, ethnicity, and achievement levels. Frequently, at the secondary level of schooling in particular, students are "streamed" or "tracked" according to criteria related to achievement. Often, only the college-bound or academically talented are the recipients of global education programs. But global education is appropriate for all students, particularly if we see one of its values as helping to develop an electorate able to select wisely national leadership which must deal with both domestic and international issues. Planners of global education curricula must overcome the sometimes justified criticism that theirs is an "elitist" subject and do all that is possible to make the curriculum appropriate for all types of students.

COMPREHENSIVENESS

By comprehensiveness we mean the extent to which all options have been examined and those considered to be most desirable carefully made an integral part of the curriculum. This is particularly important if the goal is development of global perspectives, since basic concepts and processes of global education should be further developed in areas such as literature and science. Unless the concept of comprehensiveness is carefully considered in curriculum planning, the impact of a global education curriculum will be considerably less than what it could be.

During the planning process, the answer to each curricular question must be examined for comprehensiveness. A literature program which deals only with American and English literature was not comprehensively planned when content was selected. Literature from many other regions of the world should become part of the content if the global education curriculum is to have maximum impact upon student learning. Also, a curriculum in which the activities call for students only to read or talk about cross-cultural understanding is limited. If it is to be comprehensive, the students should interact directly with people and institutions of various cultures. If evaluation in global education is comprehensive, it will include evaluation of attitudes as well as of knowledge and cognitive abilities. Goals and objectives will include all those essential in helping students develop global perspectives for viewing their world. A wide range of resources will be available to support the development of all desired learnings. Teachers will have a comprehensive repertoire of methods from which they can select the one most appropriate for the intended purpose. Similarly, all other curricular questions must be checked to see if they have been answered as comprehensively as they can effectively be.

The need for comprehensive planning of global education programs has been emphasized throughout this book. A thoughtful, systematic procedure for examining the answer to each curricular question to check for comprehensiveness is needed if global education is to have the desired impact upon students.

THE HIDDEN CURRICULUM

There is increasing recognition that an informal or implicit curriculum accompanies explicitly planned curricula. This is commonly referred to as the hidden curriculum. We know that students learn much more at school and in the community than what is deliberately intended for them to learn. They learn many things by observing the rules of the school and classroom, ways in which content is presented or omitted, disciplinary techniques, rewards given, expectations of the teacher, the use of authority, role behavior of the teacher, implicit messages of materials, and the social interactions in the classroom. The hidden curriculum operates at a level of consciousness much lower than that of the explicit or intended curriculum. Thus, the learnings achieved through it are less likely to be openly identified and desirably molded. Some of the effects of the hidden curriculum may be more insidious, less desirable, and have greater cumulative impact because they are unexamined. Curriculum specialists and other educators are beginning to call attention to the importance of the hidden curriculum and to suggest that it deserves as much attention as the formally planned curriculum so that unintended learnings do not contradict intended goals.

Many of the previous chapters discussed how the hidden curriculum makes either a positive or negative contribution. Students in the Middleston schools learn from the hidden curriculum that they are important enough to be invited to the superintendent's house for dinner, trusted enough to have freedom of movement in their school and to show visitors around, and responsible enough to help plan their education. Torney suggests that the open classroom atmosphere and the encouragement of student discussion and participation in classroom affairs can significantly affect what is learned in civics education. The hidden curriculum in these examples is, in fact, being used to help foster desired learning.

Some aspects of the hidden curriculum do not foster desired learnings and may, in fact, operate against what we hope will be learned. Torney identifies negative factors in the hidden curriculum such as the use of national symbols to foster an exclusive allegiance to a single country and denial of the existence of conflict as content is presented about political systems. Morris points out how materials can inadvertently teach undesirable outcomes through the phrasing of questions and changes in chapter titles. Such implicit messages in the hidden curriculum can be examined and directed toward desirable outcomes only as we come more fully to understand what is actually being taught through the hidden curriculum and how the possibility for undesirable learnings can be at least minimized if not eliminated.

IMPLEMENTING THE CURRICULUM

When all the preceding elements of an effective, challenging curriculum are successfully incorporated into curriculum planning, there remains yet another major problem which must be confronted: how to get the curriculum into the school and classroom. All subject areas must resolve this problem, but global education has had a particularly difficult time with it. As Joyce and Nicholson point out, it is not only the content of global education that can be an object of controversy; often the very basic question of whether or not global education as such should be part of the school's curriculum is in dispute.

Through some expensive and painful lessons during the curriculum reform decade of the 1960s, we learned that simply developing exemplary curricula is not enough to bring about a change or an innovation. There are other critical factors which must be dealt with before schools or classrooms are affected. Gross and his associates have pointed to five structural elements which need to be in place before any innovation can be successfully brought about in a school.[11] These are:

1. Clarity on the part of the staff about the innovation

2. Capability of the staff to perform a new role model

3. Availability of necessary resources

4. Compatible organizational arrangements

5. Staff motivation

Thus, there are psychological, sociological, organizational, and even political factors which must be considered by those interested in turning carefully planned programs of global education into realities.

We believe this book can be a valuable resource to help school faculties deal with the elements listed above. Various chapters help to define and make clear the changes needed to plan and implement an effective global education program. They present views of what ought to be in global education and of what currently exists, both in a positive and negative sense. The Middleston schools offer one vision of how a global education program might look. Morris, King, and Rhinesmith describe programs which exist in schools and in communities. Chapter 3 and the present chapter report some negative aspects of the curriculum which should be avoided or overcome. These discussions can contribute significantly in helping a school staff become clear about what changes and innovations are needed.

This book can help establish new roles for teachers through its descriptions of how teachers act in various programs. The Andersons also suggest new behaviors for superintendents and principals, who must be vital parts of an effective global education program. These descriptions should assist a staff in deciding what new roles they should develop and provide training for. Some of what is discussed as being needed in effective global education programs may have to be incorporated into the pre-service work of teachers. Others might become the central thrust of in-service work for a given period of time. Ultimately, each teacher and administrator must have the opportunity to develop all the needed role behaviors through some means or other.

Each chapter identifies resources of many types to be drawn upon for global education. Notes in many of the chapters suggest additional resources, and the Annotated Bibliography provides further help. Clearly, there are many resources cited in this volume that a school staff could use in developing a global education program.

This chapter and others suggest organizational arrangements and rearrangements which could make the structures of the school and classroom compatible with the goals and objectives of a global education program. The schools of Middleston are organized much differently from traditional schools, and some of these changes may need to be in place, as Gross suggests, before a global education curriculum can be implemented.

The problem of staff motivation which Gross cites is really the central thesis to which this volume is addressed. The imperatives of Joyce and Nicholson are compelling support for the development of global education programs. Becker clearly indicates what is already occurring in terms of global interdependence and provides strong evidence for making the understanding of this and other aspects of a global perspective a central thrust of the curriculum. The problems involved in developing curriculum cited in this chapter and the barriers described by Torney should provide a sobering reminder of the difficulties of the task, but the authors of this volume have attempted to impress upon the readers, be they staffs of local schools, district personnel, curriculum specialists, parents, or other concerned citizens, the need to engage in the necessary tasks.

The importance of global education has been established by others in this book. What we have attempted to do in this chapter is to point out the curriculum considerations which must be taken into account by planners of global education programs in our schools. Global education needs its "advocates." Hopefully, they will be thoughtful and informed ones.

NOTES

1. The first stage of this project is described in John I. Goodlad, M. Frances Klein, Jerrold M. Novotney, Kenneth A. Tye, and Associates, *Toward a Mankind School: An Adventure in Humanistic Education,* McGraw-Hill, New York, 1974.

2. These objectives are based on Benjamin S. Bloom et al. (eds.), *Taxonomy of Educational Objectives, Handbook I: The Cognitive Domain,* McKay, New York, 1956; and David Krathwohl, Benjamin S. Bloom, and Bertram Masia, *Taxonomy of Educational Objectives, Handbook II: Affective Domain,* McKay, New York, 1964.

3. Ralph W. Tyler, *Basic Principles of Curriculum and Instruction,* University of Chicago Press, Chicago, 1950; John I. Goodlad, "The Teacher Selects, Plans and Organizes," in *Learning and the Teacher,* ASCD Yearbook, Association for Supervision and Curriculum Development, Washington, D.C., 1959, pp. 36–60; and James D. Raths, "Teaching without Specific Objectives," in *Curricular Concerns in a Revolutionary Era,* ASCD, Washington, D.C., 1971, pp. 20–26, also in *Educational Leadership,* vol. 38, April 1971, pp. 714–20.

4. Bruce Joyce and Marsha Weil, *Models of Teaching,* Prentice-Hall, Englewood Cliffs, N.J., 1972.

5. Marsha Weil and Bruce R. Joyce, *Information Processing Models: Expanding Your Teaching Repertoire,* Prentice-Hall, Englewood Cliffs, N.J., 1977; Marsha Weil, Bruce R. Joyce, and Bridget Kluwin, *Personal Models: Expanding Your Teaching Repertoire,* Prentice-Hall, Englewood Cliffs, N.J., 1977; and Marsha Weil and Bruce R. Joyce, *Social Models: Expanding Your Teaching Repertoire,* Prentice-Hall, Englewood Cliffs, N.J., 1977.

6. The issue of integrating curriculum is fully discussed in National Society for the Study of Education, *The Integration of Educational Experiences,* Fifty-seventh Yearbook, Part III, University of Chicago Press, Chicago, 1958.

7. Bloom et al. (eds.) op. cit.; Edward J. Furst, *Constructing Evaluation Instruments,* Longmans, New York, 1958; and N. E. Gronlund, *Constructing Achievement Tests,* Prentice-Hall, Englewood Cliffs, N.J., 1968.

8. See, for example, Marvin E. Shaw and Jack M. Wright, *Scales for the Measurement of Attitudes,* McGraw-Hill, New York, 1967. The research studies listed in the Annotated Bibliography are an additional source of global attitude scales.

9. Richard E. Gross, "The Status of the Social Studies in the Public Schools of the United States: Facts and Impressions of a National Survey," *Social Education,* vol. 41, no. 3, pp. 194–200, 205, March 1977.

10. Kenneth A. Tye, "The Culture of the School," in Goodlad, Klein, Novotney, Tye, and Associates, op. cit.

11. Neal Gross, Joseph B. Giacquinta, and Marilyn Bernstein, *Implementing Organizational Innovations: A Sociological Analysis of Planned Educational Change,* Basic Books, New York, 1971.

CHAPTER NINE

Looking Ahead—An Agenda for Action

Robert Leestma*

U.S. Office of Education

*The views and ideas expressed in this chapter are those of the author and do not necessarily reflect the position or policy of the U. S. Office of Education.

T he preceding chapters say a number of significant things about the world and about education. They deal with global facts of life as well as with educational facts of life. The focus is on the great need for education to reflect much more adequately than it currently does the unity and diversity of humanity, the interdependence of nations and peoples, the need for international cooperation, and the role of individuals and schools in helping to shape an acceptable future. The book as a whole endeavors to suggest some ways to come to grips with the challenge of developing a humanistic education appropriate to the reality of interdependence on an ethnically diverse and culturally pluralistic planet with finite natural resources.

The concept of global education views the earth and its inhabitants as interacting and interdependent. It recognizes that nations and peoples are closely linked in a variety of ways, including through ethnic heritage, religion, communications systems, trade, monetary systems, science, and transnational organizations. The globalization of the human condition is interweaving the destinies of all nations and peoples at an accelerating rate and affecting many aspects of life. Global education involves multidisciplinary perspectives about the extended human family, the existing condition of mankind and the planet, and foreseeable consequences of present trends and alternative choices. It is concerned with global dynamics—the relationships between individuals, mankind, and the planet, and how these dynamics are changing our lives.

Rooted in and motivated by a compelling blend of altruism and enlightened self-interest, global education is concerned with the survival of the human species, with the prospect of the fuller development of each individual, and with enhancement of the quality of life for all. It is concerned with both the individual and humankind; with community, nation, and world; and with a humanistic approach to the ecosystem of the planet, to the interaction of humankind and the environment in both its living and nonliving aspects.

Some of the crucial facts and needs and some of the relevant propositions and perspectives involved in dealing with these concerns may be summarized as follows:

- The future is not what it used to be. The human race is beginning to share a contemporary common history and increasingly faces a common destiny. No nation has a separate future anymore.

- The future we face inevitably will be more international than the past. Global interdependence is a pervasive reality and probably irreversible. In nationalistic terms, neither manifest destiny nor self-sufficiency is what it used to be.

- The future is now. Nuclear proliferation and interdependence are present facts of life. The new frontiers include inner space— understanding humankind, interdependence, and intergenerational responsibility—and international cooperation for the common good.

- The boundary lines between problems commonly labeled "foreign" and "domestic" are often artificial and misleading. We must learn to see world problems and issues from a global perspective.

- The United States is both national and international and will remain so. There is no way we can opt out of the world. All Americans are also citizens of the world. We share with the rest of the human race the same planet, some fundamental problems which can be solved only by transnational cooperation, and ultimately a common destiny.

- It is essential for every citizen to understand more about the ethnic diversity and cultural pluralism of the world at large. For both educators and students, getting to know and communicate with people from other cultures at home and abroad is of fundamental importance for personal growth as well as for the survival and progress of mankind.

- The reduction of ethnocentrism, both personal and national; the development of a sense of the world as a set of interconnected and interdependent economic, environmental, social, and political systems; and acceptance of the ethic of intergenerational responsibility are clearly three of the educational imperatives of our time. They should be among the principal objectives in the general education of every student.

- The development of literacy in global problems and issues, appropriate concern for international cooperation, and functional competency in intercultural relations are among the categorical imperatives of citizenship for the modern world, for students at all levels in the educational system as well as for adults in and out of formal continuing education programs.

- Concern for international human rights is an integral part of global education because human rights are fundamental to the achievement of human potential. The subject is also of special importance because of its natural relationship to the American creed, its contribution to the development of a global perspective, and its long-term consequences for effective citizenship in an interdependent world.

• National security today involves more than military preparation. Global education is one of the essential new dimensions.

• The fate of global facts and perceptual frameworks in a world still made up of ethnocentric nations and peoples depends to an important extent upon what educators choose to do about the challenge. Educators bear great responsibility for helping generate a critical mass of citizens capable of recognizing the global age, its impact on their future life, and their role as American citizens in an interdependent world.

• Although formal educational policies and programs and systemwide support services are always desirable and often necessary, educators can do much on their own to develop and communicate global perspectives. In the end, a great deal of the effectiveness of the educational renewal effort depends on the capability and commitment of the individual teacher, functioning as a teacher in the classroom and as a concerned citizen in the community.

• Through global education schools can make a critical difference in helping shape the national destiny as well as in contributing to the survival of mankind. If a school does not provide a suitable program in global education, it is shortchanging its students. Global education is not just an idea whose time has come but an imperative for the global age.

The foregoing list does not do justice to all aspects of global education nor to the sense of urgency that humanity's predicament requires, but it helps highlight some of the key themes and perspectives that education at all levels must soon start to take seriously if impact is to be achieved soon enough to provide the crucial margin of difference.

Global education is concerned with the full range of possible educational outcomes: awareness, knowledge, empathy, attitudes, and skills. It seeks to develop the ability to analyze, to communicate, and to contribute to problem solving. It places a special emphasis on generating a commitment to action as a citizen in one's own society and on becoming an effective participant in the emerging world society. And it recognizes the need for more effective involvement in international cooperation by all categories of participants—individuals, communities, organizations, and nations.

Thus the agenda for global education is neither modest nor trivial. It is packed with first-order issues and problems and has a compelling urgency for every citizen of every nation—for our own good now and for the good of succeeding generations. This is particularly true for Americans who, from one point of view, not only have the most to lose in total way of life, but who also literally are inextricably bound up in global interdependence because of our national economy, political system, and stage of development—because of America's extensive and sometimes unique role in the world and its future and because of the world's multifarious involvement in America's past, present, and future.

EARLIER VISIONS

Historical perspective is often helpful in dealing with new challenges. Sometimes it takes a while for education to catch up with an early vision. An insight of Francis Bacon (whom Loren Eiseley aptly called, in the title of a recent book, *The Man Who Saw Through Time*) almost 400 years ago is worth noting in our present context:

> For the history that I require and design, special care is to be taken that it be of wide range and made to the measure of the universe. For the world is not to be narrowed till it will go into the understanding (which has been done hitherto), but the understanding is to be expanded and opened till it can take in the image of the world.
> —Francis Bacon, *The Parasceve*

As is increasingly apparent, the achievement of a global perspective throughout education at all levels is the most urgent common challenge now confronting educators around the world.

Education must provide the opportunity for every student to transcend the limitations of his or her immediate time and place. It should help broaden each student's life space to encompass humankind, global issues, and the foreseeable future. Every student should have access to a more world-centered educational program that will help prepare him or her for responsible participation in an interdependent world.

While Sputnik provided the first impetus from space for major forward movement in international education in the United States (Title VI of the National Defense Act of 1958), Astronaut Frank Borman of Apollo 8 gave the world its first human perception from space of the oneness of mankind, the organic relationship of people and planet, and the sense of a common destiny. Here is how he described his feelings as he rounded the moon in 1968 on the last orbit and headed back toward earth:

> The view of the earth from the moon fascinated me—a small disk, 240,000 miles away. It was hard to think that that little thing held so many problems, so many frustrations. Raging nationalistic interests, famines, wars, pestilence don't show from that distance. I'm convinced that some wayward stranger in a space-craft, coming from some other part of the heavens, could look at earth and never know that it was inhabited at all. But the same wayward stranger would certainly know instinctively that if the earth were inhabited, then the destinies of all who lived on it must inevitably be interwoven and joined. We are one hunk of ground, water, air, clouds, floating around in space. From out there it really is "one world."

Education is only now beginning to translate this global perception into programs that will help enhance whatever common destiny may lie ahead. As we begin to apply the perspectives of Bacon and Borman through global education, we will find ourselves embarked on a course that is likely to engage us as educators and citizens for the rest of our lives. In the process we should gain an enriched view of our local communities, the larger world of humankind, and the planet we all share.

POLICY IMPLICATIONS

In no country today does the logic of education yet correspond very closely to the intrinsic logic of world conditions, events, and issues. Given the nature of the present and the foreseeable future, every educational system should devote increased attention to the global facts of life. The facts about global education are clear enough. One does not have to load the dice to make the case. Given the growing pervasiveness of the United States in the world and the world in the United States, given the extensive local manifestation of this role in literally every community and state throughout the country, and given the increasingly visible reality of global interdependence and intergenerational responsibility, it is clear that the range of concerns covered by the concept of global education constitutes educational imperatives rather than options. Global issues and transnational problems are realities that need to be addressed directly and urgently, with determination and imagination. They are not merely ideals to be pursued in fair weather and on leisure time. Policies for global education need to be framed accordingly.

Intercultural/international learning begins early. It needs to be nourished all along the line. Global education thus requires a comprehensive set of policies which cover all grade levels and subject areas, methods and materials, teacher selection and in-service training, research and evaluation, community relations, and the rest of the spectrum of educational concerns and conditions. The policies need to be both clear and strong and reflect a compelling sense of urgency. They need to reinforce and undergird existing efforts and stimulate and support new ones. They need to help both educators and the public develop a general awareness and then an informed consciousness about global issues and interdependence, about the implications of these for the future of our society and humankind, and about the responsibilities of the schools in preparing students for active citizenship in an interdependent world. Attitudinally, the policies should lead to a basic respect for the earth and its peoples, a sense of stewardship for human use of the planet and of obligations to future generations for planetary maintenance and improvement, and a belief in the potential of international cooperation for dealing with transnational problems.

It should be noted that policy cannot be the exclusive concern of "policymakers." There are few individuals in our society who do not have a stake in the kind, scope, and quality of global education needed in the American educational system and therefore few who do not have a stake in the formulation of policy for global education. The reality of interdependence alone affects the entire nation, and thus the interest and support of the entire nation can be mobilized. Policymakers need to take into account a wide range of professional, public, government, and business sectors and constituencies.

Given the scope and significance of the challenge to which global education is a response, it is clear that policies must support substantial change on a broad front. Policies must be clear and strong enough to make possible large-scale progress throughout the school curriculum and throughout teacher education and should remain open to continuing review. The policies needed would have both voluntary and mandatory aspects, with the latter enforced through appropriate regulations and accountability provisions.

From the beginning, policies should encourage giving greater visibility to global education concerns and establishing coordinator roles in institutions and agencies, should foster close cooperation between schools and communities, should encourage and assist expanded opportunities for international experience for teachers and students, and should foster linkages and international cooperation with programs and related organizations in other countries.

Finally, it should be clear that global education and its policy implications for educational renewal are not limited to institutions or organizations nor only or primarily to teachers. The continuing professional renewal of educators at all levels and in all roles is central to the effectiveness of the kind of program needed. No single exposure or once-and-for-all pre-service or in-service training effort is going to be sufficient, because the subject matter and the relationships among the various aspects will continue to change. Recurrent education on the content and dynamics of global education for a changing world should become the norm from now on for all who claim education as a profession.

A DECADE OF DEVELOPMENT

If global education is as fundamental and imperative as this book maintains, it is clear that we have to widen the scope of our efforts and greatly accelerate the pace. It is not necessary to agree on all the details of the concept or of program implementation to realize that a strong, broadly based, nationwide commitment to a *decade of development in global education* by educators at all levels is needed if enough is going to happen to make a difference in national citizenship awareness and action.

The vision and commitment needed to enable American education to come to grips with the world, interdependence, and the great issues facing mankind cannot be successful if pressed by educators alone. The challenge must be shared by those in leadership roles throughout society, whether teachers, administrators, curriculum specialists, or educational policymakers; by those in underlying academic disciplines, organizations of teachers and other educational personnel, teacher education, the publishers or producers of instructional materials; and by leaders in community, business, organized labor, government, and communications media.

One way to focus attention on the dimensions of the task before us is to lay out a draft agenda for action. Here is one such effort as a basis for stimulating a broader discussion of the subject. It endeavors to be ambitious, but realistic. It is not complete but is intended to be illustrative of scope, content, and pace. It is not a statement of Federal policy, plan, or intent, nor does it attempt to speculate on what the Federal role should be. It is not in any way a Federal prescription or recommendation nor does it imply Federal funding. It is simply one educator's attempt to identify some of the dimensions of the challenge for educational renewal in an age of global interdependence. The primacy of state and local authority, responsibility, and control is explicit or implicit throughout.

The agenda is divided into phases and steps, all of which could be accomplished before the decade of the 1980s draws to a close if a strong enough national will and consensus develop.

PHASE 1, PREPARATORY PERIOD—BY 1980:

- Every state education department and most school systems and teacher education programs would have a collection of some basic references on global education and would have provided opportunities for selected staff members to become aware of the global education concept, some relevant research, successful programs elsewhere, and local possibilities.

- In-service education programs would be available in every region of the country to begin to acquaint teachers and others with the global education concept.

- A survey of the role of the world in the community, region, or state and vice versa would have been conducted, planned, or under consideration in a majority of states.

PHASE 2—BY THE MID-1980s:

- Study groups would be at work in a sizable proportion of state education departments, local school systems, and teacher education institutions to analyze and enrich existing curricula, requirements, and materials from a global perspective.

- In-service education opportunities would be available in the majority of states, including through teacher centers.

- Pre-service education programs would be offering some orientation to global education, at least as an option.

- Initial research agendas would be established and studies and surveys begun.

- A national baseline survey of the knowledge and attitudes of students, teachers, administrators, parents, and community leaders on global education concerns would be completed.

- Every state education department and a sizable proportion of school districts would become involved in an international educational exchange program for students and/or staff.

- State and local school board policy statements would be giving explicit support to global education.

- National public awareness and local community support would be growing, in part, because of increased attention to global problems and issues in the mass media, particularly television, and in the schools.

PHASE 3—BY 1990:

- Teachers in every state would have access to in-service education programs for global education, at least at the awareness level.

- Good case-study material on the initiation or improvement of global education programs in a variety of school and community situations would be becoming widely available.

- All school districts, state education departments, and pre-service teacher-education programs would have access to information clearinghouses and resource centers on global perspectives in education.

- Teacher certification requirements in a sizable number of states would begin to reflect global education concerns.

- State curriculum requirements in a sizable number of states would begin to reflect global education objectives.

- School accreditation requirements would begin to reflect attention to global education.

- Local, state, and national assessments of educational progress would include attention to global education concerns.

- Textbooks and other educational materials would increasingly provide more adequate treatment of global issues and perspectives.

Thus, by 1990, it would be hoped that the great majority of school districts, state education departments, and teacher education programs would be incorporating extensive and effective attention to global education concerns throughout the curriculum; that the majority of teachers would be aware of and knowledgeable about global education concerns and be making some contribution to achieving appropriate global education objectives in schools; that the majority of school systems and all state education departments, particularly those concerned with large numbers of students, would be linked directly in one way or another with communities and educational programs in other countries and be participating regularly in international exchange programs for both students and teachers; that the majority of teachers and students would have opportunities for some form of direct experience with multicultural situations and global issues at home or abroad; that the great majority of students across the country would have access to effective programs of global education; and that the cumulative progress of the total movement would be sufficient to generate self-sustaining momentum, growth, and improvement.

The scenario is subject to infinite variation, of course, depending upon a host of variables, beginning with one's assessment of the national state of readiness; one's estimate of the leadership available, of the profession's willingness to change in the direction of global education, and of the amount of resources needed that can be mobilized and shared; and one's personal sense of challenge and optimism. At this stage, the foregoing rough sketch is intended only to stimulate an open examination of what might be possible rather than to forecast the shape of any broad concensus on actions or allocation of roles and responsibilities that might emerge from wide debate. Whatever the outcome, such a broad-gauged planning exercise is clearly one of the needed next steps.

Can global education meet the challenge? Can schools lead, at least to some extent, instead of follow society? Can they form the productive partnership with the community that the global education concept and the needs of the times require? Time will tell. But the challenge of interdependence alone is clear enough and the properties of global education set forth in this book persuasive enough that, I believe, educators will find a way to utilize the concept, approaches, and materials of global education to strengthen American education across the board and make it more relevant to the new age that is upon us.

If most teachers have the opportunity to become aware of the global facts of life and then set about doing what they can within their own professional and community contexts, there is little doubt that schools can make a significant difference in how the emerging generations of citizens meet the global issues of humanity and contribute to shaping the future in which the human race will share a common destiny.

In reality, whether most people have recognized it yet or not, we are living on an increasingly unstable fault line. Various global problems are reaching proportions where singly or in combination they can have seismic effects throughout the world. The difference between the major transformation of human affairs now in process and previous eras of great change is that the future is becoming recognizable while it is still on the way. We already can see, or soon learn, how the phenomenon of global interdependence is changing our lives. There is still time to help shape the future. A more world-centered education is an indispensable part of this process.

The national mood—the beginnings of an awakening to interdependence and related global issues—and the educational moment seem to be coming together. There is movement and momentum in global education. There is no point in prosecuting the past nor in fearing the future; rather, our task is to develop an understanding of present realities and to become more sensitive to the future consequences of existing trends that, left unfaced, do not bode well for the nation or for humanity.

If we fail to meet the challenge of coming to grips with the global facts of life, history will not deal lightly with our generation of educators. We have had sufficient early warning to help shape a better future to mobilize ideas and energies soon enough to make a significant difference in how it all turns out.

Annotated Bibliography: Global Perspectives in Education

Selected and Compiled by Lillian K. Drag

Part I: Imperatives and Issues

Part II: Instructional Materials:
Teaching Methods and Learning Activities

Part III: Sources for Additional Materials

Part IV: Pertinent Periodicals

Part V: (a) Projects and Programs
(b) Agencies Sponsoring International and Intercultural
Exchanges,List Developed by Stephen Rhinesmith

Part VI: Research Studies

T his selected list of readings was compiled to reflect, support, and supplement the ideas about global education presented in the body of this work. It is intended to provide the reader with a well-balanced and broad picture of what is being said and done in the field of educating for world-mindedness and to offer further background for those interested in implementing programs. Frequently the annotations cite related references. We have intentionally omitted reference to studies of particular geographical, cultural, or political units in order to underscore the "global" emphasis in this book. Most of the material listed has been published within the past ten years although a few, still useful, older works are included.

This bibliography is arranged in six parts. Part I deals with philosophical considerations, key concepts, and principles undergirding global perspectives in education. Rationales for promoting world-mindedness in schools, fundamental issues, and imperatives for determining priorities are discussed in the titles listed. Some selections examine the educational process, and others provide data on the world situation. This section, therefore, may be helpful to the educator who is considering becoming involved, already planning for, or in the process of implementing a global education program. Part II lists instructional materials and is directed to two audiences, the teacher and the student. The selections are classroom-oriented, emphasizing practical rather than theoretical aspects of global awareness. A sampling of student texts is provided, but trade books (nontextbooks) are omitted. Further readings and materials for students may be found in Part III, along with guides to simulations, games, and multimedia items and a list of addresses of organizations that can supply further information and classroom aids. Further reviews of the literature are also listed for those administrators, curriculum workers, teachers, and researchers who wish to extend their knowledge of the field. Part IV is more than a listing of periodical titles, for the annotations frequently spell out specific articles directly related to global issues. It is for this reason that so few articles are listed in other sections of the bibliography. Part V is divided into two sections: (*a*) Projects and Programs and (*b*) Agencies Sponsoring International and Intercultural Exchanges. The Projects and Programs section focuses specifically on various groups involved in promoting world-mindedness and global awareness, carrying out educational programs, and producing materials for classroom use. In some instances, a selective listing of their publications is provided in the annotation. Part VI lists Research Studies which have examined various aspects of global education.

Part I: Imperatives and Issues

Agan, Raymond J., and Joseph Hajda (eds.): *Curriculum for Man in an International World,* International Education Year Conference, 1970, Kansas State University, Topeka, 1971.

Contributions by Harold Taylor, Franklin Parker, and Donald Robinson, among others. Arthur J. Lewis, "Continuing Education for World Affairs," charts the relationship between information and attitudes. He proposes "Earth Survival Centers" to promote both.

Anderson, Lee F.: *Improving Global Education in the Nation's Schools: An Analysis of the Problem and Some Proposals for Action,* paper delivered at the National Council for the Social Studies Annual Meeting, Washington, D.C., 1976. Available from the Mid-America Program, Indiana University, 513 North Park, Bloomington, Ind. 47401.

Suggests that culture building, institutional development, technology development, language development, and intellectual development are more fundamental aspects for improving global education than changes in school curriculum or education of teachers.

————: *Schools as Travel Agencies: Helping People to Move Up, Down, and Sideways through Human Culture,* Social Science Education Consortium, Inc., no. 199, packet M, Boulder, Colo., 1977.

Presents a view of how the concept of culture can be fostered in children by developing the meaning of "macroculture" as a "perspective from which to look upon culture as a generic phenomenon."

Association for Childhood Education International: *Children and Intercultural Education: Overview and Research, Part II,* ACEI, Washington, D.C., 1974.

Contains John A. Carpenter and Judith V. Torney, "Overview — Beyond the Melting Pot to Cultural Pluralism," and Donald C. La Due and others, "Selected Research on Intercultural-International Education." This is part of a three-booklet kit which serves as a guide to developing appreciation for cultural diversity.

————: *Learning to Live as Neighbors,* ACEI, Washington, D.C., 1972.

A carefully chosen collection of articles reprinted from Childhood Education *arranged under three classifications: general philosophy, methodology, and case studies. Selected to review ideas related to a new three-year "Project: Neighbors Unlimited," focusing on international and intercultural relations in school, home, and community. See also, the Association's* Suggestions for Implementing Project: Neighbors Unlimited, *ACEI, Washington, D.C., 1972.*

Association for Supervision and Curriculum Development: *Education for Peace: Focus on Mankind,* prepared by the ASCD 1973 Yearbook Committee, George Henderson (chairman and ed.), ASCD, Washington, D.C., 1973.

Peace education in this work includes social justice, social change, ecological balance, and economic welfare, all viewed from a global perspective. Focuses on the ethical implications and the action orientation required of the student in the study of the mutual interdependence of the systems of man.

Bailey, Stephen K.: "International Education: An Agenda for Global Interdependence," *The College Board Review,* vol. 97, Fall 1975.

"This nation needs . . . an internationally informed citizenry . . . that is adequately aware of its relationship to the rest of the world, prepared to support as well as criticize the tough decisions which leaders must make, and capable of contributing to the necessary dialogue of a functioning democracy and an emerging world order."

Becker, James M.: *Education for a Global Society,* Phi Delta Kappa Educational Foundation, Bloomington, Ind., 1973. (Fastback no. 28.)

Presents some of the imperatives for a global society, perceives the need for transnational participation, and provides guidelines for promoting global education in schools.

————: *An Examination of Objectives, Needs, and Priorities in International Education in U.S. Secondary and Elementary Schools,* Lee F. Anderson, Project Coordinator, James M. Becker, Director, United States Office of Education, 1969. Also available from ERIC.

An extensive nationwide study resulting in the propositions that curricula develop in students knowledge and understanding of the world system, a view of the earth as a single planet, man as a single species of life, and his social system as one of many alternatives. Suggests the need for students to examine their own feelings, sensitivities, and values; learn to work effectively with others; and assume responsibility for their own actions. Appendixes include papers prepared by key persons in education and the social sciences; summary of recommendations from Harold Taylor's The World and the American Teacher; *and "Needed Research and Development in International Education," by James Becker and Lee Anderson.*

————: *International Education for Spaceship Earth,* Foreign Policy Association, Thomas Y. Crowell, New York, 1968.

A short survey of the larger study cited above which summarizes the relationship between man and his environment, needed changes in education, obstacles to change, and strategies for change. See also King, David C., listed in Part II, Instructional Materials, referring to same project.

Becker, James M., and Maurice A. East: *Global Dimensions in U.S. Education: The Secondary School,* Center for War/Peace Studies,* New York, 1972.

Discusses recent developments as related to the international dimension of the curriculum. Provides an analysis of trends, needs, and resources to improve international content and teaching strategies.

Becker, James M., and Howard D. Mehlinger (eds.): *International Dimensions in the Social Studies,* 1968 Yearbook, National Council for the Social Studies, Washington, D.C., 1968.

Proposes that world affairs permeate all social studies, indicating what is being done, the emphasis needed, and useful resources. Discusses area studies, simulation techniques, case method, government programs, and world affairs councils.

Benedict, Ruth: *Patterns of Culture,* Houghton Mifflin, Boston, 1961. (Paperback.)

A classic on cultural anthropology for teacher reference. Readable and still valid though first published in 1934.

Bhagwati, Jagdish N. (ed.): *Economics and World Order: From the 1970's to the 1990's,* Free Press, New York, 1972. (Paperback.)

Originating in the World Order Models Project, these papers deal

---

*Now Center for Global Perspectives.

with the gap between the rich and poor nations, prospects of narrowing that gap, and the problems of world order and policy.

Bobrow, David B.: *International Relations: New Approaches,* Free Press, New York, 1972.

Shows how the study of international relations has changed, requiring an interdisciplinary perspective. Suggests a framework for evaluating traditional as well as the newer approaches. Illustrates newer methods. Secondary and college levels.

Bohannan, Paul: "Our Two-Story Culture," *Saturday Review,* vol. 55, Sept. 2, 1972, pp. 40–41.

One "story" is a large-scale world, primarily economic and political; the other "story" is a small-scale world of family and community. The difficulty lies in communication between the two stories, at the same time avoiding fear among microcultures. It takes intercultural education and civil rights based on equality and justice to negotiate the stairs between the two cultures.

Bohannan, Paul, et al.: *A Preliminary Review of the Intercultural Dimension in International/Intercultural Education, Grades K–14,* Social Science Education Consortium, no. 156, packet M, Boulder, Colo., 1973.

Offers a general model for international/intercultural education after examining rationale and objectives. Discusses the current state of the field, reviewing desirable programs.

Brameld, Theodore: *The Climactic Decades: Mandate to Education,* Praeger, New York, 1970.

Stresses the need for more adequate teaching about world affairs, education for future-centeredness, issue-focused curricula, teaching for involvement in sociopolitical affairs.

————: *The Teacher as World Citizen: A Scenario of the 21st Century,* 1974 Kappa Delta Pi lecture, ETC Publications, Palm Springs, Calif., 1976. (Paperback.)

Describes the kind of world the author hopes mankind might achieve by the year 2000 written as if by a citizen of the "World Community of Nations."

Brown, Ina C.: *Understanding Other Cultures,* Prentice-Hall, Englewood Cliffs, N.J., 1963. (Paperback.)

A helpful text on cultural anthropology to provide teachers with the needed frame of reference (cultural patterning) for learning about other peoples.

Brown, Lester R.: *In the Human Interest: A Strategy to Stabilize World Population,* Norton, New York, 1974.

Singles out the problem of overpopulation to stress the need for a cooperative effort at all levels, local, national, and supranational, in order to solve it. Teacher background material.

————: *The Interdependence of Nations,* Foreign Policy Association, Headline Series, no. 212, New York, October 1972.

Adapted from the author's World without Borders *(see entry below for fuller annotation), this booklet is useful in introducing the issue of nation-state and world organization to the novice.*

————: *World Population Trends: Signs of Hope, Signs of Stress,* Worldwatch Institute, Worldwatch Paper No. 8, Washington, D.C., 1976.

Reviews population trends over the last half decade, indicating that the world's population will not double in size before leveling off. By 1985 more than a billion people may live in countries with an essentially stable population. Documents the hunger and nutritional stress that afflicted the Indian subcontinent and parts of Africa. Discusses "the fatal legacy of inadequate food reserves."

————: *World without Borders,* Vintage Books, Random House, 1972.

Brown sees the need for an educational effort designed to provide a better understanding of the relationship between persistent problems confronting people at the local or national level and the cooperative "supranational" efforts needed to solve these problems. A source for developing teacher awareness of an interdependent world.

Brown, Lester R., et al.: *By Bread Alone,* Praeger, New York, 1974.

Discusses the imminent global food crisis and need to counteract it by population control, change in diet of the affluent, augmenting present food supply, and taking a worldwide approach to solution of the problem.

Buergenthal, Thomas, and Judith V. Torney: *International Human Rights and International Education,* U.S. National Commission for UNESCO, Washington, D.C., 1976.

Analyzes the 1974 UNESCO Recommendation concerning Education for International Understanding, Cooperation and Peace, and Education relating to Human Rights and Fundamental Freedoms. Stresses the educational implications of this important policy statement bearing on vital contemporary issues. Relates the history of international education efforts and reviews new approaches. Contains information about the human rights activities of international and regional organizations.

Calderwood, James D.: *The Developing World: Poverty, Growth and Rising Expectations,* Scott, Foresman, Glenview, Ill., 1976. (Paperback.)

Focuses on tensions, problems, and challenges resulting from the division of the world between the rich and poor nations. Emphasis is on the commonality of people's problems and on the interrelationships and interdependence of peoples and countries in the world. Teaching guide available.

Center for International Education: *Sundry Papers,* University of Massachusetts, School of Education, Amherst, 1970.

Three major thrusts of the Center are reflected in these collected papers: cross-cultural training, the teaching of non-Western studies in United States schools, and education for national development.

Council of Chief State School Officers: *Civic Literacy for Global Interdependence,* Council of Chief State School Officers, Committee on International Education, Washington, D.C., 1976.

An important statement from an influential educational body supporting study for attainment of global perspectives in American schools.

Dubos, René: *A God Within,* Scribner, New York, 1972.

Place is an important symbol for man, which seems to indicate to the author that smaller rather than larger political units are preferable. "As we enter the global phase of human evolution it becomes obvious that each man has two countries, his own and planet earth."

———: *So Human an Animal,* Scribner, New York, 1968.

A readable and important book designed to illustrate that each individual is unique in the ways his person responds to his environment; that all experiences leave their mark, especially very early influences; that "human beings are as much the product of their total environment as of their genetic endowment." Sees the present system on a suicidal course which can be averted with a science of human life. "Man makes himself through enlightened choices that enhance his humanness."

Eckholm, Erik: *Losing Ground: Environmental Stress and World Food Prospects,* Norton, New York, 1976. (Paperback.)

Gives an eyewitness report on the vast damage now being done to the earth. Sees disaster unless worldwide land-use reforms are instituted.

Falk, Richard A.: *A Study of Future Worlds,* Free Press, New York, 1975. (Paperback.)

Proposes an integrated world policy based on present political realities developing a strategy for moving from the present to the 1990s. Details structures and functions of new world organizations designed to eliminate poverty, war, environmental imbalance, and injustice.

————: *This Endangered Planet: Prospects and Proposals for Human Survival,* Vintage Books, Random House, New York, 1971.

Shows the interrelationship of war and violence with such problems as population growth, pollution, depletion of natural resources, poverty, and the denial of human rights. Proposes a world order as the solution, moving toward strong international institutions away from the nation-state system.

Faure, Edgar, et al.: *Learning To Be: The World of Education Today and Tomorrow,* International Commission on the Development of Education, UNESCO, Paris; George G. Harrap and Co., London, 1972.

Report of the "critical reflection by men of different origins and backgrounds seeking . . . for over-all solutions to the major problems involved in the development of education in a changing universe." Faure's preamble offers a rationale for developing world-mindedness. Chapter 8, "Elements for Contemporary Strategies," indicates the range of improvements and reforms and gives principles, considerations, recommendations, and illustrations of specific innovations from various of the twenty-three countries involved.

Galbraith, John Kenneth: *Economics, Peace, and Laughter,* Houghton Mifflin, Boston, 1971.

Twenty-six essays, first of which is "Economics and the Quality of Life" (which is not dependent on how much we produce). "Economics as a System of Belief" restates central ideas of The New Industrial State *and responds to criticisms. Makes a case for "producer sovereignty" in contrast to "consumer sovereignty."*

Three models of underdevelopment, effects of poverty on national behavior, and prescriptions for our foreign aid programs are given.

Global Dimensions in U.S. Education, Center for War/Peace Studies,* New York, 1972.

Four studies published jointly by the Education Commission of the International Studies Association, the Committee on Pre-Collegiate Education of the American Political Science Association and the Center for War/Peace Studies: The Elementary School, *by* Judith V. Torney *and* Donald N. Morris; The Secondary School, *by* James M. Becker *and* Maurice A. East *(see listings under authors' names for annotations);* The University, *by* Maurice Harari; *and* The Community, *by* William C. Rogers *(annotated listing under author's name).*

Global Education: Helping Secondary Students Understand International Issues, Institute for Development of Educational Activities (I|D|E|A|), Dayton, Ohio, 1974.

Report of an international seminar sponsored by the Charles F. Kettering Foundation and Gottlieb Duttweiler Institute of Zurich, Switzerland, in cooperation with the National Commission on the Reform of Secondary Education. Report prepared by William P. Shaw.

Goals for Mankind: A Report to the Club of Rome on the New Horizons of Global Community, ed. Ervin Laszlo et al., Dutton, 1977.

Deals with three questions: "What do today's separate governments and societies want to accomplish? How compatible are these operative aspirations with the overarching goals of a humane and healthy earth community? What basic helps and hindrances are there to closing the gaps between shortsighted ambitions and long range preservation of our common household?" (See entries below under Meadows, under Mesarovic and under Tinbergen for annotations of earlier reports to the Club of Rome.)

Goldschmidt, Walter: *Exploring the Ways of Mankind,* 2d ed., Holt, New York, 1971.

A cultural anthropology reference to provide the necessary background for understanding the commonalities of peoples from diverse cultures. Easy to read.

Goodlad, John I., and Associates: *Toward a Mankind School: An*

---

*Now Center for Global Perspectives.

Adventure in Humanistic Education, McGraw-Hill, New York, 1974.

Reports the initiation of an attempt to identify some of the basic ideas of the concept of mankind, their significance for teachers and children, their relationship to the culture of the school, and the experimental translation of these ideas into a curriculum for children. Annotated bibliography included.

Goodman, Mary Ellen: *The Individual and Culture,* Dorsey, Homewood, Ill., 1967.

Examines the interrelationship between the nature and means of human development and the nature and impact of culture on the individual. Presents basic concepts dealing with individual autonomy versus cultural determinism as used by anthropologists and sociologists. See also Goodman's The Culture of Childhood: Child's Eye Views of Society and Culture, *Teachers College, New York, 1970.*

Griffin, Willis H., and Ralph B. Spence: *Cooperative International Education,* Association for Supervision and Curriculum Development, Washington, D.C., 1970.

The Great Education proposed here "must deal with attitudes." Some of the authors' basic assumptions: "New insights into human behavior; increasingly refined concepts of social change; and invention of new means of communicating, teaching and learning make possible" a vastly superior education.

Haavelsrud, Magnus (ed.): *Education for Peace: Reflection and Action,* IPC Science and Technology Press, Guilford, Surrey, England, 1975.

Contains thirty articles from twenty countries, dealing with substantive and methodological aspects of peace education, from early childhood to adulthood. What is peace education? Why is it needed? How should it be achieved? Where is it needed most? These basic questions are answered from different cultural viewpoints.

Hall, Edward T.: *The Silent Language,* Fawcett, New York, 1959.

Develops the concept of cultural universalism, supporting the view that both human qualities and human culture are "universal." Proposes a theory of culture with colleague George Trager based on the conviction that culture is communication and communication is culture. Identifies ten kinds of basic human activities (Primary Message Systems) based on anthropological studies. See also Hall's The Hidden Dimension, *Doubleday, New York, 1969.*

Handleman, John R., H. B. Shapiro, and J. A. Vasquez: *Introductory Case Studies for International Relations: Vietnam, the Middle East, and the Environmental Crisis,* Rand McNally, Chicago, 1974.

Provides a set of theoretical concepts for interpreting global issues. Conceptual frameworks, applicable at three levels of sophistication, are used to examine issues in the case studies provided. A college text which may add to the secondary teacher's understanding of international relations.

Hansen, Roger D., and the Staff of the Overseas Development Council: *The U.S. and World Development: Agenda for Action, 1976,* Praeger, New York, 1976.

Assesses current issues and decisions facing the United States in its relation with the developing countries. Comparative statistics, especially economic data, are up-to-date on the world situation. Includes, for instance, a table on World Energy Consumption, by types of energy, 1960–1990.

Hanvey, Robert G.: *An Attainable Global Perspective,* Center for War/Peace Studies,* New York, 1975. Commissioned by the Center for Teaching International Relations, University of Denver.

Describes certain modes of thought, sensitivities, intellectual skills and explanatory capacities necessary for attaining a global perspective: Dimension 1, Perspective consciousness; Dimension 2, State-of-the-planet awareness; Dimension 3, Cross-cultural awareness; Dimension 4, Knowledge of global dynamics (the world as a system); Dimension 5, Awareness of human choices; Dimension 6, Ethical awareness. Suggests teaching strategies and offers sample lessons. See also, Hanvey's "Explorations in the Emergent Present," Intercom, no. 77, Winter 1974–75.

Harman, Willis W.: "Policies for National Reunification," *Journal of Creative Behavior,* vol. 4, Fall 1970, pp. 283–293.

Presents six propositions (hypotheses) relating to the present state of society and the probable future course of events. Basic premises of "New Age" culture include an image of man as a part of a whole and capable of the "communion with nature prerequisite to resolving the planet's ecological problems, the fraternity to fellow man without which social problems will resist solution, and the supremely meaningful task of human evolution to eliminate the anomie of our time."

---

*Now Center for Global Perspectives.

Hartwig, Gerald (ed.): *Intercultural and International Education in the Schools of North Carolina,* Center for International Studies, Duke University, Durham, N.C., 1977.

A report on the efforts of a group of educators to improve global perspectives in North Carolina.

Hayden, Rose L.: *International Education: Putting Up or Shutting Up,* American Council on Education, International Education Project, Washington, D.C., 1975.

Sees the need for new curricular and research models to update traditional international education programs in order to respond to contemporary challenges.

————: *The World and Your School District,* American Council on Education, International Education Project, 1975.

Provides suggestions for updating every child's basic education in order to educate for life in a future globally oriented society. Gives examples of leadership activities for people at the local level for attaining that goal.

Heilbroner, Robert L.: *An Inquiry into the Human Prospect,* Norton, New York, 1974.

A frankly subjective, pessimistic reply to the question, "Is there hope for man?" Cites external challenges: population overload (impossible to curb) leading to urban disorganization leading to "iron" governments; nuclear warfare, rise in international tensions; environmental deterioration, global thermal pollution. Examines the response in avoiding these threats and "in coping with the dangerous tendencies of industrial civilization itself": individual capabilities for change and lack of social organization.

Henderson, James L.: *Education for World Understanding,* Pergamon, New York, 1968.

Sketches a blueprint for an educational system designed to develop the consciousness of the universal in man using the most promising sources of international cooperation today. Specifically recommended are Chapter 2, "Pre-secondary School Possibilities," for children between six and fifteen and Chapter 5, "The Terrestrial Teacher," expressing the psychology of such a teacher, with multinational examples. Chapter 6, "The Promise of Collective Memories," describes the types of human behaviors that govern the conduct of world affairs.

Hill, Christopher (ed.): *Rights and Wrongs: Essays on Human Rights,* Penguin, Baltimore, 1969.

Case histories reveal disregard for human rights. Discusses philosophical principles underlying the question of human rights and reviews international organizations involved in redressing human wrongs.

Hines, Paul D., and Leslie Wood: *A Guide to Human Rights Education,* National Council for the Social Studies, Washington, D.C., 1969.

Includes milestones in the history of human rights, human rights since 1945, basics for human rights, and teaching ideas. Appendix includes human rights documents and a selected bibliography.

Hirschfeld, Gerhard: *The People: Growth and Survival, First Cycle,* Aldine, Chicago, 1973. (Published for the Council for the Study of Mankind.)

Defines "the people" and attempts to explain why they "have never attained lasting freedom, security, and self-determination — briefly, dignity." Makes specific proposals for the creation of a mankind-oriented society, inviting response from readers, pro and con. Provocative.

Howe, James W., and the Staff of the Overseas Development Council: *The U.S. and the Developing World: Agenda for Action, 1974,* Praeger, New York, 1975.

Assessment of current issues and decisions facing the United States in its relation with the developing countries. Includes statistics on world economic relationships. See also entry under Hansen, Roger D.

Hunkins, Ralph H.: "Education for International Understanding: A Critical Appraisal of the Literature," doctoral dissertation, Indiana University, University Microfilms, Ann Arbor, Mich., 1968.

Notes problems of defining and describing what is meant by educating for international understanding. Focuses on several different rationales offering suggestions for improving the literature, which in turn might make actual classroom practices more rational. Develops a paradigm and criteria for appraising various positions taken in the literature. A useful work for clarifying goals of education for international understanding.

Hunt, Maurice P., and Lawrence E. Metcalf: *Teaching High School Social Studies,* 2d ed., Harper & Row, New York, 1968.

Sees the teacher's task as that of helping each student improve his own capacity for perception. Defines learning as an expansion of insight, a moving to higher levels; effective learning takes place in situations where beliefs and attitudes are challenged, where some-thing is at stake. Provides a sound rationale for the reflective method of teaching.

International Education Project: *Education for Global Interdependence,* American Council on Education, Washington, D.C., 1975.

Incorporates findings of task forces on Diffusion, Overseas Professional Skills Reinforcement, Language Competence, Transnational Collaborative Research, and Library Resources. Makes policy recommendations for improved support of international education with respect to federal and state governments, foundations, and the educational community.

Kenworthy, Leonard S.: *The International Dimension of Education,* Association for Supervision and Curriculum Development, Washington, D.C., 1970.

Examines aspects of change in the world, the need for "internationally-minded individuals," and implications for teaching including strategies and materials. Spells out characteristics of quality international programs for elementary and secondary schools.

Kimball, Solon T.: *Culture and the Educative Process: An Anthropological Perspective,* Teachers College, New York, 1974.

Stresses need for all peoples to understand their relation to nature, to one another, and to other cultures in order to solve world-order problems.

Kluckhohn, Clyde: *Mirror for Man,* Premier Books, Fawcett World Library, New York, 1970. (Paperback.)

A classic cultural anthropology text useful for teacher background material.

Kothari, Rajni: *Footsteps into the Future: Diagnosis of the Present World and Design for an Alternative,* Orient Longman, New Delhi, 1974.

One of the basic studies of the World Order Models Project concerned directly with the world order questions which underlie the problems of interdependence. Each of the studies is made by autonomous teams of scholars and intellectuals in different regions throughout the world who come up with different answers.

Kurtz, Paul: *The Fullness of Life,* Horizon Press, New York, 1974.

In Part III, "Prospects for the Future," the author stresses the global consciousness of the humanist outlook. Teacher background material.

Leestma, Robert: "Global Education," *American Education,* vol. 14, June 1978, pp. 1–8. *Presents a strong case for the importance of global education in today's curriculum. Suggests pertinent themes: Unity and diversity of mankind, international human rights, global interdependence, intergenerational responsibility, and international cooperation.*

Low, Robert G., and Lawrence E. Metcalf (eds.): *The Individual and World Order: Human Rights and Responsibilities,* World Law Fund, New York, 1971.

Selected readings which highlight the problems of individual rights and responsibilities, especially in war situations.

Macdonald, James B., Bernice J. Wolfson, and Esther Zaret: *Reschooling Society: A Conceptual Model,* Association for Supervision and Curriculum Development, Washington, D.C., 1973.

Provides a much-needed theoretical base for world-minded schools by restructuring the sociocultural, psychological, and transactional dimensions of schooling. Sociological dimensions of liberation, pluralism and participation undergird the proposal for "higher levels of self-esteem, commitment, responsibility, freedom, and an ever-expanding awareness of the world."

Man's Home, United Nations, New York, 1972.

Five pamphlets produced to provide background information for participants in The United Nations Conference on Human Environment. They serve to justify international involvement in development, creation of a worldwide monitoring system, problems of cities, use and abuse of resources, and pollutants. Specific recommendations of the conference are found in Environment: Stockholm, *United Nations, New York, and* The Message from Stockholm, *American Association of University Women, Washington, D.C. 20037.*

Massialas, Byron G. (ed.): *Political Youth, Traditional Schools: National and International Perspectives,* Prentice-Hall, Englewood Cliffs, N.J., 1972.

Surveys the political attitudes and knowledge of children and youth in the United States and thirteen other countries. Contributors focus on the role of education in political socialization. Offers recommendations for needed changes in school curriculum, organization, and classroom practice.

Maxwell, Elizabeth H.: *Experiments in International Education,* UNESCO, Paris, 1969.

Describes the work of the Conference of Internationally-Minded Schools which included teachers' conferences, young people's camps, festivals of the arts, study courses, drama tours, international magazines, travel bursaries, interschool exchanges and associations. Affiliated in August 1969 with the International Schools Association.

Mead, Margaret: *Family,* photographs by Ken Heyman. Collier, New York, 1971.

Pictures taken in over forty countries carry text by Dr. Mead on human roles and relationships. (This is the paperback edition of Family of Man.*) See also Margaret Mead and Key Heyman:* World Enough: Rethinking the Future, *Little, Brown, Boston, 1975.*

Meadows, Donna H., et al.: *The Limits to Growth: Report to the Club of Rome,* Universe Books, New York, 1972.

Reports the application of system dynamics to the problem of a global ecological crisis. Identifies the general trends in the area of population, food production, industrialization, pollution, and consumption of nonrenewable resources over a 200-year period (1900–2100). Foresees a severe, possibly catastrophic decline in both world population and industrial capacity should the existing trend of exponential growth continue.

Mendlovitz, Saul H. (ed.): *On the Creation of a Just World Order: Preferred Worlds for the 1990's,* Free Press, New York, 1975.

Members of the World Order Models Project from Japan, India, Africa, Western Europe, Latin America, China, and the United States offer their ideas of what the world could be like and how steps can be taken now toward that world.

Mershon Center, Ohio State University: *A Research Project on the Role of Schools in National and International Political Learning,* Ohio State University, Columbus, 1974. (Mimeographed.)

See entry in Part VI, Research Studies, under Alger, and in Part V, Projects and Programs, entry under Transnational Intellectual Cooperation Program for annotations.

Mesarovic, Mihajlo, and Eduard Pestel: *Mankind at the Turning Point: The Second Report to the Club of Rome,* Dutton, New York, 1974. (Paperback.)

Study of the interactions of a world divided into ten interdependent regions in various scenarios extending fifty years into the future, using computers and "multilevel hierarchical systems theory." Concludes that long-term solutions must incorporate global approaches: controlled, differentiated growth to balance world population, food, energy, and wealth distribution. More optimistic than the first report to the Club of Rome, The Limits to Growth, *by Meadows et al. See* Goals for Mankind, *cited earlier, and* Tinbergen, *cited below, for more recent reports to the Club of Rome.*

Metcalf, Lawrence E.: "Developing and Applying Humane Values," *Issues in Secondary Education,* ed. William Van Til, Seventy-fifth Yearbook, Part II, National Society for the Study of Education, University of Chicago Press, Chicago, 1976, chap. IV.

Within this chapter Metcalf discusses "Today's Value Crisis—Its Global Nature," leading to the need for man in the twenty-first century to be a transnational person with commitments to supranational institutions. Delineates five global problems: ecological imbalance (includes air pollution), war, growing disparity between rich and poor nations, absence of democratic government, and the violation of human rights by many governments. Stresses value-oriented discussion of personalized attitudes and choices in order to advance moral growth and mental health.

Mische, Gerald, and Patricia Mische: *Toward a Human World Order,* Paulist Press, Ramsey, N.J., 1977.

Stresses the need for release from the "National Security Straight-jacket" in order to attain feasible world order alternatives based on more humane and socially just values. Outlines grass-roots strategies.

Moraes, Dom: *Voices for Life: Reflections on the Human Condition,* Praeger, New York, 1975.

A fine collection of essays contributed by eminent men from different countries and diverse disciplines expressing individual views of human problems yet sharing a common concern for humanity.

Morehouse, Ward: *Citizen Understanding and Action,* Institute for World Order, New York, 1976.

Suggests ways to change people's attitudes with regard to peace by means of proven behavioral techniques.

————: *A New Civic Literacy: American Education and Global Interdependence,* Interdependence Series, no. 3, Aspen Institute for Humanistic Studies, Princeton, N.J., 1975.

Schools have the opportunity to shape a more compatible world by facing the realities of global interdependence. Cites key interdependence issues needing to be stressed in order to develop a new and stronger civic literacy.

————: *Organizational Atlas on the Diffusion of International/Inter-cultural Education,* Interim Report by the Foreign Area Materials Center, State Education Department, University of the State of New York, Albany, revised October 1974.

Describes existing efforts on an "organizational map" which includes consumers or users, producers, diffusion techniques, and geographical scope (regional, state, or national).

National Association of Independent Schools: *The Wingspread Report on New Dimensions in the Teaching of the Social Studies,* NAIS, Ad Hoc Committee on the Social Studies, Racine, Wis., 1968.

Suggests elements of the global problem which must be confronted by teachers and students for survival in world of today: the international order, black studies, the balance of nature. Cites changes needed in classroom procedures and school structure as well as teachers and their training.

The National Commission on the Reform of Secondary Education: *The Reform of Secondary Education: A Report to the Public and the Profession,* B. Frank Brown, Chairman, McGraw-Hill, New York, 1973.

Report of a conference which includes a chapter devoted to the recommendation that all secondary school students should receive a basic global education.

National Council for the Social Studies: "Curriculum Guidelines for Multiethnic Education: Position Statement," *Social Education,* October 1976, Special Supplement.

An NCSS Task Force developed these guidelines for designing and implementing sound ethnic studies programs and for integrating schools' curricula with ethnic content. Focus is on ethnic pluralism rather than on cultural pluralism in describing the ideal characteristics of school environments and goals which each school can aim for. Includes program evaluation checklist. Deals directly with the issue of the responsibility of education to foster diversity.

National Society for the Study of Education: *The United States and International Education,* ed. Harold G. Shane, Sixty-eighth Yearbook, Part I, University of Chicago Press, Chicago, 1969.

Chapter III by C. Arnold Anderson, "Challenges and Pitfalls in International Education," and Chapter XI by Harold Shane are especially noteworthy in pursuing education in world affairs. Shane uses Hall and Trager's "universals" (cited under Hall, above) to develop a "culture ring" model as a basis for curriculum development.

National Task Force on Citizenship Education: *Education for Responsible Citizenship: The Report of the National Task Force on Citizenship Education,* B. Frank Brown, Director, McGraw-Hill, New York, 1977.

Chapter 12, "The Crisis of Global Transformation, Interdependence, and the Schools," by Saul H. Mendlovitz, Lawrence Metcalf, and Michael Washburn, develops the need for world-order thinking in all civic education and suggests how to proceed with that development.

Nesbitt, William A., and Charles Bloomstein: "Should the Nation-State Give Way to Some Form of World Organization?" in National Council for the Social Studies, *Controversial Issues in the Social Studies: A Contemporary Perspective,* ed. Raymond H. Muessig, 45th Yearbook, NCSS, Washington, D.C., 1975, pp. 261–303.

Suggests a five-step model: (1) perspective or overview to provide student with sufficient historical background; (2) analysis, to give the student some grasp of contemporary world problems; (3) projection—extrapolating what is most likely to happen; (4) examination of alternatives; (5) strategies. Lists pertinent materials under the first four steps.

Overly, Norman V., and Richard D. Kimpston (eds.): *Global Studies: Problems and Promises for Elementary Teachers,* Association for Supervision and Curriculum Development, Washington, D.C., 1976.

A brief is made for greater exposure in the schools to the realities of increasing interdependence in the world today. Focus is on the role of the teacher in using global studies as an encompassing organizer for general education. Useful chapter, "Resources for Teachers," includes classroom resources for children with level indicated.

Phi Delta Kappa Conference on World Education, Glassboro, New Jersey: *Man's Changing Values and a World Culture: New Directions and New Emphases for Educational Programs, Report . . . ,* U.S. Department of Health, Education, and Welfare, ERIC, Washington, D.C., 1972.

Objectives of the conference: to examine the values of our changing world; to recognize the growing need for a world culture; to see how our changing values help or hinder development of a world culture; and to find new directions for existing educational pro-grams. Offers five suggested workshop presentations on new direc-tions and emphases.

Phi Delta Kappa Teacher Education Project on Human Rights: *A Guide for Improving Teacher Education in Human Rights,* University of Oklahoma, Norman, 1971.

Designed to improve pre-service and in-service programs in the area of basic human rights and values. Gertrude Noar did most of the writing. Includes foundations for a human rights program in education, specifics of institutional and teacher behavior in human rights, practical approaches to the teaching of human rights, and an extensive bibliography.

The Planetary Bargain: Proposals for a New International Economic Order to Meet Human Needs, report of an international workshop convened in Aspen, Colorado, July 7–August 1, 1975, Aspen Institute for Humanistic Studies, Program in International Affairs, Princeton, N.J., 1977.

A policy paper outlining elements of international bargaining and proposing reform of the international system.

Polak, Fred L.: *The Image of the Future,* translated and abridged by Elise Boulding, Jossey-Bass, San Francisco, 1973.

A historical survey of Western man's way of thinking about the future, providing a look at the broad sweep of the processes leading to the impending "common global heritage on earth." Polak argues that the main dynamic in development has been contributed by images of the future, suggesting that failure to create new future images can result in a stagnancy in which innovation applies only to means and no longer to ends.

Preston, Ralph C. (ed.): *Teaching World Understanding,* Prentice-Hall, New York, 1955.

An early collection of ideas for developing understanding of the people of the world among young people. Based on the Quaker objective: the development of a deep respect for human personality wherever and however it may be found.

———: *Teaching Social Studies in the Elementary School,* 3d ed., Holt, 1968.

Incorporates many of the ideas proposed in Teaching World Understanding, *cited above.*

Pusch, Margaret D.: "The Cultural Connection: Foreign Students in the Schools," in David S. Hoopes (ed.), *Readings on Intercultural Communication,* vol. 5, *Intercultural Programming,* University of Pittsburgh, Intercultural Communications Network, Pittsburgh, 1976, pp. 158–164.

Describes a program in Syracuse, New York, designed to provide an opportunity for elementary school pupils to learn about other cultures through interaction with people from these countries (foreign students attending Syracuse University).

Reischauer, Edwin O.: *Toward the 21st Century: Education for a Changing World,* Knopf, New York, 1973.

Argues that a global perspective needs to be developed "if mankind is to survive. . . ." "Education . . . is not moving rapidly enough to provide the knowledge about the outside world and the attitudes toward other people that may be essential for human survival within a generation or two." Feels that international cooperation has the potential to solve world problems if supported by an informed citizenry that is educated in a "new and radically different way."

Robinson, Donald W., et al.: *Promising Practices in Civic Education,* National Council for the Social Studies, Washington, D.C., 1967.

Chapter 6, "Developing a Committed and Involved Citizenry," includes a number of school practices, background conditions, and examples of outstanding teachers contributing to the goal of "National Pride and International Cooperation."

Rogers, William C.: *Global Dimensions in U.S. Education: The Community,* Center for War/Peace Studies,* New York, 1972.

Brief history and critical review of the efforts to involve adults in continuing education about world affairs and international relations. Sees the local community as the institution for continuing education in world affairs, listing the many organizations used for this purpose, the variety of programs offered and an analysis of content of these programs, and the resources (human, library, financial).

Sanders, Irwin T., and Jennifer Ward: *Bridges to Understanding,* Carnegie Commission on Higher Education, New York, 1970.

Describes international programs of American colleges and universities, indicating how few of them are related to high schools and other community groups.

---

*Now Center for Global Perspectives.

Schumacher, E. F.: *Small Is Beautiful: Economics As If People Mattered,* Harper & Row, New York, 1973. (Paperback.)

Presents arguments for limiting growth and gives case studies of effective action in this area. Questions the suitability of the nation-state to handle such limitation. The chapter entitled "The Greatest Resource—Education" considers education as a cultural institution: "Our task—and the task of all education—is to understand the present world, the world in which we live and make our choices."

Selected Readings in Citizen Education, prepared for a national conference on "Education and Citizenship: Responsibilities for the Common Good," Kansas City, September 1976, sponsored by the U.S. Office of Education.

Indicates that preparation for responsible citizenship today requires multidisciplinary efforts encompassing global dimensions.

Social Education. See Part IV, Pertinent Periodicals, for specific titles and numbers, briefly annotated.

Starratt, Robert J.: "Curriculum Theory: Controversy, Challenge, and Future Concerns," *Heightened Consciousness, Cultural Revolution, and Curriculum Theory,* ed. William Pinar, McCutchan, Berkeley, Calif., 1974.

Identifies global survival as an area of neglect in both theory and practice. Curriculum theorists need to describe the kinds of experience that will "promote the development of personal, sociopolitical, and academic skills necessary to cope with the global challenge. . . ."

Taylor, Harold: *The World as Teacher,* Doubleday, New York, 1969.

"About the education of teachers in an understanding of the world and its problems, and about some possibilities that exist for changing the world through what teachers do in it." Based on a two-year study of teacher education institutions.

Thompson, Laura: *The Secret of Culture,* Random House, New York, 1969.

Like the works by Benedict, Ina Brown, Goldschmidt, and Kluckhohn cited earlier, this popular treatise provides basic understandings in the field of cultural anthropology.

Tinbergen, Jan, Antony J. Dohman (ed.), and Jan van Ettinger (director): *RIO: Reshaping the International Order, A Report to the Club of Rome,* Dutton, New York, 1976.

Experts in the fields of food production, monetary systems, international trade, arms control, natural resources, and the human environment recommend a new international order focusing on the world's poorest people and what rich nations can do to help them.

Toffler, Alvin: *The Eco-Spasm Report,* Bantam, New York, 1975. (Paperback.)

Presents some shocking scenarios of the world scene in an effort to stimulate new directions and more rational planning.

Torney, Judith V., and Donald N. Morris: *Global Dimensions in U.S. Education: The Elementary School,* Center for War/Peace Studies,* 1972.

Reviews important studies of international attitudes and attitude formation in children. Describes several current programs in the U.S. attempting to improve international content in elementary school curricula. The authors view the period of middle childhood as especially important in the formation of attitudes.

Toward the Achievement of Global Literacy in American Schools, Council of Chief State School Officers, Washington, D.C., July 1976.

A report on the Wingspread workshop on problems of definition and assessment of global education.

UNESCO: *The Associated Schools Project: An Appraisal,* presented at the International Meeting of Experts on the UNESCO Associated Schools Project, Levis, Quebec, September 29–October 7, 1973. (Processed.)

Describes the organization of the project in fourteen of the sixty-two countries involved. Analyzes the results of a questionnaire addressed to teachers and students on progress and problems. Section III, "Conclusions and Recommendations," attempts to provide a synthesis of findings.

———: *Desirability of Adopting an International Instrument on Education for International Understanding, Cooperation and Peace,* UNESCO General Conference, Seventeenth Session, Paris, 1972.

Examines the historical background of international education

---

*Now Center for Global Perspectives.

efforts; definitions and content of education for international understanding; the present portion of education in member states; and the feasibility of formulating new standards. Appendix I is a recommendation on future directions. Appendix II presents some definitions.

————: *International Understanding at School,* UNESCO, Paris, 1971.

Traces the history of the UNESCO Associated Schools Project in Education for International Understanding and Cooperation. Sums up the experience to date of the selected primary and secondary schools and teacher-training institutions, and describes some pilot projects. Emphasis is on the importance of the atmosphere of the school: "The principles of human rights should be reflected in the organization and conduct of school life, in classroom methods, and in relations between teachers and students and among teachers themselves." See also International Understanding at School *in Part IV, Pertinent Periodicals.*

————: *Some Suggestions on Teaching and Human Rights,* UNESCO, Paris, 1968.

A brief summing up of practical experience by teachers and schools in various countries as they attempted to promote better understanding of the principles of human rights. Appendix includes the Universal Declaration of Human Rights.

UNESCO. Canadian Commission for UNESCO: *Occasional Paper, No. 2,* Ottawa, January 1972.

Describes the Associated Schools Project in Canada: objectives, history, participation, conditions necessary for success, representative topics studied in school curriculum, and extracurricular activities.

UNESCO General Conference, eighteenth session, 1974: *Recommendation concerning Education for International Understanding, Cooperation and Peace, and Education Relating to Human Rights and Fundamental Freedoms,* UNESCO, Paris, 1974.

Guiding principles are developed for education for international understanding based on the premise that the educational process is the entire process of social life of the individual in national and international communities.

UNESCO. International Commission on the Development of Education. See Faure, Edgar, et al. in this section.

U.S. Department of State: "Toward a Strategy of Interdependence," *Special Report,* no. 17, Washington, D.C., July 1975.

A slightly edited version of Lincoln P. Bloomfield's chapters I and III of vol. I in a four-volume study, Analyzing Global Interdependence, *by the Center for International Studies of MIT. Part I discusses the semantics of interdependence; types of interdependence such as environmental, security, and economics; interdependence as a fact in food, trade, foreign investment, multinational corporations, and nonfuel mineral resources; interdependence as a "good," interdependence as a "bad"; interdependence as perception and as balance. Part II develops policy options offering five alternatives and finally developing a possible U.S. interdependence policy.*

U.S. House of Representatives. Committee on Education and Labor: *International Education: Past, Present, Problems and Prospects,* Selected Readings to Supplement H. R. 14643, October 1966.

Events and forces influencing the development of programs. Gives the bases for future programs considered by the U.S. government. Although the International Education Act of 1966 was passed, no appropriations were made to support it.

U.S. National Commission for UNESCO: *American Education in a Revolutionary World: Role of the States,* New York, n.d.

Proposes that opportunities and resources for the study of other peoples and cultures should have equal priority with science, mathematics, and other fields.

Utah State Board of Education: *Position Paper on International Education,* Salt Lake City, November 1976.

Brief but pointed statement supporting implementation in the public schools of promising new practices and instructional programs. See Focus on Man, Social Studies for Utah Schools *in Part II, Instructional Materials, for example of curriculum efforts.*

Wagar, W. Warren: *Building the City of Man: Outlines of a World Civilization,* Grossman, New York, 1971.

Analyzes failings of modern civilization and proposes a new world order for the future. Chapter 6, "Education," discusses work as growth; learning in and out of the educational establishment; centering on the person and education in values; schools and values; the free academy; and cognitive synthesis (integration of human knowledge).

Walsh, John E.: *Intercultural Education in the Community of Man,* The University Press of Hawaii, Honolulu, 1973.

Thesis is that we must develop an overarching world culture made up of common values and perceptions and including shared traditions and a common language. Current cultures would be maintained as well. Examines the problems of intercultural education and offers suggestions as to how to proceed.

Ward, Barbara: *This Lopsided World,* Norton, New York, 1968.

Writer-economist Ward contrasts the people of the rich and poor nations as she does in Spaceship Earth, *Columbia, New York, 1966;* Five Ideas That Changed the World, *Norton, 1959; and* The Rich Nations and the Poor Nations, *Norton, 1962. See also her report on the Habitat conference,* The Home of Man, *Norton, 1976.*

Ward, Barbara, and René Dubos: *Only One Earth: The Care and Maintenance of a Small Planet,* Norton, New York, 1972.

Social, economic, and political aspects of global issues such as misuse of resources, pollution, overpopulation, unbalanced development, and urbanization are examined.

Wax, Murray L., Stanley Diamond, and Frederick O. Gearing (eds.): *Anthropological Perspectives on Education,* Basic Books, New York, 1971.

A set of original essays together with an international bibliography useful for teacher background material.

Wulf, Christoph (ed.): *Handbook on Peace Education,* International Peace Research Association, Education Committee, Frankfurt am Main–Oslo, 1974.

Includes contributions from all parts of the world involving the issues of conflict theory, development theory, and international structures. Part II explains peace education in more concrete terms. Part III, "Reports on Approaches to Peace Education in Different Countries," describes practices.

Part II: Instructional Materials: Teaching Methods and Learning Activities

Abraham, Herbert J.: *World Problems in the Classroom: A Teacher's Guide to Some United Nations Tasks,* UNESCO, Paris, 1973.

Information and study suggestions on peace and security, disarmament, human rights, social justice, development, population, and environment are presented in compact form to facilitate teaching. Indicates what is being done through the United Nations system to deal with these problems.

Abrams, Grace C., and Fran C. Schmidt: *Learning Peace: A Resource Unit,* Jane Addams Peace Association, Philadelphia, 1972.

Intended to help the teacher in grades 7–12 teach about and for peace. Activities for students deal with self-assessment of personal attitudes, examination of conflicts and their resolution, investigation of twentieth-century international peace organizations, and investigation of alternatives to war. References to media, literature, and organizations are cited.

Alger, Chadwick F., and David G. Hoovler: *Perceiving and Evaluating Your Actual and Potential Routes for International Involvement,* Transnational Intellectual Cooperation Program, Mershon Center, Ohio State University, Columbus, 1976.

Adult-level learning package includes discussion, exercises, and exemplary materials to heighten awareness and effectiveness in daily participation in international affairs. See also Part VI, Research Studies.

Anthropology Curriculum Project, University of Georgia: *A Sequential Curriculum in Anthropology for Grades 1–7: Concepts of Culture, Grades 1 and 4; The Development of Man and His Culture, Grades 2 and 5; Cultural Change, Grades 3 and 6;* University of Georgia, Athens, 1965–1970.

A program developed for use in elementary grades that emphasizes the comparative dimension of world cultures.

Anthropology Curriculum Study Project, American Anthropological

Association: *Patterns in Human History,* Macmillan, New York, 1971.

A course of study, blending anthropology and history, designed to assist teachers unfamiliar with anthropology. Teaching kits include teaching plan, record, filmstrip, study prints, masters, and readings. Cultural mapping is used to focus on the long-range development of human societies and human nature.

Asimov, Isaac: *Earth: Our Crowded Spaceship,* John Day, New York, 1974.

Discusses the problems we face as population increases and energy sources, food, and land become more scarce. Profusely illustrated with charts, maps, photographs, it is designed for ages seven to sixteen.

Association for Childhood Education International: *Children and International Education,* ACEI, Washington, D.C., 1972.

A portfolio of ten leaflets providing an array of resources available to help develop in children and teachers a knowledge and appreciation of others. See also the association's program, Project: Neighbors Unlimited, *developed to encourage world-mindedness, which produced a survey of the international-intercultural dimensions of curriculum useful for elementary and secondary schools.*

Becker, James M.: *Teaching International Relations,* ERIC Clearinghouse for Social Studies/Social Science Education, Interpretive Series No. 6, Superintendent of Documents, GPO, Washington, D.C., n.d.

Brief overview of the field offering goals and purposes; some approaches, scope, and suggested emphases. Appendix contains a selected bibliography and sources for information.

Bliss, Betsy (ed.): *Concern: Poverty* and *Concern: Race,* Silver Burdett, Morristown, N.J., 1975.

Two booklets of a series provide high school teachers with materials for discussion: photos, drawings, songs, firsthand accounts, data, etc. A Leader's Guide provides discussion questions with suggestions on how to lead a discussion and use materials.

Center for Latin American Studies, University of Florida: *Cross-Cultural Inquiry: Value Clarification Exercises,* Gainesville, Fla., 1974.

"Short, incomplete case studies in which the student is forced to project himself into a decision-making situation, and then, through ... questions that follow, to justify" the decision made.

The strategy attempts to place North American students in the shoes of Latin Americans.

Center for War/Peace Studies:* *Approaches to Conflict and Change,* David C. King, program director, Thomas Y. Crowell, New York, 1972.

A series of eight 3–4 week units for helping teachers deal with critical issues and concepts involved in significant international concerns.

———. *Guide to Selected Curriculum Materials.* (See Part III, Sources for Additional Materials.)

———. *Media on Conflict, Change and Interdependence.* (See Part III.)

———. *Patterns of Human Conflict,* Schloat Productions, Tarrytown, N.Y., 1973

A teaching package for grades 9 through 12; includes filmstrips, cassettes, student booklets, and teacher's guide dealing with all levels of conflict: personal, intergroup, national, and international. Problem-solving approach and critical thinking emphasized.

———. *The Quality of Life.*
Futuristic approach to life styles, environment, etc.

———. *So You Want to Teach About . . .,* 1974.
Ten papers. Offer guidelines and brief lessons on conflict in United States history, interdependence, survival, etc.

———. See also *Intercom* entry in Part IV, Pertinent Periodicals.

Clark, James I.: *Peoples and Cultures Series,* McDougal, Littell, Evanston, Ill., 1976.

Series includes volumes on Latin America, Western Europe, Eastern Europe, the Soviet Union, the Mediterranean, Africa, India, Southeast Asia, China, and Japan. Provides up-to-date, substantive material from a world-centered view. Attractive format, profusely illustrated paperbacks.

"Columbus in the World, the World in Columbus," Brief Reports Nos. 1–20, April 1974–January 1976, Transnational Intellectual Cooperation Program (TICP), Mershon Center, Ohio State University, Columbus.

---

*Now Center for Global Perspectives.

Information concerning Columbus; involvement in the world through contacts in business, industry, church, ethnic groups, the university, etc., is presented in tabular, statistical form, concisely and in a neutral way. Directed by Chadwick F. Alger. (See Part V, Projects and Programs, for further details on TICP.) This packet is a condensed version of longer research reports which are also available.

Comstock, Margaret: *Building Blocks for Peace,* Jane Addams Peace Association, Philadelphia, 1973.

A concise handbook for kindergarten teachers presents units organized around concepts of relating and sharing. Contains suggested books, songs, films, and activities. Objective: increasing a child's awareness of her feelings, her relationships, and "the world."

Concepts and Inquiry: Learner-Verified Edition II, Allyn and Bacon, Boston, 1974–1976.

K–8 program includes paperback texts, filmstrips, vocabulary building exercises, puzzle and game masters, and guides. Presents children and their ways of life in other lands using a sequential and cumulative approach.

Discovering the World: An Adventure in Global Understanding, Grades K–5, Spoken Arts, New Rochelle, N.Y., 1970.

A multimedia human relations program designed to develop world-mindedness in children.

Dufty, David, et al.: *Looking Around Corners: The Intercultural Explorers Guide,* Reed Education, Sydney, 1975.

A product of the Intercultural Studies Project, Department of Education, University of Sydney, this volume offers help in understanding better a country one is visiting, exploring it more fully, and appreciating it more deeply whether the journey is in fact or in imagination using materials available in the classroom. For secondary students and teachers.

————. *Seeing It Their Way: Ideas, Activities, and Resources for Intercultural Studies,* Reed Education, Sydney, 1975.

The basic ideas book of the Intercultural Studies Project cited in annotation above. Looks at how the outside world views Asia and studies misconceptions, assumptions, and attitudes. Suggests ways to modify these views and to reach the goals of cultural interaction and understanding.

Experiences in Inquiry: HSGP and SRSS, prepared by the High

School Geography Project (sponsored by the Association of American Geographers) and Sociological Resources for the Social Studies (sponsored by the American Sociological Association), Allyn and Bacon, Boston, 1974.

Provides samples of the materials produced by HSGP and SRSS useful in the education of teachers in inquiry methods. Format encourages active involvement of teachers in the inquiry process. Selections include some useful in developing global understandings.

Exploring Human Nature, Education Development Center, Inc., Social Studies Program, Cambridge, Mass., 1975.

A year-long upper high school course looks at the question of human aggression: Is it inevitable? What are its roots, its cultural manifestations? Asks: How can insights into human behavior be applied to social questions?

Families around the World and *Teacher's Guide,* Project Social Studies Center, University of Minnesota, Minneapolis, 1972.

Deals with concepts of culture, role, and socialization through the study of family patterns. Provides the basis for further study of community, political systems, and culture values. SRA/CBS has issued a filmstrip series with same title.

Fersh, Seymour (ed.): *Learning about Peoples and Cultures,* McDougal, Littell, Evanston, Ill., 1974.

Short, pithy selections; strong, poignant, and relevant illustrations; and substantive text in the interesting format provide students with a fresh look at human beings in their own culture as well as other cultures. Grades 8–12.

Field Staff Perspectives, InterCulture Associates, Thompson, Conn., 1974.

Modules of study related to understanding cultures around the world developed by the American Universities Field Staff contain readings, cassettes, exercises, study prints, and simulations. Examples of modules: Man at Aq Kupruk: A Village of Northern Afghanistan; Southeast Asia: Amidst Diversity Is Unity Possible? Perspectives on Africa; Urbanization: Cities around the World.

Ford, Richard: *Tradition and Change in Four Societies: An Inquiry Approach,* Holt, New York, 1974.

The four societies studied are China, emphasizing political change; India, concentrating on economic development; Brazil, dealing with race relations; and West Africa, on urbanization. Explores the human issues and values. Grades 9–12.

Fraenkel, Jack, Margaret Carter, and Betty Reardon: *Peacekeeping,* Random House, New York, 1974. (Perspectives in World Order Series).

Uses models and scenarios to enable students to understand the United Nations, League of Nations, and a future limited world government based on mutual deterrence and world law. Paperback high school text with teacher's manual.

Fyson, Nance Lui: *The Development Puzzle: A Sourcebook for Teaching about the "Rich World/Poor World" Divide, and Efforts towards "One World" Development,* 4th ed., Voluntary Committe on Overseas Aid and Development (VCOAD), Parnell House, London SW1, 1974.

A loose-leaf servicebook, updated each year, includes introductory information on current issues, problems, and facts of developing countries; lists of publications and audiovisual aids; articles on ideas for teachers; suggestions on sources for speakers, exhibitions, etc. Gives prices, addresses, and order forms. See Part V, Projects and Programs, for further information on VCOAD.

————. *Latin America and the Caribbean; Africa; Asia: Resources for World Geography,* Voluntary Committee on Overseas Aid and Development, London, 1975.

Three workbooks designed for fourteen-to-sixteen age group contain brief factual data, stories, case studies, discussion on problem areas. Attractive format, illustrated with photographs, stimulates reader to examine issues.

Garbarino, Merwyn S., and Rachel R. Sady: *People and Cultures,* Rand McNally, 1975.

Cultural diversity is explored using five case studies of particular cultures. Designed to develop insights into the meaning of culture through interpreting visual evidence and value clarification techniques.

Geography Curriculum Project, University of Georgia: *Population Growth and World Food Resources,* University of Georgia, Athens, 1977.

Explores relationships between demographics and food availability. Investigates population growth as a technical resource problem and as a cultural problem. Applies ideas and concepts through the study of selected countries of the world.

Gibson, John S.: *The Intergroup Relations Curriculum: A Program for Elementary School Education,* Lincoln Filene Center for Citizenship and Public Affairs, Medford, Mass., 1969.

Gives background of the center's research and development program (see entry in this section under Lincoln Filene Center). Provides key understandings, activities, and methods for elementary level.

Glen Falls (New York) City Schools: *Project Survival: International Education for the Seventies in Glen Falls,* Glen Falls City Schools, Glen Falls, N.Y., 1970.

Includes a Working Paper *and* Teachers' Survival Kit. *Primary goal is to develop an increased understanding of the world as a global system and mankind as a single human community. (K–12) Antecedent program is described in Bulletin No. 35 of the National Council for the Social Studies,* Improving the Teaching of World Affairs: The Glen Falls Story, *and Curriculum Series No. 13,* Bringing the World into Your Classroom.

Goodson, W. R., et al.: *Adventure on a Blue Marble: Approaches to Teaching Intercultural Understanding,* Southern Association of Colleges and Schools, Atlanta, Georgia, 1969.

Discusses various instructional approaches to international understanding including case studies. Gives addresses of all foreign embassies in the United States, lists sources for international correspondence, and provides a bibliography.

Graves, N. (ed.): *Teaching Materials on Population, International Understandings and Environmental Education,* UNESCO, Paris, 1975.

Prepared by the Commission on Geography in Education of the International Geographical Union. Material is presented in three ways: straightforward didactic account of a topic; detailed suggestions of how to teach it in a stated context; and pupil resources. Extensive use of photographs, diagrams, pictures, maps, and graphs.

High School Geography Project, sponsored by the Association of American Geographers.

Developed a ninth- and tenth-grade level course, Geography in an Urban Age, *published by Macmillan, New York, consisting of six sequential units containing separate softcover books for teacher and students with supporting teaching materials. Also developed teacher-education kits to help in analyzing teaching strategy and applying the strategy to a new situation.*

Holt Databank System, Holt, New York, 1976.

> *An integrated K–6 program with texts, visuals, media, tests, and guides. Common problems offer opportunities for developing empathy.*

Institute for Education in Peace and Justice: *Educating for Peace and Justice,* 3d ed., St. Louis, Mo., 1975.

> *A teacher's manual for use in teaching global awareness, conflict resolution, and the development of alternatives. Loose-leaf format facilitates division into units. Includes methods and resources, geared to secondary level with a few units for earlier years.*

Institute for World Order: *World Food and Hunger Studies,* Institute for World Order, Transnational University Program, New York, 1976.

> *A curriculum guide on food, economic justice, and development including sample course outlines, annotated bibliography, multimedia guide, and a list of key organizations.*

Intercom. See Part IV, Pertinent Periodicals, for selected titles, briefly annotated.

The Inter-dependence Curriculum Aid, The World Affairs Council of Philadelphia, John Wanamaker Store, Third Room Gallery, 13th and Market Streets, Philadelphia, Pa. 19107, n.d.

> *A curriculum guide for secondary schools treating eight areas: food and nutrition, global economy, human rights, oceans, peace and disarmament, resources scarcity, science and technology, and world law and international institutions.*

Kenworthy, Leonard S.: *Social Studies for the Seventies in Elementary and Middle Schools,* Xerox Publications Division, Stamford, Conn., 1973.

> *A teacher's text which introduces the student to the world much earlier than most texts. Deals with world-mindedness in chapters devoted to "Studying the World—General," and "Studying Personal Problems and Problems of the Local Community, the United States, and the Rest of the World." Useful methods and materials are included for teaching each topic.*

Kenworthy, Leonard S. (ed.), et al.: *Helping Boys and Girls Discover the World: Teaching About Global Concerns and the United Nations in Elementary and Middle Schools,* the UNESCO Associated Schools Project of the U.S.A., United Nations Association of the U.S.A., 1978.

Booklet format offers questions and answers dealing with philosophy, practical suggestions, promising practices, and helpful resources for teachers and parents.

King, David C.: *International Education for Spaceship Earth,* Foreign Policy Association, New Dimensions, no. 4, Thomas Y. Crowell, New York, 1970.

Based on the Foreign Policy Association study cited in Part I, Imperatives and Issues, under Becker. Part I is a digest of the full report: educational needs for "spaceship earth" where all inhabitants have a common destiny and earth is a single interlocked world system; obstacles to change. Part II offers strategies for change, experimental curriculum projects, and innovative teaching methods. Useful readings and bibliographies throughout with a chapter on use of simulation games.

King, Edith W.: *The World: Context for Teaching in the Elementary School,* Wm. C. Brown, Dubuque, Iowa, 1971.

Calls for an emphasis on the international dimension of education beginning in the very early years. Describes and outlines many practical examples for furthering world-mindedness in the classroom, particularly through the arts, literature, and social studies curricula. Suggestions are for parents and teachers as well as children. Bibliography and appendixes provide excellent resources.

Kinghorn, Jon R., and William P. Shaw: *Handbook for Global Education: A Working Manual,* Charles F. Kettering Foundation, Dayton, Ohio, 1977.

Provides a step-by-step guide for directing a "We Agree" Workshop in Global Education including goal-setting, action to implement goals, and pertinent materials for follow-up activities. Written primarily for educators working in kindergarten through grade twelve. See also, School Improvement through Global Education in Part Va Projects and Programs.

Kurfman, Dana G. (ed.): *Developing Decision-making Skills,* 47th Yearbook, National Council for the Social Studies, Arlington, Va., 1977.

Deals with skills in thinking (conceptualizing, generalizing, applying, and evaluating); information gathering (questioning, observing, reading maps and graphs, and "purposeful" reading); and group processes. Models for teaching decision-making skills in elementary and secondary schools are also provided. Skills, strategies, and concepts developed pertain to the development of a global perspective.

Larson, Jo Ann: *Children of the World: A Series of Nine Television Programs for Elementary Students,* United Nations Children's Fund, New York, 1973.

A guide to nine 30-minute videotape programs which depict a child's life in different countries, thereby pointing out similarities and differences that exist for all humans. The guide presents instructional objectives; previewing, viewing, and postviewing techniques; and supplementary materials.

Lincoln Filene Center for Citizenship and Public Affairs, Tufts University: *Ideology and World Affairs: A Resource Unit for Teachers,* Lincoln Filene Center for Citizenship and Public Affairs, Medford, Mass., 1963.

Published for the Northeastern States Youth Citizenship Project (nine states). Based on key understandings developed by John S. Gibson, suggested materials and activities were developed cooperatively, organized, and tested by many teachers. Democratic, communist, and totalitarian ideologies are examined here and abroad in the Afro-Asian and Latin American worlds as well as the Western world. Though dated, this unit may be useful as a model for developing current materials. See also Gibson, previously cited in this section.

McBride, John: *Teaching International Development: A Monday Morning Manual,* Community Alternatives, Vancouver, B.C., Canada, 1974.

Offers lesson strategies and student development projects for the following themes: population, hunger, literacy, aid, and trade. Resources are also listed.

McNeill, William H.: *The Ecumene: Story of Humanity,* Harper & Row, New York, 1973.

A high school world history text which provides a global perspective for studying various world societies.

Magnelia, Paul F.: "The Inter-Nation Simulation and Secondary Education," *Journal of Creative Behavior,* vol. 3, Spring 1969, pp. 115–121.

The author found that this type of simulation exercise was effective at secondary school level. He found it to have the capacity to reach out and involve students of supposed low ability.

Man: A Course of Study, Education Development Center, Cambridge, Mass., 1970.

This conceptually based program was designed for upper elemen-

tary students to expand awareness of the interdependence of global society and the commonalities of mankind. Multimedia.

Management Institute for National Development: *Global Development Studies: A Model Curriculum for an Academic Course in Global Systems and Human Development at the Secondary and Undergraduate Levels of General Education,* MIND, New York, 1974.

An experimental model centering on the global nature of today's social, political, and business affairs in order to help students understand the realities of global systems, interdependencies, and imbalances. Suggests use of surveys, interviews, research, and group discussion to develop conscious attitudes toward one's own beliefs and the beliefs and conceptions of others. Organizations and relevant periodical literature are listed and pertinent bibliographies with source information are provided.

Massialas, Byron G., and Jack Zevin: *World Order,* World History through Inquiry, Rand McNally, Chicago, 1970.

Depicts the changing nature of war and possibilities for dealing with it, considering both historical and futuristic aspect.

————. *Two Societies in Perspective,* World History through Inquiry, Rand McNally, Chicago, 1970.

Uses visual evidence to encourage students to hypothesize about differing conceptions of warfare and to contrast two societies, Britain and China.

Metcalf, Lawrence, and Robert Low: *Individual Responsibility,* Crises in World Order, Random House, New York, 1974.

Explores in-depth questions on rights and responsibilities of individuals, raising moral issues.

Michigan Department of Education: *Guidelines for Global Education,* Lansing, Mich., 1978.

This state guide provides definitions, goals, strategies, and resources to develop programs for involving educators and students in the dynamics of global interdependence. Accompanied by Global Education bibliography which includes sources and annotated materials listings.

Mid-America Program for Global Perspectives in Education: *Guidelines for World Studies and Checklist for World Studies,* Indiana University, Social Studies Development Center, Bloomington, Ind., 1974.

Provides information on processes, procedures, and materials in the field. Clarifies some of the available options with suggestions and experiences to assist in developing global education programs, courses, or units.

―――. *Your State in the World,* Indiana University Social Studies Development Center, Bloomington, Ind., 1977.

A resource handbook developed for the Council of Chief State School Officers that identifies ways to point up relationships between individuals, groups, and agencies in a community and in the world. A number of states including Illinois, Kentucky, and Indiana have developed their own version of this handbook. Based on the Columbus in the World project.

Mitsakos, Charles L. (ed.): *The Family of Man* series, Selective Educational Equipment, Inc., Newton, Mass., 1971.

Community study kits with artifacts, based on the work of University of Minnesota Project Social Studies, are activity-centered, multimedia kits designed to improve student understanding of families and communities around the world and their interrelationship.

Mix, New World Issues Series, rev. ed., Harcourt Brace Jovanovich, New York, 1975.

Cross-cultural approach to humanity through varied and cosmopolitan readings: prose, poetry, songs, and other expression. Reading level grades 9–12.

Moyer, Joan E.: *Bases for World Understanding and Cooperation: Suggestions for Teaching the Young Child,* Association for Supervision and Curriculum Development, Washington, D.C., 1970.

Focus is on process skills with selected generalizations to serve as guidelines for teachers. Suggestions for varied opportunities for experiences (action proposals) contributing to the understanding of the generalizations are offered. Stresses the need for parents and teachers to work together and the importance of a world-minded teacher.

"The Needs of Man," available from Zen-Du Productions, P.O. Box 3927, Haywood, Calif. 94540.

A colorful wheel device correlating human needs such as food, social institutions, and interdependence with suggested project activities. Geared to intermediate and middle school levels.

Nesbitt, William A.: *Interpreting the Newspaper in the Classroom:*

Foreign News and World Views, 2d ed., Foreign Policy Association, New York, 1971.

Chapter headings; "Some Barriers to Reality"; "The Process and Processing of News"; "Evaluating the Press"; " . . . A Case Study"; "The School: Function, Techniques, Resources"; and "Readings."

————. *Teaching about War and Its Control: A Selective Annotated Bibliography for the Social Studies Teacher,* 1972. For annotation see entry in Part III, Sources for Additional Materials.

———— (ed.). *Data on the Human Crisis: A Handbook for Inquiry,* New York State Education Department, Center for International Programs, New York, 1972.

Data in the form of graphs and statistics on major world problems—past, present, and future. Teacher's Guide *includes suggestions for data inquiry experiences—just what teachers need.*

Nesbitt, William A., and Norman Abramowitz: *Teaching Youth about Conflict and War,* ed. Charles Bloomstein, Teaching Social Studies in an Age of Crisis, no. 5, National Council for the Social Studies, Washington, D.C., 1973.

Concept and value questions are raised leading to guidelines for structuring one's own views as well as others'. Provides a framework to stimulate class discussion and aid in organizing and analyzing data. Suggested study topics with sources for materials, a game for involving students, and annotated pertinent materials for students and teachers are given.

Nesbitt, William A., and Andrea Karls: "Teaching Interdependence: Exploring Global Challenges through Data," *Intercom,* no. 78, June 1975.

This issue is a cooperative project with the Center for International Programs and Comparative Studies of the New York State Education Department, growing out of a handbook for inquiry, Data on the Human Crisis. *Data used concern world military interdependence, food, energy, environmental pollution, control of the seas, etc. Uses Columbus, Ohio, as case study in "One City's Links with the World."*

Noon, Elizabeth: *Media-Supported World Affairs Seminars,* American Association of School Librarians, Chicago, 1971.

Demonstrates six uses for world affairs discussion through partial transcripts of six seminars that were carried on by high school groups using library media centers. Discussions were spontaneous and unrehearsed and each was on a "hot" subject at the time:

America's position on China, the Allende election in Chile, the Arab-Israeli conflict, and others.

Oswald, James M.: *Earth: A Planet in Crisis,* Institute for World Order, New York, 1974.

A Transnational Curriculum Project kit including an activities manual, materials set for classroom use and exercises to be used in unit on "fluid geography," and, a film "Population and the Quality of Life." See also Oswald, James M., June R. Chapin, and Roger La Raus: Planet Earth, *Houghton Mifflin, Boston, 1976.*

————. *Earthship: Fluid Geography of Three-Dimensional Spaceship Earth,* Manual for Teachers, Phase I, part A, Institute for World Order, New York, 1972.

A brief outline of objectives and classroom activities to develop "earthmanship," the improvement of understanding, communications, and relationship among peoples on "spaceship earth." Exploratory material based on geographic concepts.

————. *Intercultural Social Studies Project for Secondary Schools: Annual Report,* American Universities Field Staff, Hanover, N.H., 1973.

Reports the first year of a two-year developmental project (1972–1974) initiated jointly by the American Universities Field Staff and the Institute of International Studies, USOE. The project created a culture studies network involving 103 teachers and their students who field-tested multimedia embracing fifty "field staff perspectives." See also Oswald's: A Pedagogical Framework for Intercultural Studies, *American Universities Field Staff, Hanover., N.H., 1974.*

Our Working World, Science Research Associates, Chicago, 1973.

Grades 1–6 program with texts, student problem books, media, satellite kits, tests, and guides focusing on how individuals work in the world and showing need for interdependence and responsibility.

People and Technology, Education Development Center, Cambridge, Mass., 1972.

Global interdependence is stressed in unit on the Volta River Dam in Ghana. Benefits and disadvantages of technology can be explored on a global level. For upper elementary grades.

People: Cultures, Times, Places, Addison-Wesley, Menlo Park, Calif., 1976.

K–8 program includes tests, media kits, and guides. Emphasis on global education is evidenced by its focus on the needs and wants of people through time and in various locales.

Peoples and Cultures Series, McDougal, Littell. See entry under Clark for annotation.

Perryman, Donald: *Weighing Arguments,* Civic Education Services, Inc., Washington, D.C., 1969.

Useful booklet for teachers and students asks and responds to these questions: Can you identify value choices? How do we resolve value conflicts? How do we weigh factual claims? What difficulties with logic and language need to be overcome?

Pickus, Robert, and Robert Woito: *To End War,* World Without War Council, Berkeley, Calif., 1974.

A comprehensive guide and annotated compilation of current books on all topics affecting the problems of war and peace. Provides a rationale for study in this area.

Pittsburgh Board of Public Education: *International Relations: Course of Study, Scholars Program,* Department of Curriculum and Instruction, Pittsburgh, 1968.

Stresses need for greater social, economic, and scientific interdependence. Five course units presented:
  I. *The United States Pursuing Its National Interests in World Affairs*
  II. *The U.S.S.R. Striving for Security and Leadership in World Affairs*
  III. *Communist China Attempting to Return to Its Former Eminence and Power in Asia*
  IV. *The New (Western) Europe Evolving around the Common Market and NATO*
  V. *The U.S. Striving for Peace, Security, Freedom, and Welfare for All Peoples within a Framework of National Interests and a Polarized World*

Public Issues Series/Harvard Social Studies Project, Grades 9–12, American Education Publications, Columbus, Ohio, 1971.

A series of paperbacks adapted from the Harvard project conducted by Donald W. Oliver and Fred M. Newmann that employs controversial case studies to motivate students in vital public issues and help them analyze and discuss persisting human dilemmas. Oliver and Newmann authored the accompanying teaching guide, Cases and Controversy, *emphasizing conflict of values and emergent values. Forces student to look at his personal value system.*

Remy, Richard C., et al.: *International Learning and International Education in a Global Age,* National Council for the Social Studies Bulletin No. 47, Washington, D.C., 1975.

Practical suggestions for teachers interested in implementing global education in their classrooms.

Saltonstall, Caroline (ed.): *Point of View,* Curriculum Project on International Development, Cambridge, Mass., 1976.

An experimental kit of discussion material consisting of twenty-five short quotations illustrating many different values with regard to development. For small-group discussion.

Schroeder, Fred E. H.: *Joining the Human Race: How to Teach the Humanities,* Everett/Edwards, Deland, Fla., 1972.

Aimed at secondary school humanities courses. Wants to make students feel they have a share in achievements and problems of all men. Uses an interdisciplinary approach with a history emphasis.

Silver Burdett Social Science, Silver Burdett, Morristown, N.J., 1976.

Key global concepts are introduced in texts, masters, tests, film-strips, individualized learning packages, problem-solving booklets, and guides, grades 1–6. Offers abundant opportunities for cross-cultural comparisons.

Simile II, P.O. Box 1023, La Jolla, Calif.

Guns or Butter, Powderhorn, Conflict, and Star Power are simulation games which put students in present-day predicaments such as dealing with nuclear weapons, living with a limited world government, and unequal distribution of resources in order to develop empathic understandings. For further information and sources concerning games see various entries in Part III, Sources for Additional Materials.

Sister Cities International: *Establishing a Sister City School Affiliation Program,* Sister Cities International, Washington, D.C., n.d.

A brief pamphlet describing characteristics of a school-affiliation program and techniques for getting it started. Uses school-to-school linkages across national borders to further students' global awareness.

The Social Sciences: Concepts and Values, Harcourt, Brace, Jovanovich, New York, 1975.

*Core concepts from varied disciplines that develop a global per-
spective are presented for K–6. Texts, filmstrips, activity books,
prints, tests, and guides are included. This series continues
(grades 7–9) with* Man in Culture, *based on anthropological
concepts;* Man in His Environment, *ecology-oriented unit; and*
Man's Economic World, *showing increasing national economic
specialization in a world that is growing more interdependent.*

Sociological Resources for the Social Studies, sponsored by the
American Sociological Association, Allyn and Bacon, Boston,
1969–1974.

Three kinds of instructional materials: Episodes in Social Inquiry
*series, twenty-three short inquiry units representative of the field of
sociology;* Inquiries in Sociology, *a one-semester sociology course
for eleventh or twelfth grade;* Readings in Sociology *series, seven
paperbacks consisting of professional readings, rewritten for the
high school student. Also developed an accompanying* Instructor's
Guide *and optional transparencies.*

Southwest Educational Development Laboratory: *Multicultural
Social Education Program–First Year: People Are Both Alike and
Different, 8,* Southwest Educational Development Laboratory,
Austin, Tex., 1969.

*An experimental unit for grade 8 designed to provide the opportu-
nity "to develop rational understanding of cultural diversity."
Activities attempt to illustrate the common humanity of people.*

Spurgin, John H., and Gary R. Smith: *Global Dimensions in the
New Social Studies,* Social Science Education Consortium, no.
165, packet M, Boulder, Colo., 1973.

*An analysis of fourteen packages of available social studies mate-
rials that contain components appropriate for global education to
assist teachers and curriculum planners. Appendix contains annotated texts of simulation games with global dimensions and global
education centers, projects, and organizations.*

Srinivason, Lyra: *Cross Cultural Study Prints: A New Aid to Teaching World Cultures,* InterCulture Associates, Thompson, Conn.,
1977.

*A kit developed for teaching world history and world cultures
courses from grade 5 through secondary school. Packet consists of
thirty-one photos taken around the world plus a response work-*

sheet for elementary students. See entry under InterCulture Associates in Part III, Sources for Additional Materials.

Stadsklev, Ronald: *Handbook of Simulation Gaming in Social Education,* 2 vols., University of Alabama, Institute of Higher Education Research and Services, 1974.

Part 1, Textbook, addresses itself to such concerns as, "What Is a Simulation?" "How Should One Be Used?" "Why Use It?" Part 2, Directory, answers the question, "Where Are the Materials?"

Stavrianos, Leften: *A Global History of Man,* Allyn and Bacon, Boston, 1970. (Paperback)

This text provides students with information about human similarities in order to provide a way of looking at various world societies.

Summerfield, Geoffrey (ed.): *Man: For High Schools,* McDougal, Littell, Evanston, Ill., 1971.

A series of literature texts designed to develop an awareness of what it is like to be alive in the twentieth century, a sense of life's possibilities, and the idea of the universality of man. Outstanding contemporary authors are included. Grades 9–12.

The Taba Program in Social Science, Addison-Wesley, Menlo Park, Calif., 1972–1974.

Developmental treatment of concepts through four levels of learning. Concepts are causality, conflict, cooperation, cultural change, difference, interdependence, modification, power, societal control, tradition, and values. Concerned with helping students identify with people in different cultures, disagree constructively with others, and develop open-mindedness and tolerance of other people's ideas. Grades K–7.

Tankard, Alice D.: *The Human Family, Human Rights, and Peace: A Source Book for the Study and Discussion of the Universal Declaration of Human Rights,* Center for Teaching About Peace and War, Wayne State University, Detroit, 1973.

A clear and graphic presentation understandable by children and adults.

Teaching about Interdependence in a Peaceful World, United States Committee for UNICEF, New York, 1976.

An elementary teacher's kit which relates global concepts to child's own experience with units on world food supply, worldwide health, and the delivery of mail, using simulation and role-playing activities. A companion teacher's kit, Teaching about the Child and World Environment, *offers three more units on the interrelatedness of natural forces and human activities. Both cite books for children as well as resources for teachers. Also available are* Teaching about Spaceship Earth, *a role-playing experience with plans for eight hours of lessons;* Teaching about the Rights of the Child, *posters, wall sheet, bibliographies, and official "Declarations";* UNICEF World Puzzle, *a 20-inch-diameter circle design showing children at play on a world jungle gym.*

Utah State Board of Education: *Focus on Man: A Prospectus, Social Studies for Utah Schools,* Utah State Board of Education, Salt Lake City, 1972.

Takes the traditional expanding communities approach, but the guiding questions asked about selected focal points at various levels may offer suggestions for pertinent activities, especially in areas of recognition of the dignity and worth of the individual; the use of intelligence to improve human living; and the effective development of moral and ethical values.

Victor, David, and Richard Kraft: *Global Perspectives Handbook,* Mid-America Program for Global Perspectives, Bloomington, Ind., 1976. (Experimental Edition.)

Provides classroom activities and resources to increase global awareness in students. Pertinent materials, films, and books are listed. Suggests ideas for teacher-developed activities.

Windows on Our World, ed. Lee F. Anderson, Houghton Mifflin, Boston, 1976.

A kindergarten through sixth-grade level social studies textbook program with four overarching goals: to develop children's understanding of themselves as individuals, as members of groups, as human beings, and as inhabitants of earth. Book 5, "The United States," by David C. King and Charlotte C. Anderson, contains a chapter, "The United States in the Global Community," which uses material compiled by the Columbus in the World *project cited earlier. Book 4, "Planet Earth," and Book 6, "The Way People Live," also present the global perspective clearly and forcefully, stressing world interdependence and peaceful cooperation.*

Wolsk, David: *An Experienced-centered Curriculum: Exercises in Perception, Communication, and Action,* Educational Studies and Document Set No. 17, Unipub, New York, 1975.

Describes a UNESCO-sponsored experimental project designed to develop and apply a new approach to education for international understanding. Based on need for deepened understanding for human motivation and behavior, it is intended for eleven-to-eighteen-year-olds. Various techniques for involvement are used: critical incidents, simulations, role playing, interview surveys, community action projects, and others.

Wood, Jayne Millar: *Focusing on Global Poverty and Development: A Resource Book for Educators,* Overseas Development Council, Washington, D.C., 1974.

A useful, loose-leaf, comprehensive collection of materials to help teachers integrate studies of global development and interdependence into existing courses. Content engages secondary students in learning about world poverty and interdependence; attitudes, values, processes, and change; and development from the economic and environmental standpoint. Attains a cross-cultural perspective by treating both domestic and international views of each topic. Background essays and readings provide means for implementing the teaching suggestions made. Extensive additional materials are listed.

The World of Mankind, Follett, Chicago, 1973.

Texts, reinforcement activities, tests, and guides are provided in this program for grades 1–8. Global concepts may be extended by the in-depth cultural studies at several levels stressing commonalities.

The World Without War Game, World Without War Publications, 7245 South Merrill Avenue, Chicago, Ill. 60649.

Students experience group conflict dynamics that present them with realistic alternatives to war.

Part III: Sources for Additional Materials

The African-American Institute, School Services Division, 833 United Nations Plaza, New York, N.Y. 10017.

Inexpensive teacher materials: elementary and secondary kits, packets for librarians, resource guides, and mini-modules.

American Friends Service Committee, 15 Rutherford Place, New York, N.Y. 10003.

Asia Society, 112 East 64th Street, New York, N.Y. 10021.

Maintains liaison with many of the university outreach programs on Asian Studies, publishes and distributes a bimonthly bulletin and other informational materials.

Association for Childhood Education International, 3615 Wisconsin Avenue, N.W., Washington, D.C. 20016.

See Childhood Education *in Part IV, Pertinent Periodicals, and entry under the Association in Part I, Imperatives and Issues, for specific annotations.*

Basa, Patricia, and Tony Codianni: *Global Perspectives: A Bibliography,* Mid-America Program for Global Perspectives in Education, Social Studies Development Center, Bloomington, Ind., 1976.

Lists and annotates resources and suitable classroom materials with a "planetary" perspective. Selections emphasize interrelatedness of world problems and issues. Section I, Resources for Teachers, includes books and pamphlets, bibliographies of resources, articles, and sources for additional material. Section II, Resources for Classroom Use, includes readings, multimedia, simulations, and additional sources. Section III, resources produced by selected projects and organizations for teachers and for classroom use.

Becker, James M.: "International Studies," chap. 16 in *Guide to Reading for Social Studies Teachers,* National Council for the Social Studies, Washington, D.C., 1972.

Cites selected literature on global perspectives, international relations, international development, foreign policy, international organizations, and world law and world order.

Big Blue Marble Alphaventure, Suite 319, 717 Fifth Avenue, New York, N.Y. 10022.

Distributes materials based on TV show, "Big Blue Marble."

Buggey, Jo Anne, and June Tyler: "Global Education in Elementary Schools," *Social Education,* vol. 41, no. 1, January 1977.

The authors, experienced teachers, have selected and annotated resources for use by students and teachers including social studies series; supplementary materials including multimedia kits, simulation games, and activity materials; and teacher sources.

Center for War/Peace Studies*: *A Guide to Selected Curriculum Materials on Change, Conflict, Identity, Interdependence, Power and Authority, Values, and Valuing,* Curriculum Materials Program, Center for War/Peace Studies, New York, 1973.

The guide is distributed in six conceptual units, but each contains a listing of all the materials tested with complete indexes. Represents three years of work by the Diablo Valley Education Project and the Mt. Diablo Valley Unified School District, Concord, Calif. Junior and senior high school materials. See also the Center's Media on Conflict, Change, and Interdependence, *1974.*

Charles, Cheryl L., and Ronald Stadsklev (eds.): *Learning with Games: An Analysis of Social Studies Educational Games and Simulations,* The Social Science Education Consortium and ERIC Clearinghouse for Social Studies/Social Science Education, Boulder, Colo., 1973.

Offers sources and resources for games and simulations and analyzes seventy games.

Cottingham, Jane, and Marilee Karl: "Development Education," *Educational Documentation and Information: Bulletin of the International Bureau of Education,* fiftieth year, no. 201, fourth quarter, 1976.

An international list of resources connected with development education including printed materials, films, slides, tapes, and teaching kits, listed alphabetically by institutions for the most part. Section II lists actual teaching materials. Fully annotated.

Davison, Susan E. (ed.): *Gaming: An Annotated Catalogue of Law-Related Games and Simulations,* Special Committee on Youth Education for Citizenship, Working Notes, no. 9, American Bar Association, Chicago, Ill., 1975.

---

*Now Center for Global Perspectives.

*Describes more than 125 simulation games indicating grade level,
distributor, date, price, number of players, time, and annotation.
Part I, Basic Concepts of Law, and Part V, The Political Process,
contain items pertaining to the international arena.*

Dougall, Lucy: *War/Peace Film Guide*, 2d ed., World Without War
Council, Berkeley, Calif., 1973.

*Describes and evaluates many of the outstanding films on war,
international development, the arms race, and other related areas.*

ERIC/CHESS, Clearinghouse for Social Studies Education, 855
Broadway, Boulder, Colo. 80302.

*ERIC is a nationwide information system with clearinghouse in
major fields of study. ERIC/CHESS has produced items on world
studies:* Off the African Shelf: An Annotated Bibliography;
Teaching International Relations; Global Dimensions in the New
Social Studies; A Preliminary Review of the Intercultural Dimension in International/Intercultural Education, Grades K–14.
Keeping Up, *a free newsletter, contains new publications, articles,
and a selection of abstracted documents. Also:* Directory of Contacts for International, Educational, Cultural, and Scientific
Exchange Programs *pertaining to Part Vb, Agencies Sponsoring
International and Intercultural Exchanges.*

Fowler, Kathryn M.: *Hunger: The World Food Crisis*, National
Science Teachers Association, Washington, D.C., 1977.

*Consists of a series of annotated bibliographies, one for teachers
and one for students, along with separate guides to organizations,
films, and other materials, K–12.*

Global Education Associates, 552 Park Avenue, East Orange, N.J.
07017.

Hadjisky, Margellen G. (comp.): *Peace Education in the Primary
Grades: The Young World Citizen, A Bibliography and Sample
Activities, K–3*, Wayne State University, 1973. Available from
EDRA, Computer Microfilm International Corp., P.O. Box 190,
Arlington, Va. 22210.

Hollister, Bernard C., and Deane C. Thompson: *Grokking the
Future: Science Fiction in the Classroom*, Pflaum/Standard, Dayton, Ohio, 1973. (Paperback.)

*Suggestions for readings, exercises, and questions on such topics
as ecology, population, social order, prejudice, economic trends,
and future cities.*

Horn, Robert E.: *The Guide to Simulations/Games for Education and Training,* rev. ed., Information Resources, Lexington, Mass., 1977.

Comprehensive and current listing of about 1,400 items useful for schools, businesses and community groups. Includes complete demonstration session to introduce simulation gaming.

Howard, Norma K.: *Cultural and Cross Cultural Studies: An Abstract Bibliography,* University of Illinois, ERIC Clearinghouse on Early Childhood Education, Urbana, Ill., 1974.

References selected from Research in Education *(RIE) and* Current Index to Journals in Education *(CIJE) deal with cultural differences, preschool education and day care, and elementary education.*

InterCulture Associates, Box 277, Thompson, Conn. 06277.

Multicultural, ethnic, and international education materials developed or imported for classroom use include books, multimedia kits, audiovisual materials, instruments, artifacts, and curriculum materials. Issues InterCulture News *free of charge.*

International Education Resources: A Summary of OE-Funded Research Projects and Reports Available through the Educational Research Information Center, 1956–71, Institute of International Studies, U.S. Office of Education, 1972.

A helpful source of information for works issued before most of the publications cited in this bibliography.

Keating, Charlotte M.: *Building Bridges of Understanding between Cultures,* Palo Verde Pub. Co., Tucson, Ariz., 1971.

A bibliography of children's literature fully annotated and grouped under topic by three levels of schooling. Selected to develop an understanding and appreciation of the world's cultural diversity.

Mangrulkar, Latika: *World Order Values: A Bibliography for Young Children,* Center for Teaching About Peace and War, Wayne State University, Detroit. n.d.

Mid-America Program for Global Perspectives in Education: *Selected Sources of Information, Materials, and Teaching Ideas,* Social Studies Development Center, 513 North Park Avenue, Indiana University, Bloomington, Ind. 47401.

National Council for the Social Studies, 1515 Wilson Boulevard, Arlington, Va. 22209. Previous address was Washington, D.C.

Nesbitt, William A.: *Teaching about War and Its Control: A Selective Annotated Bibliography for the Social Studies Teacher*, New York State Education Department, Center for International Programs, New York, 1972.

An aid to the teacher in considering both what to teach about war and peace and how best to teach it. Topics include nationalism, U.S. foreign policy, modern war, and ethics and morality. Calls attention to the value of using films, simulations, and case studies as well as using data and scenarios. Although the publication date is not current, the ideas and suggestions for action are timeless.

Newmann, Arthur: *Select Bibliography: International Education*, University of Florida, Gainesville, 1971. (Mimeographed.)

Background readings developed for the author's course in International Education at the University of Florida. Headings used: Universal Man, World Community, Perception, and Communication.

Office of International Postal Affairs, U.S. Postal Headquarters, Washington, D.C. 20260.

Pellowski, Anne: "Internationalism in Children's Literature," in May Hill Arbuthnot and Zena Sutherland, *Children and Books*, 4th ed., Scott, Foresman, Glenview, Ill., 1972, part seven.

Planetary Citizens, 777 United Nations Plaza, New York, N.Y. 10003.

Promotes the idea of the oneness of humanity. Distributes sticker: "Planetary Citizens: One Earth, One Humanity, One Destiny," matching buttons, passports, and T-shirts.

Social Studies School Services, 10000 Culver Boulevard, Culver City, Calif. 90230.

A convenient commercial clearinghouse for purchasing classroom materials in the area of international education, global perspectives, and world affairs. Specializes in the distribution of innovative items other than standard texts.

Stone, Frank A.: *Multicultural and Worldminded Teaching*, University of Connecticut, School of Education, World Education Project, Storrs, Conn., n.d.

A useful annotated bibliography focusing on elements in a world-minded program and teaching for global perspectives.

Tysse, Agnes N. (comp.): *International Education: The American Experience—A Bibliography, vol. 1, Dissertations and Theses,* Scarecrow Press, Metuchen, N.J., 1974.

Includes foreign student study in the United States, activity of Americans overseas, American schools abroad, and Peace Corps information.

United Nations, Office of Public Information, External Relations Division, Room 1045B, United Nations Plaza, New York, N.Y. 10017

United Nations Association of USA, 833 UN Plaza, New York, N.Y. 10017.

United Nations Children's Fund (UNICEF). See United States Committee for UNICEF.

United Nations Development Program, Division of Information, Room 5404, United Nations, New York, N. Y. 10017.

United States Committee for UNICEF, 331 East 38th Street, New York, N.Y. 10016.

The U.S. national committee for UNICEF. Provides school services in the form of publications and materials: teachers' kits, books, filmstrips, slides, displays, and promotional aids. See Part II, Instructional Materials, entry under Teaching about Interdependence, *for annotations on teachers' guides.*

United States Office of Education, 330 Independence Avenue, S.W., Washington, D.C. 20201.

Issues publications through Superintendent of Documents, U.S. Government Printing Office. Institutional Development and International Education, headed by Robert Leestma, offers program services.

World Council for Curriculum and Instruction, Box 171, Teachers College, Columbia University, New York, N.Y. 10027.

Teacher information.

World Health Organization, Room 2235, United Nations, New York, N.Y. 10017.

Part IV: Pertinent Periodicals

AFFHF Bulletin, American Freedom from Hunger Foundation, Inc., Washington, D.C. Monthly. $5/yr.

See annotation for American Freedom from Hunger Foundation in Part Va, Projects and Programs.

Alternatives: A Journal for World Policy, South Point Plaza, Lansing, Mich. 48910. Quarterly. $15/yr.

An offshoot of the Institute for World Order's "World Order Models Project" (see Part Va, Projects and Programs). Provides a forum for global issues and for developing and encouraging models of alternative futures.

Asia Bulletin, Asia Society, Inc., 112 East 64th Street, New York, N.Y. 10021. Bimonthly. $15/yr.

"Dedicated to deepening American understanding of Asia and stimulating thoughtful trans-Pacific intellectual exchange."

Atlas: World Press Review, Atlas World Press Review, 230 Park Avenue, New York, N. Y. 10017. Monthly. $14/yr.

Key articles of interest to U.S. readers from the foreign press about world issues or about U.S. decisions as seen by non-Americans. Important for providing points-of-view differing from our own.

Bulletin of the Atomic Scientist: Science and Public Affairs, Educational Foundation for Nuclear Science, Kent Chemical Laboratories, 1020 E. 58th Street, Chicago, Ill. 60637. Monthly. $18/yr.

Each issue contributes articles on the quality of life in the world today.

Center Focus: News from the Center of Concern, 3700 13th Street, N.E., Washington, D.C. 20017.

See Center of Concern *in Part Va, Projects and Programs, for purposes.*

Childhood Education, Journal of the Association for Childhood Education International, Washington, D.C. Issued 6 times per year. $18/yr.

Frequent issues on pertinent topics, especially the issues of March 1965, "The World and the Classroom," October 1965, "Building on Cultural Differences"; January 1969, "Beyond Ourselves toward Deeper Understanding"; May 1971, "The World House: Building a Qualitative Environment for All the World's Children"; and February 1973, "Children and War," by Norma Law.

Communique, Society for Intercultural Education, Training and Research, Georgetown University, Washington, D.C. 20057. $5/yr.

Newsletter reports programs, research, and new ideas in the field of cross-cultural human relations and cross-cultural training. Cites events, materials, and organizations concerned with these topics.

The Cooperator, joint publication of the International Cooperation Council and the Cooperators, Northridge, Calif.

See Part Va, Projects and Programs, for purpose of the International Cooperation Council. The Cooperators are now beginning a major effort to form a universal religion.

Crisis Paper, Atlantic Information Centre for Teachers of London. Issued 6 times or more a year. $8. Subscription address: Atlantic Information Centre for Teachers, Atlantic Council of U.S., 1616 H St., N.W., Washington, D.C. 20006.

Significant contemporary crises which generate an international reaction are examined by providing a selection of news commentary from the world press. Sent by air mail from London. The Centre acts as a clearinghouse on methodologies and curricula in world affairs teaching. It also publishes The World and the School *three times annually for $14. Each issue provides an in-depth treatment addressed to secondary school teachers.*

Development Education Exchange Papers (DEEP), FFH/Action for Development, FAO, Rome, Italy.

Published bimonthly to facilitate the exchange of ideas and material among those involved in planning and running educational programs. Available from Unipub, Box 433, Murray Hill Station, New York, N.Y. 10016.

Development Forum, United Nations, New York, N.Y. 10017. Free.

Published monthly by the Centre for Economic and Social Information (CESI) "to promote knowledge of and interest in the international development process by a many-sided presentation of news and reportage, facts and debate." January/February 1977, vol. 5., no. 1, contains an index for years 1975 and 1976.

Educational and Psychological Interactions, Bulletin from Department of Educational and Psychological Research, School of Education, Malmö, Sweden.

See the following issues: no. 39, March 1973: "Social Development and Student Democracy: Notes on Two Research Projects," ed. A. Bjerstedt; and no. 48, May 1974, "World Citizen Responsibility: Assessment Techniques, Development Studies, Material Construction, and Experimental Teaching," by E. Almgren and E. Gustafson. Also entry in Part VI, Research Studies, under Yebio.

Educational Leadership, Journal of the Association for Supervision and Curriculum Development, Washington, D.C. $25/yr. membership.

See issues of March 1968, "Cross-National or International Education"; November 1969, "International Cooperation in Education"; and December 1975, "Multicultural Curriculum: Issues, Designs, Strategies."

ERIC/CHESS, Clearinghouse for Social Studies/Social Science Education, 855 Broadway, Boulder, Colo. 80302.

A segment of the nationwide information system, Educational Resources Information Center (ERIC), designed to keep educators current in their field. This publication occasionally includes a current awareness bulletin, Looking at . . . , on a particular topic.

Focus on Asian Studies, Association for Asian Studies, Service Center for Teachers of Asian Studies, Ohio State University, Columbus. Quarterly. $2/yr.

A newsletter to promote increased attention to Asian studies in elementary and secondary education. Reports activities of organizations, teaching ideas, related materials and books. Annotated.

Foreign Policy Magazine, 155 Allen Blvd., Farmingdale, N.Y. 11735. Quarterly. $12/yr.

A publication of the Carnegie Endowment for International Peace.

The Futurist: A Journal of Forecasts, Trends and Ideas about the Future, World Future Society, Washington, D.C. Bimonthly. $15/yr.

Reports in-depth coverage of what is happening throughout the world—developments in psychology, technology, communications, arts, science, education, etc. "World Trends and Forecasts" is a special section. In the June 1974 issue, "The World of 1994," Margaret Mead, Glenn Seaborg, John Platt, Theodore Gordon, Willis Harman, and Roy Amara discuss the areas of art, medicine, economics, space travel, city life, and education in the future.

Headline Series, Foreign Policy Association, 345 East 46th Street, New York, N.Y. 10017. Published five times a year, $1.40/copy.

Booklets give brief but thorough treatment of topics dealing with U.S. foreign policy, world problems, study of foreign countries. Titles include: Dollars, Jobs, Trade, and Aid; The Interdependence of Nations; Rethinking Economic Development; The UN and World Order; Future Worlds; The U.S., Interdependence and World Order; Our Daily Bread; Interdependence and the World Economy.

Ideas and Action Bulletin, FFH/AD, FAO, 00100 Rome, Italy. Published bimonthly. Free. Available from Unipub, Box 433, Murray Hill Station, New York, N.Y. 10016.

FFH (Freedom from Hunger), AD (Action for Development), and FAO (Food and Agriculture Organization) are all UN–affiliated. Articles include those written by Third World personnel directly involved in development efforts, giving the reader a feeling for "the way things are." Cites useful educational materials and news of related organizations worldwide.

Intercom, Center for Global Perspectives (formerly the Center for War/Peace Studies), 218 East 18th Street, New York, N.Y. 10003. Quarterly. $6/yr., single copies $1.75.

A guide to the world affairs field addressing a single topic in each issue to provide completely self-contained teaching units. Emphasis is on practical teaching suggestions and materials useful in secondary schools unless otherwise indicated. Many classroom activities are open-ended and present a variety of viewpoints. See following entries for selected titles, briefly annotated (in numerical order).

———. "Education on War, Peace, Conflict and Change," no. 65, 1970.

———. "Teaching about Population," no. 72, May 1973. *Analytical look at problems indicates complexities involved and provides basis for various options for global action.*

———. "Multinational Corporations: The Quiet Revolution?" no. 74, Spring 1974. *Stresses impact on global economic interdependence.*

———. "Teaching Global Issues through Simulation," no. 75, Summer 1974. *Includes complete instructions for "The Road Game" and describes the "Planet Management Game" published by Houghton Mifflin and "Baldicer," John Knox Press, among other games relating to international affairs.*

———. "Explorations in the Emergent Present," by Robert Hanvey, no. 77, Winter 1974–1975. *Discusses the limits of global growth, including food and energy, and the disagreements concerning their future effects. Contains five classroom studies.*

———. "Teaching Interdependence: Exploring Global Challenges through Data," no. 78, June 1975. *See entry under Nesbitt and Karls in Part II, Instructional Materials.*

———. "Teaching Toward Global Perspectives, II," no. 79, October 1975. *Offers a variety of techniques for classroom activities.*

———. "America in the World," by David C. King, no. 80, February 1976. *Includes readings, data, fictional accounts, and role plays.*

———. "Women and Men: Changing Roles in a Changing World," by Andrea B. Karls, no. 81, April 1976. *Cites African, Muslim, Latin American, Chinese, Indonesian, and U.S. women.*

———. "Environmental Issues and the Quality of Life," by David C. King and Cathryn J. Long, no. 82, July 1976. *Stresses the highly interdependent aspects of life today, the real conflicts in each environmental issue, and the social dimension involved.*

———. "Shaping the Environment," by David King and Cathryn Long, no. 83, September 1976. *How humans can shape their environment with examples of students in an inner-city-school program.*

———. "Education for a World in Change: A Working Handbook for Global Perspectives," no. 84/85, November 1976. *Teaching suggestions include lesson plans for K–12 and well-written teacher background information. Many classroom activities use fiction and science fiction as a base. First section, dealing with the concept of global education, offers perspectives on the twenty-first century, avenues for change, goals and objectives, and important aspects for development of the global perspective.*

———. "Global Perspectives: The Human Dimension, Part 1—Self-Knowing and Human Knowing," no. 86, April 1977. *Sample lessons demonstrate ways students can achieve the knowing and caring about themselves and about humanity through language arts, music, art, social studies, and science experiences.*

———. "Global Perspectives: The Human Dimension, Part 2—Planet-Knowing and Planet-Caring," no. 87, August 1977. *A humanistic, cross-disciplinary approach emphasizes relationships between the self and other humans and an understanding of the world.*

The Inter Dependent, United Nations Association UNA–USA, 345 E. 46th Street, New York, N.Y. 10017. Monthly. Student rate $4, others $5/yr.

Lists sources of classroom materials for teaching about global affairs and offers insight into major and minor world order concerns. Newspaper-style journal.

International Education, University of Tennessee, College of Education, Knoxville. Biannual. $4/yr.

Vol. 4, no. 2, 1974/1975, contains an article by Frank A. Stone, "World-minded Learning," pp. 7–19, which considers various definitions, teaching elements in a world-minded program, and global teaching techniques.

International Educational and Cultural Exchange, publication of the U.S. Advisory Commission on International and Cultural Affairs, U.S. Government Printing Office, Washington, D.C. $2/yr.

Deals with all aspects of student exchange for secondary and higher education levels.

International Interaction, bulletin of the International Education Project, American Council on Education, One Dupont Circle, Washington, D.C. 20036. Published monthly. Free.

Primarily higher education coverage; contains professional articles and information.

International Peace Research Newsletter, vol. 11, no. 1 and 2, Spring 1973, special issue on peace education, Christoph Wulf, guest editor.

Contains three parts: Reports on two conferences, information about various peace education projects throughout the world, and news of related events.

International Peace Studies Newsletter, Center for Peace Studies, The University of Akron, Akron, Ohio 44325.

Describes current peace studies programs, curriculum workshops, newsletters and journals, and varied peace-oriented activities.

International Understanding at School, Unipub, Box 433, Murray Hill Station, New York, N.Y. 10016.

Published twice a year for the UNESCO Associated Schools Project. No. 25, June 1973, the 20th Anniversary issue, gives an overview of the program's evolution, an appraisal, and describes specific schools' projects from fourteen countries of the sixty-two taking part (900 Associated Schools).

The Link (formerly the SSEC Newsletter), Social Science Education Consortium, Boulder, Colo. $5/yr.

Macroscope, Transnational University Program, Institute for World Order, 1140 Avenue of the Americas, New York, N.Y. 10036. Free.

An occasional newsletter noting briefly resource materials, activities, programs, and meetings.

Memos, Global Development Studies Institute, P.O. Box 522, 14 Main Street, Madison, N.J. 07940. Published six times a year. $2/yr.

A newsletter for teachers of global studies provides up-to-date information and annotated listings of pertinent materials for classroom use and teacher background information.

New Dimensions, Foreign Policy Association/Thomas Y. Crowell, New York.

A series of booklets suggests how social studies teachers can enrich their teaching, especially about world affairs. Topics already covered: Simulation Games, Foreign News and World Views, Teaching the Comparative Approach to American Studies, International Education for Spaceship Earth, Teaching about War and War Prevention.

News and Notes on the Social Sciences, publication of the Office of the Coordinator for School Social Studies, 306 Memorial West, Indiana University, Bloomington, Ind. 47401. Published twice a year. Free.

Includes useful notes on books, curriculum projects, and free and inexpensive materials including those on global education. Brief teacher-written articles, news and notes of conferences, and forthcoming events are included.

Newsletter, Society for Citizen Education in World Affairs, 1511 New Hampshire Avenue, N.W., 9th floor, Washington, D.C. 20036. Published six times a year. $10/yr.

Deals with information concerning organizations and activities in the field of world affairs, including materials being produced.

Phi Delta Kappan, Phi Delta Kappa, Bloomington, Ind. Published monthly, September through June. $10/yr.

Contains frequent articles with global perspective. Vol. 51, no. 5, January 1970, and vol. 49, no. 4, December 1967, are issues devoted to International Education.

Saturday Review, Saturday Review Magazine Corporation, P.O. Box 10010, Des Moines, Iowa 50340. Biweekly. $14/yr.

Norman Cousins, a world-minded citizen, often editorializes on the world situation in addition to the magazine's frequent articles discussing world affairs.

Simulation/Gaming/News, Box 3039, University Station, Moscow, Idaho 83843. Published five times a year. $4/yr.

Lists books, games, conferences, etc., on simulations and games for the classroom. Includes articles on use of simulations and reviews new materials and action in the field.

Social Education, National Council for the Social Studies, Washington, D.C. Seven issues annually (October through May). $15/yr.

Reports on new curriculum projects, social studies research, techniques, approaches, etc., of social studies education in elementary and secondary schools. See following entries for selected titles (arranged chronologically), briefly annotated.

————. "International Education for the Twenty-first Century," vol. 32, no. 7, November 1968.

An expanded issue devoted to the international dimension of the social studies curriculum with a view to what schools should offer students. Much of the writing is based on the Foreign Policy Association study, An Examination of Objectives, Needs and Priorities . . . , ed. James M. Becker, cited in Part I.

————. "International Relations: Ideas and Issues," vol. 34, no. 1, January 1970.

Discusses the question: "Are National Self-Interests and World Peace Compatible?" Communication analysis, the world population crisis, influence of the military-industrial complex, disarmament and realism, and a space-age curriculum are also discussed.

————. "Special Issue: Global Hunger and Poverty," Jayne Millar Wood, guest editor, vol. 38, no. 7, November/December 1974.

Provides background information and techniques and resources for teaching. Robert McNamara, Lester Brown, and George McGovern write on the situation at home and abroad. Noted educators in the field also contribute articles: James Becker, David King, Donald Morris, James Oswald, the editor, and others. Andrea Karls lists sources and resources.

————. "Global Education: Adding a New Dimension to Social Studies," vol. 4, no. 1, January 1977.

Articles include Gerald W. Marker's "Global Education: An Urgent Claim on the Social Studies Curriculum," containing useful current information on the world situation; Sallie Whelan's "Peoria and the World . . . ," detailing classroom experiences; and the section "Global Education in Elementary Schools," keynoted by Charlotte Anderson and Lee Anderson's article presenting a definition of and rationale for global education, followed by Donald Morris on "Implications for Curriculum and Instruction" and a selected bibliography of classroom materials.

Society for Citizen Education in World Affairs Newsletter, 1511 New Hampshire Avenue, N.W., Washington, D.C. 20036. Bimonthly. $10/yr.

Provides firsthand resource materials and a wide range of organizational news. Emphasis is on continuing education.

Spectrum, Student Advisory Committee on International Affairs, 1717 Massachusetts Avenue, N.W., Suite 503, Washington, D.C. 20036.

Bimonthly newsletter on foreign policy issues of domestic interest.

Sustenance: The Newsletter of the Action Center, The Action Center, 1028 Connecticut Avenue, N.W., Washington, D.C. 20036.

A Project of The Institute for World Order, the Action Center mobilizes young people for food, justice, and development.

Teachers College Record, Teachers College, Columbia University, New York.

Special issue, "Hand in Hand for World Understanding," vol. 70, no. 6, March 1969.

Topics in Culture Learning, Culture Learning Institute, 1777 East-West Road, Honolulu, Hawaii 96822. Free.

A journal-like publication with articles focusing heavily on Asian cultures with particular attention given to learning processes and educational contexts. Volume 4 devotes a major section to "Cross-Cultural Research—A Variety of Perspectives."

Transition, Institute for World Order, Inc., 1140 Avenue of the Americas, New York, N.Y. 10036. Bimonthly.

Promotes values of peace, social justice, economic well-being, and ecological balance through education. Vol. 3, no. 5, November 1976, features an interview with Rajni Kothari, who has worked on the Institute's World Order Models Project.

UNICEF News, UNICEF Information Division, United Nations, New York, N.Y. 10017. Published four times a year. $6/yr.

Centers on children around the world, each issue addressing a world-wide problem. For example, the 1976, no. 3, issue deals with "Coping with Change" by discussing the effects of changing society on family structures in six developing societies. An aid in helping students understand the universal basic human needs which transcend national boundaries. Extensive photographs.

United Nations Publications, available from Unipub, Box 433, Murray Hill Station, New York, N.Y. 10016.

Including periodicals such as UNESCO Courier, World Health, ILO Panorama, *etc.*

War on Hunger, U.S. Agency for International Development (AID). Monthly magazine.

Free from Publications Division, Office of Public Affairs, AID, Room 4953, State Department Building, Washington, D.C. 20523.

Ways and Means of Teaching about World Order, Institute for World Order, 1140 Avenue of the Americas, New York, N.Y. 10036.

A quarterly newsletter containing practical classroom strategies. Newsletter no. 17, March 1975, "Earthship," offers sample activities from a manual of thirty activities on the development of basic perceptual and conceptual skills. "Teaching about Global Hunger" is title of no. 18, June 1975.

The Whole Earth Papers, Global Education Associates, 552 Park Avenue, East Orange, N.J. 07017. $10/yr.

A monograph series which explores specific human issues in the context of global interdependencies.

World Agricultural Situation, published by U.S. Department of

Agriculture, three times a year. Free. Write to Publications Service, Economic Research Service, Room 0054, South Building, U.S. Dept. of Agriculture, Washington, D.C. 20003.

Contains data and analyses about current problems and yields, suggests future trends, and issues special reports of seven world regions.

The World and the School. See *Crisis Paper* in this section for further information.

World Education Reports, World Education, 1414 Sixth Avenue, New York, N.Y. 10019. Published three or four times a year. $5/yr.

Topical reading in the field of nonformal education in developing countries.

World Issues, Center for the Study of Democratic Institutions, Santa Barbara, Calif. Published five times annually. Dues $15/yr.

Membership publication along with the bimonthly The Center Magazine.

Worldwatch Papers, Unipub, Box 433, Murray Hill Station, New York, N.Y. 10016.

A continuing series describing the research of the Worldwatch Institute, directed by Lester R. Brown (see Part Va, Projects and Programs, for further information). Issued to date:
"The Other Energy Crises: Firewood," Erik P. Eckholm, no. 1, September 1975. *Indicates that more need for wood than ever before requires massive tree planting programs and search for alternative fuel sources.*
"The Politics and Responsibilities of the North American Breadbasket," Lester R. Brown, no. 2, 1975. *Proposes a global food strategy for U.S. and Canada.*
"Women in Politics: A Global Review," Kathleen Newland, no. 3, 1975. *Documents both the problems and progress, particularly at the local level.*
"Energy: The Case for Conservation," Denis Hayes, no. 4, 1976. *Examines opportunities for energy conservation in transport, food production, heating and lighting systems, and waste disposal.*
"Twenty-two Dimensions of the Population Problem," Lester R. Brown et al., no. 5, 1976.
"Nuclear Power: The Fifth Horseman," Denis Hayes, no. 6, 1976. *Examines issues to be faced by increased use of nuclear power.*
"The Unfinished Assignment: Equal Education for Women," Patricia L. McGrath, no. 7, 1976. *Traces worldwide development of new educational opportunities for women.*

"World Population Trends: Signs of Hope, Signs of Stress," Lester R. Brown, no. 8, 1976. *Analyzes the stabilization of population growth rates.*
"The Two Faces of Malnutrition," Erik Eckholm, no. 9, 1976. *Proposes nutrition strategies to reduce the negative effects of undernutrition and overnutrition.*
"Health: The Family Planning Factor," Erik Eckholm and Kathleen Newland, no. 10, 1977. *Documents need for reasonable limit to family size and proposes a comprehensive health program.*
"Spreading Deserts—The Hand of Man," Erik Eckholm and Lester R. Brown, no. 11, 1977.

Yearbook of International Organizations, Union of International Associations, Brussels.

Yearbook of the United Nations, Unipub, New York.
Published annually, provides comparative statistical information on the nations of the world.

Yearbook of World Problems and Human Potential, Union of International Associations, Brussels. First edition, 1976.

Part V*a*: Projects and Programs

AFS International/Intercultural Programs, 313 East 43d Street, New York, N.Y. 10017.

Provides family-living and school experiences in the United States for teen-aged students from Europe, Asia, Africa, the Middle East, and Latin America and similar experiences abroad for American teen-agers.

American Freedom from Hunger Foundation, Inc., 1717 H Street, N.W., Washington, D.C. 20006.

Source of information and materials on developing nations, drawing together news and research notes on the issue of hunger. Publishes AFFHF Bulletin.

American Universities Field Staff, 3 Lebanon Street, Hanover, N.H. 03755.

An independent educational organization specializing in cross-cultural studies. Produces materials designed for secondary classes: Field-staff Perspectives *and "Culture Study Films."*

The Amherst Project, Richard H. Brown and Van R. Halsey (eds.), Addison-Wesley, Reading, Mass., 1970–1974.

Curriculum materials using inquiry approaches for the study of history in secondary schools include three units useful for teaching a global perspective. The studies use primary sources to inquire about the nature, methods, and implications of history.

Anthropology Curriculum Project and Geography Curriculum Project, University of Georgia, 107 Dudley Hall, Athens, Ga. 30602.

Curriculum materials produced emphasize an international dimension. Topics on cultures, cities, regions have content drawing on areas and cultures in a comparative framework. See Part II, Instructional Materials, for specific titles.

Aspen Institute for Humanistic Studies. Publications are available from Aspen Institute Publications, 360 Bryant Street, P.O. Box 1652, Palo Alto, Calif. 94302.

An international nonprofit organization concerned with suggesting ways of dealing with current issues from a human-centered point-of-view. One of its major programs is the Program in International Affairs, which issues occasional papers, some of them listed in this bibliography.

Bay Area China Education Project (BACEP), Berkeley-Stanford Joint Center.

One of the NDEA-sponsored university outreach programs on Asian Studies that provide a variety of materials and services to teachers. Maintains liaison with the Asia Society. Other similar programs are the University of Michigan's Project in Asian Studies Education (PASE), Ann Arbor, and the Service Center for Teachers of Asian Studies, Ohio State University, Columbus.

Carnegie-Mellon Project: *Tradition and Change in Four Societies,* Carnegie-Mellon Institute, Pittsburgh, 1968.

A tenth-grade course using an inquiry approach to aid students in gaining some ideas of how race relations in this country are unique and ways in which they are similar to those of other multiracial societies. See Ford entry in Part II.

Center for Conflict Resolution, 731 State Street, Madison, Wis. 53703.

A nonprofit educational organization offering workshops, consultation, intervention, and a resource center on conflict, group process, and problem solving. Sponsors conferences and disseminates information on peace-related issues and social concerns. Issues CCR Newsletter.

Center for Global Perspectives (formerly Center for War/Peace Studies), 218 East 18th Street, New York, N.Y. 10003. A program of the New York Friends Group.

A research, development, and consulting agency concerned with education about our global society. Works with and through educational institutions and voluntary organizations in the United States. Publishes Intercom *(see Part IV, Pertinent Periodicals) and* War/Peace Report, *a bimonthly publication. See also Global Perspectives: A Humanistic Influence on the Curriculum in this section.*

The Center for International Programs and Comparative Studies, Ward Morehouse, Director, State Education Department of New York, Albany, N.Y. 11224.

Created to encourage the development of programs to study other societies and cultures such as those in Asia, Africa, Eastern Europe, and Latin America. See, for example, entries in Part II,

314

Instructional Materials, under Nesbitt (ed.) and Nesbitt and Karls.

Center for Latin American Studies, University of Florida, Gainesville.

One of the National Defense Education Act (NDEA) area studies centers (others focus on Africa and Asia) designed to train graduate-level students in the cultures, languages, and social systems of the developing world. "Outreach" programs attempt to disseminate research in usable form to schools stressing nontraditional materials for elementary and secondary social studies. See entry in Part II, Instructional Materials, for specific example. The Latin American Center at the University of California at Los Angeles, another of the NDEA centers, developed a network at the junior college level. The Institute for Latin American Studies at the University of Texas at Austin focuses in a similar vein on public agencies. See Chapter 7 for further details.

Center for Peace Studies, University of Akron, Akron, Ohio 44325. See *International Peace Studies Newsletter* in Part IV, Pertinent Periodicals, for annotation.

Center for Teaching International Relations (CTIR), Graduate School of International Studies, University of Denver, Denver, Colo. 80208.

A joint project with the University of Denver School of Education, Graduate School of International Studies, and the Center for Global Perspectives. The purpose of the Center—to develop international studies at the secondary level—is carried out through institutes, curriculum development, a Materials Distribution Center, and other informational services. Topics include conflict resolution, the global environment, use of evidence in decision making, newspaper analyses, etc.

Center for War/Peace Studies. See Center for Global Perspectives.

The Center for World Education, College of Education and Social Services, University of Vermont, Burlington, Vt.

Free newsletter contains useful information about teaching strategies and materials on teaching about global issues or international studies.

Center of Concern, 3700 13th Street, N.E., Washington, D.C. 20017.

An ecumenical and independent public interest group established by the Jesuits in 1971 that works through newsletters, conferences, workshops, and educational materials to sensitize the public to global issues, especially concerning Third World rights and perspectives. See Center Focus *in Part IV, Pertinent Periodicals, for newsletter information.*

Columbus in the World, the World in Columbus. See Transnational Intellectual Cooperation Program in this part and Part II, Instructional Materials, entry under "Columbus in the World," for further detail.

Connecticut Schools Project on International Education, 1973–1976.

A pilot project of the Center for War/Peace Studies investigating how a variety of schools can work together to facilitate the changes needed for increasing global perspectives in curricula. The Institute for Educational Development of New York City was involved in initial stages.

Consortium on Peace Research, Education and Development (COPRED), Institute of Behavioral Science, University of Colorado, Boulder, Colo. 80302.

Promotes transnational relations for assistance and support. Linkages to other like-minded organizations form a communication network for the peace research/education/action community.

Culture Learning Institute, 1777 East-West Road, Honolulu, Hawaii 96822.

An institute of the East-West Center emphasizing cross-culture relationships and intercultural communication.

Dag Hammarskjöld Foundation, Övre Slottsgatan 2, 75220 Uppsala, Sweden.

Publishes the periodical Development Dialogue: A Journal of International Development Corporation.

Diablo Valley (California) Education Project.

Initiated as a "laboratory" of the Center for War/Peace Studies with the intent to develop a curriculum guide through a series of areawide teacher workshops stressing affective development as the basis for educating citizens to deal with world problems. Inspired a network of cooperating school and community organizations with the Diablo Valley team providing resource services for greatly expanded activities focused on world-centered learning. (See Chapter 7 for further detail.) Part III, Sources for Additional Materials, annotates the Center for War/Peace Studies: A Guide to

Selected Curriculum Materials ... , *a product of the Diablo Valley Education Project and the Mt. Diablo Valley Unified School District, Concord, Calif.*

The Directory of Resources in Global Education, Interorganizational Commission on International Education, % Jayne Millar Wood, Overseas Development Council, 1717 Massachusetts Avenue, N.W., Washington, D.C. 20036, 1977. Free. See also listing under Overseas Development Council in this section.

Information concerning what fifty-two key organizations are doing in the area of global studies, contact persons, and resources.

Food and Agriculture Organization of the United Nations.

Issues a bibliographic catalog on: World Food Situation, Agriculture, Economics and Statistics, Fisheries, Forestry and Forest Industries, Nutrition, Legislation, FAO official records, Vocabularies, Directories, etc. For further information, contact Unipub, Inc., 650 First Avenue, P.O. Box 433, Murray Hill Station, New York, N.Y. 10016.

Foreign Policy Association, 345 East 46th Street, New York, N.Y. 10017. A private, nonprofit, nonpartisan organization aiming to develop an informed public on major foreign policy issues through education.

Issues Headline Series, New Dimensions Series *(see Part IV, Pertinent Periodicals), and* Great Decisions, *a yearly publication which compiles short articles on a set of current topics, published by Allyn and Bacon.*

Freedom from Hunger Campaign/Action for Development (FFHC/AD, also FFH/AD), Food and Agricultural Organization (FAO), 00100 Rome, Italy.

Promotes public awareness through publications (see Development Education Exchange Papers *and* Ideas and Action Bulletin *in Part IV, Pertinent Periodicals). Supports educational initiatives furthering an exchange of ideas and materials. Sponsors in-depth research on the attitudes and motivations of people in industrialized countries toward aid and development cooperation.*

Global Development Studies Institute, P.O. Box 522, 14 Main Street, Madison, N.J. 07940.

Focus is on the introduction of global education at the secondary school and introductory college levels. Provides occasional papers for consideration of underlying concepts of global development. Publishes Memos *six times a year for teachers.*

Global Perspectives: A Humanistic Influence on the Curriculum.

Operated by the Center for Global Perspectives, cited earlier, the function of the project is to suggest ways to provide the best education for students, K–12, who will be spending their adult lives in the twenty-first century. Developing curriculum based on four concepts: interdependence, conflict, communication, and change.

Global Studies Project, Indiana University, Social Studies Development Center, 513 North Park, Bloomington, Ind. 47401.

Attempting to develop a planetwide perspective through a course on world geography for seven grades. Approaches global concerns through personal world of the students in modules such as family, food and energy, communication, social justice, work, and global perspectives.

Harvard Social Studies Project, Harvard University, Cambridge, Massachusetts.

Produced a series of issue-oriented unit books to help secondary-level students to clarify and deal with their own positions on public issues. Emphasis is on social sciences, law, and philosophy. See Public Issues Series/Harvard Social Studies Project *in Part II, Instructional Materials, for annotation.*

High School Geography Project (HSGP). See Part II, Instructional Materials, for annotation describing publications under Experiences in Inquiry and High School Geography Project. Sponsored by the Association of American Geographers.

Human Relations Education Project of Western New York.

A regional, cooperative project in the Buffalo-Niagara Falls metropolitan area (forty school districts involved) to improve the teaching of human relations through curriculum development and in-service education activities. Stresses respect for the dignity of every individual and development of more effective personal relationships. Study guides and bibliography K–12 have been developed.

The Humanities Project, Laurence Stenhouse, Project Director, British Schools Council and Nuffield Humanities Project, London, England.

Among the major premises are these: that controversial issues should be handled in class with adolescents, teachers should not promote own views, mode of inquiry should have discussion rather than instruction as its core, discussion should protect divergence of view rather than consensus, and teachers should have responsibility for quality and standards in learning.

The Institute for Education in Peace and Justice, 3700 West Pine Street, St. Louis, Mo. 63108. See Part II, Instructional Materials, for publication information.

Institute for Latin American Studies, University of Texas, Austin.

One of three National Defense Education Act (NDEA) area studies centers, this one proposes to bring together a variety of public agencies that deal with education. Focus is on familiarizing elementary and secondary teachers with Latin American culture, concepts, and history through several miniresource centers set up around the state of Texas. Short-term training seminars provide updated classroom materials.

Institute for World Order, Inc., 1140 Avenue of the Americas, New York, N.Y. 10036.

A private foundation in the field of general public education and community action. Develops curriculum materials, devises teaching methodology, and trains teachers in use of materials and methods, grades 7–12. Materials are inquiry-oriented in approach, stressing preferred world systems based on values of peace, social justice, economic welfare, and ecological balance. See also World Order Models Program, *which follows in this part.*

Intercultural Studies Program.

A curriculum research and development project funded by the University of Sydney and the Asian Studies Coordinating Committee. Aim of the program is to help teachers and students develop a curriculum which is intercultural rather than ethnocentric. See entries under Dufty et al. in Part II, Instructional Materials, for products of the program.

Intercultural Understanding Project, Melvin H. Samuels, Project Director, Allegheny County Board of School Directors, Pittsburgh, 1971.

Initiated in 1968, a Title III, ESEA program designed to develop a more open-minded attitude toward people of other cultures, to develop a more world-minded view. Introductory unit, "The American Teen-Age Sub-Culture," begins the development of basic concepts and skills elaborated in subsequent units. Secondary level. Materials developed for each unit, e.g., "Japan: World Cultures Unit."

International Cooperation Council, 8570 Wilshire Blvd., Beverly Hills, Calif. 90211.

Long-range objective: To foster the emergence of a new universal man and civilization based upon unity in diversity among all peoples. Cooperating organizations consist of religious and secular groups. Issues Spectrum *and* The Cooperator *(see Part IV, Pertinent Periodicals) jointly with the Cooperators.*

International Education Project, American Council on Education, One Dupont Circle, Washington, D.C. 20036.

Publishes monthly bulletin, International Interaction *(see Part IV, Pertinent Periodicals). See also entries under Hayden in Part I, Imperatives and Issues.*

The International School-to-School Experience.

A student exchange program for students as young as eleven years old, growing out of the Children's International Summer Villages program. (See Chapter 7 for further details.)

International Social Science Council: *World Models: Images of Society and Man.*

Project sponsored by UNESCO includes participants from Latin America, Eastern and Western Europe, India, the United States and U.S.S.R.

Jane Addams Peace Association, 1213 Race Street, Philadelphia, Pa. 19107. See Part II, Instructional Materials, for entries under Abrams and Schmidt and under Comstock for specific publications' annotations.

Latin American Center, University of California, Los Angeles. See entry under Center for Latin American Studies, in this section for annotation.

Mankind Project, University of California, Graduate School of Education, Los Angeles, Calif. 90024. See entry in Part I, Imperatives and Issues, under Goodlad and Associates for further detail.

Mid-America Program for Global Perspectives in Education, James M. Becker, Director, Social Studies Development Center, Indiana University, 513 North Park, Bloomington, Ind. 47401.

Aim is "to provide young people with more and better opportunities to acquire understandings and develop capacities for sound judgment necessary for an increasingly interdependent world." Primarily concerned with communication, resource mobilization, and leadership in a demonstration area including Illinois, Indiana, Kentucky, Michigan, and Ohio. Stresses interrelatedness of world problems. See also entry in Part II, Instructional Materials.

National Council for Services to International Visitors (COSERV), U.S. Agency for International Development (AID), Washington, D.C.

Federally sponsored through AID, this council acts as an umbrella organization for visitors' bureaus that organize tours, luncheons, and home visits for foreign guests. (See Chapter 7 for further detail.)

Organization for Economic Co-operation and Development, OECD Publications Center, Suite 1207, 1750 Pennsylvania Avenue, N.W., Washington, D.C. 20006.

Produces much information on development topics, issuing an annual catalog of publications with monthly supplements.

Overseas Development Council, 1717 Massachusetts Avenue, N.W., Washington, D.C. 20036.

An independent, nonprofit organization which supports in-service programs for teachers and has assembled a guide for curriculum development (see Wood, Focusing on Global Poverty *in Part II, Instructional Materials). The Council serves as a clearinghouse for information, which it publishes in the following formats:*
Development Paper Series: *pamphlets for general public use.*
Communique Series: *briefs of 6–8 pages on important issues.*
Monograph Series: *thorough professional discussions intended for people in the development field, academics, students.*
Occasional Paper Series: *studies on more specialized topics than above. See entries under Howe and under Hansen for annual publications in Part I, Imperatives and Issues.*

Oxfam, Education Department, 274 Banbury Road, Oxford, England.

Attempts to increase young people's consciousness, responsibility, and self-confidence and to link them with others in developing countries working closely with individual teachers and children, schools, local education authorities, and the youth service in the United Kingdom. Produces many educational materials described in its booklet Oxfam Educational Materials, 1976/1977.

Project Social Studies, Curriculum Center, University of Minnesota, Minneapolis.

Developed kits for activity-centered study of communities in order to promote a global perspective and an understanding of mankind. See Part II, Instructional Materials, under Families Around the World *and Mitsakos (ed.),* The Family of Man, *for annotations.*

Santa Clara Valley Project.

A pilot project of the Center for War/Peace Studies set up to establish a permanent resource in California to help schools improve their conflict management skills and strengthen the global dimension of their curricula.

School Improvement through Global Education.

A joint project of the North Central Association's Commission on Schools and the Charles F. Kettering Foundation design to integrate a global perspective in all courses in the curriculum through in-service training. Three booklets have been written by Jon Kinghorn et al.: A Guide to the Four Essential Themes; Step-by-step Guide for Conducting a "Consensus and Diversity" Workshop in Global Education; *and* Implementation Guide, *1978.*

Society for Intercultural Education, Training and Research (SIE-TAR), 107 MIB, University of Pittsburgh, Pittsburgh, Pa. 15260. *A professional association serving the needs of individuals and institutions working in the intercultural field.*

Sociological Resources for the Social Studies (SRSS). See Part II, Instructional Materials, for annotation describing publications under *Experiences in Inquiry* and *Sociological Resources for the Social Studies.* Sponsored by the American Sociological Association.

Stockholm International Peace Research Institute (SIPRI).

An independent institute set up in 1966 to contribute to the understanding of the conditions for peaceful solutions of international conflicts. Conducts scientific research, publishing books, reports, and papers based on that research. Available from Taylor and Francis Ltd., 10/14 Macklin Street, London WC2B 5NF, or the Press Secretary, SIPRI, Sveavagen 166, S-113 46, Stockholm, Sweden.

Transnational Intellectual Cooperation Program, Columbus in the World, the World in Columbus, directed by Chadwick F. Alger, Mershon Center, Ohio State University, 199 West Tenth Avenue, Columbus, Ohio 43201.

Funded by the Kettering Foundation and Ohio State University

Mershon Center, TICP has prepared a series of twenty reports on Columbus's involvement in the world. "The goal of the project is simply that of stimulating . . . more interest in international activity in Columbus by making people more aware of this activity." See also Alger entries in Part VI, Research Studies.

United Nations Educational, Scientific and Cultural Organization (UNESCO), Place de Fontenoy, 75700 Paris, France.

Emphasis is on scientific and educational advancement in the developing countries and on the problems of environment in the more developed industrial countries. Programs have attempted to improve the education systems of its member countries.

UNESCO Associated Schools Project.

Over 900 schools in sixty-two countries, 75 percent of which are secondary schools, are committed to three main themes for study: the role of the United Nations and international agencies in dealing with world problems, foreign peoples and cultures, and the principles of human rights and their application. Emphasis is on courses and projects that give a real sense of content of and of contact with another culture. Issues circular International Understanding at School.

Voluntary Committee on Overseas Aid and Development (VCOAD), Parnell House, 25 Wilton Road, London SW1.

Coordinates the education work in the United Kingdom of overseas aid charities and distributes the teaching materials they produce. It also produces materials. See Fyson in Part II, Instructional Materials, for specific titles, annotated.

World Affairs Councils.

Focus is on international relations in urban centers. See Chapter 7 for information.

World Association for the School as an Instrument of Peace, 27, Eaux-Vives, 1207 Geneva, Switzerland.

Seeks to instill in teachers an awareness of universal human values and instructional approaches to use schools as an instrument of peace. Publishes School and Peace.

World Education, 1414 Sixth Avenue, New York, N.Y. 10019.

"A private nonprofit development assistance agency which helps to design nonformal educational programs that integrate such aspects of individual and national development as health, nutrition, agriculture, family planning and literacy."

World Education Project, University of Connecticut, School of Education, Storrs, Conn.

World Federalists USA, 2029 K Street, N.W., Washington, D.C. 20006.

World Future Society: An Association for the Study of Alternative Futures, P.O. Box 30369, Bethesda Branch, Washington, D.C. 20014.

Purpose is to serve as an unbiased forum and clearinghouse for investigations of the future. Publishes The Futurist: A Journal of Forecasts, Trends, and Ideas about the Future. *Offers a book service to members, and has an introductory slide presentation and cassettes on various topics.*

World History Project, Washington International School, 3600 Macomb Street, N.W., Washington, D.C. 20008.

Developing a curriculum in world history for children from ages four through seventeen for schools throughout the world. Projected curriculum is organized in three cycles: cycle 1 introduces history through stories and geography; cycle 2 consists of four 1-year courses organized chronologically; cycle 3 courses deal with significant themes. Funded by the National Endowment for the Humanities, 1976–1977.

World Order Models Program.

A program of the Institute for World Order, cited earlier, which addresses itself to the problem of developing a model of a just world order and appropriate transition strategies to attain it. Books issued under this program and published by Free Press are: A World Federation of Cultures, *by Ali A. Mazrui;* On the Creation of a Just World Order, *ed. Saul H. Mendlovitz;* A Study of Future Worlds, *by Richard Falk; and* Footsteps into the Future, *by Rajni Kothari.*

World Studies Project, One World Trust, 37 Parliament Street, London SW1.

Aims to encourage a dual perspective in education, global and national, and to assist secondary school teachers in dealing with issues in world society such as world poverty, pollution, violence and oppression, disarmament, world law, and human rights. Holds consultations, workshops, conferences in teachers' centers, individual schools, and colleges of education. Issued Learning for Change in World Society: Reflections, Activities, Resources, *1976, and, in conjunction with publisher Thomas Nelson, a series,*

Starting Points in World Studies, *1977, which contains four pictorial booklets:* World in Conflict, Caring for the Planet, Progress and Wealth, *and* Fighting for Freedom.

World Without War Council, 1730 Grove Street, Berkeley, Calif. 94709.

Worldwatch Institute, 1776 Massachusetts Avenue, N.W., Washington, D.C. 20036.

An international research organization funded by private foundations and United Nations agencies which aims to focus public attention on emergency global issues. Publishes Worldwatch Papers *(see Part IV, Pertinent Periodicals, for specifics).*

Part V*b:* Agencies Sponsoring International and Intercultural Exchanges

Developed by Stephen Rhinesmith

Below are listed nationally recognized organizations offering travel/study opportunities on the secondary and presecondary level for students and teachers.

Sponsoring Organization	Status	Program Offerings
AFS International/ Intercultural Programs 313 East 43d Street New York, N.Y. 10017	Private Nonprofit	Students incoming/ outgoing Teachers incoming/ outgoing Domestic Intercultural
American Host Program Hotel Commodore 2100 Park Avenue and 42d Street New York, N.Y. 10017	Private Nonprofit	Teachers incoming
American Institute for Foreign Study 102 Greenwich Avenue Greenwich, Conn. 06830	Profit	Students incoming/ outgoing (presecondary also)
A Better Chance 376 Boylston Street Boston, Mass. 02116	Private	Domestic Intercultural
Boy Scouts of America North Brunswick New Jersey 08902	Private Nonprofit	Students incoming/ outgoing Tape and correspondence exchange
Council on International Educational Exchange 777 United Nations Plaza New York, N.Y. 10017	Private Nonprofit	Students incoming/ outgoing Teachers incoming/ outgoing

English-Speaking Union of the U.S. 16 East 69th Street New York, N.Y. 10021	Private Nonprofit	Students outgoing Students incoming
The Experiment in International Living Kipling Road Brattleboro, Vt. 05301	Private Nonprofit	Students incoming/ outgoing Teachers incoming
Foreign Area Fellowship Program 110 East 59th Street New York, N.Y. 10022	Private Nonprofit	Teachers outgoing
Foreign Study League 111 East 33 Street South Salt Lake City, Utah 84110	Profit	Students incoming/ outgoing (presecondary also)
Girl Scouts of the United States of America 830 Third Avenue New York, N.Y. 10022	Private Nonprofit	Students incoming/ outgoing Tape and correspondence exchange
International Christian Youth Exchange 55 Liberty Street Room 1306 New York, N.Y. 10005	Private Nonprofit	Students incoming/ outgoing
Lions Youth Exchange Program Lions International York and Cermak Roads Oak Brook, Ill. 60521	Private Nonprofit	Students incoming/ outgoing
National Association of Independent Schools 4 Liberty Square Boston, Mass. 02109	Private Nonprofit	Information on study opportunities abroad in boarding private schools
National Association of Secondary School Principals Office of Students Activities	Private Nonprofit	High school-to-high school exchanges of groups of students

1904 Association Drive
Reston, Va. 22091

National Council for Community Services to International Visitors (COSERV) Meridian House 1630 Crescent Place, N.W. Washington, D.C. 20009	Private Nonprofit	Community hosting
National Council of YMCAs 291 Broadway New York, N.Y. 10007	Private Nonprofit	Students incoming/ outgoing (camp experience)
National Education Association 1201 16th Street, N.W. Washington, D.C. 20036	Private Nonprofit	Teachers outgoing/ incoming
National 4-H Foundation 7100 Connecticut Avenue Chevy Chase, Md. 20015	Private Nonprofit	Students incoming/ outgoing (technical exchanges)
Open Door Student Exchange 180 Hempstead Turnpike West Hempstead, N.Y. 11552	Private Nonprofit	Students incoming/ outgoing To Latin America
People-to-People High School Student Ambassador Program West 422 Riverside Avenue Spokane, Wash. 99201	Private Nonprofit	Students outgoing
Rotary International 1600 Ridge Avenue Evanston, Ill. 60201	Private Nonprofit	Students incoming/ outgoing
Sister Cities International 1612 K Street, N.W. Suite 202 Washington, D.C. 20006	Private Nonprofit	Community hosting Teachers outgoing/ incoming

U.S. Office of Education Department of Health, Education, and Welfare 330 Independence Avenue, S.W. Washington, D.C. 20201	Government	Teachers outgoing Students outgoing
Youth for All Nations, Inc. 16 Saint Luke's Place New York, N.Y. 10014	Private	Correspondence exchange
Youth for Understanding 2015 Washtenaw Avenue Ann Arbor, Mich. 48104	Private Nonprofit	Students incoming/ outgoing

Part VI: Research Studies

Alger, Chadwick F.: *A World of Cities: Or Good Foreign Policies Begin at Home,* Transnational Intellectual Cooperation Program, Mershon Center, Ohio State University, Columbus, 1976.

A report to the Charles F. Kettering Foundation summarizing the rationale and work of "Columbus in the World" (see Part II, Instructional Materials, and Part Va, Projects and Programs). Discusses past images of international relations, need for change, diagnosis of Columbus as an international city, and transition strategies to alternative futures for Columbus. See also his Foreign Policies of United States Publics, *January 1975.*

———: *Your City in the World: The World in Your City,* Transnational Intellectual Cooperation Program, Mershon Center, Ohio State University, Columbus, 1977.

A detailed report on the research methods used in Columbus to discover international activities and foreign policies of people, groups, and organizations. Includes questionnaires, examples of data, etc., developed for the Columbus in the World, the World in Columbus program.

———: *Your Community in the World/The World In Your Community: Discovering the International Activities and Foreign Policies of People, Groups and Organizations in Your Community,* Transnational Intellectual Cooperation Program, Mershon Center, Ohio State University, Columbus, 1974.

A guide to the research methods used in Columbus with questionnaires, examples of data, etc., for use by groups or classes investigating the international links of their community. Full research reports also available.

Almgren, E., and E. Gustafsson: "World Citizen Responsibility: Assessment Techniques, Development Studies, Material Construction, and Experimental Teaching," *Educational and Psychological Interactions,* no. 48, School of Education, Malmö, Sweden, 1974.

Test batteries were constructed to study attitudes to foreign groups and international relations (see Yebio in this section). More negative attitudes were found among the older students, particularly toward minority groups and immigrants. Special teaching pack-

ages intended to increase students' world citizen responsibility were developed and tested, showing positive results.

Bjerstedt, Åke (ed.): "Social Development and Student Democracy: Notes on Two Research Projects," *Educational and Psychological Interactions,* no. 39, March 1973.

Contains brief summaries in English of the two Malmö projects, Social Development and Training and Student Democracy. Lists reports and publications from these projects as well as related abstracts and annotations. Highlights concerning Variable Field W—World Citizen Responsibility—are especially noteworthy.

————: "Social Development and Training in the Comprehensive School: Project Summary and Report Abstracts," *Pedagogisk Dokumentation,* no. 27, School of Education, Malmö, Sweden, May 1974.

Focuses on (1) "cooperation," (2) "resistance" (ability to make independent choices, resistance to "nonobjective" attempts to influence), and (3) "world citizen responsibility" (feeling of responsibility for developments in other countries, reduced inclination to disparage unthinkingly anything foreign, etc.). Construction and testing of measuring methods, mapping of student development, and explorations of alternatives of using educational influence are included. Found marked stereotypes in sex-role perception, increasingly negative ideas about minority groups, and some encouraging results in the desired direction following systematic measures taken.

Connell, Robert: *The Child's Construction of Politics,* International Scholarly Book Services, Beaverton, Oreg., 1971.

Accounts of how the political world is regarded by particular children who were watched and listened to patiently and given sound reassurances that what they said would in no way become the property of the school system. Contrasts these remarks with "standardized responses" of survey research.

Hess, Robert D., and Judith Torney: *The Development of Political Attitudes in Children,* Aldine, Chicago, 1967.

Presents findings of the research on the process by which an individual child develops a sense of involvement in political life, based on questionnaire data from about 12,000 elementary school children, grades 2 through 8.

Hunkins, Francis P., et al.: *Review of Research in Social Studies Education: 1970–1975,* Bulletin 49, National Council for the Social Studies, Washington, D.C., 1977.

A cooperative endeavor of the ERIC Clearinghouse for Social Studies/Social Science Education, the Social Science Education Consortium, and the National Council for the Social Studies. Striking in the paucity of references concerning global perspectives or international education.

Lambert, Wallace E., and Otto Klineberg: *Children's Views of Foreign Peoples,* Appleton-Century-Crofts, New York, 1967.

A twenty-nation study indicated children's patriotic loyalty but also their receptivity and friendliness to aliens. Delineates individual characteristics most often associated with international understanding.

Langerman, Arthur L.: *Building World Sensitivity—Fact or Fiction? An Analysis of International Education as Practiced in Ohio Schools,* Miami University, Department of Educational Administration, Oxford, Ohio, 1972.

Brief pamphlet reviews the survey which indicates the degree to which international education is being undertaken in Ohio high schools. Sums up with recommendations and guidelines for high school curriculum, staff, and activities. See following entry for full report.

————: "International Education in Ohio Secondary Schools," doctoral dissertation, Miami University, Oxford, Ohio; University Microfilms, Ann Arbor, Mich., 1972.

Questionnaire survey of programs and activities in 534 public and private Ohio secondary schools found few strong programs in international education. Only 15 percent had a stated philosophy referring to international education; most schools relied upon traditional world history, geography, and foreign language courses; and teachers were found to be inadequately prepared. See following entries under Miami University for additional references.

Miami University, Department of Educational Administration: *An Analysis of the International Education Programs in Ohio Secondary Schools,* presented to the Charles F. Kettering Foundation, Oxford, Ohio, n.d. (Processed.)

A descriptive study designed to identify courses and activities and the training and personal experience of teachers in order to determine how best to improve international education programs in Ohio.

————: *International Education in Ohio Schools,* Oxford, Ohio, 1971.

The same study as reported above issued for public consumption, suggesting ways to strengthen and expand present programs with guidelines to follow in designing new programs.

Mitsakos, Charles: "An Examination of the Effects of the Family of Man Social Studies Program in Rural Grade Children's Views of Foreign People," unpublished doctoral dissertation, Boston University, School of Education, 1977. See entry under Mitsakos (ed.) in Part II, Instructional Materials.

Nathan, James A.: "The International Socialization of Children," unpublished doctoral dissertation, Johns Hopkins University, Baltimore, June 1972.

Indicates that elementary schoolchildren, reflecting the impact of exposure to television, hold a global image of conflict, war, and chaos.

Pike, Lewis W., and Thomas S. Barrows: *Other Nations, Other Peoples,* final report conducted by the Educational Testing Service for the U.S. Office of Education, Educational Testing Service, Princeton, N.J., 1976.

A survey of student interests and knowledge, attitudes and perceptions concerning other peoples of the world.

Schmidt, Neil: "Fourth, Fifth, and Sixth Grade Students' Global Orientations: A Descriptive Study," unpublished doctoral dissertation, University of California, Los Angeles, 1975.

A selected sample of upper elementary youngsters was examined with two questionnaires that were specifically developed to build a data base about the learners' global orientation. Findings indicated that youngsters' knowledge of the world was very limited. Includes an extensive review of the literature in the field.

Smith, Lee Howard: "The Development of Worldminded Attitudes in High School Students through the Use of Anthropological Materials," doctoral dissertation, University of Minnesota, 1973; University of Microfilms, Ann Arbor, Mich., 1974.

Designed to test the changes in the world-view of students as a result of teaching them anthropological content (Patterns in Human History, Anthropology Curriculum Study Project). Found no effect. Appendix B, "The Sampson-Smith Worldmindedness Scale."

Targ, Harry R.: "Children's Developing Orientations to International Politics," *Journal of Peace Research,* vol. 7, 1970, pp. 79–97.

Survey of 244 fourth, fifth, and sixth graders illustrates how young people see their own nation as good. Discusses the child's belief, evaluations, and expectations. Findings indicate that most adolescents become political "realists" justifying war.

Tolley, Howard, Jr.: *Children and War: Political Socialization to International Conflict,* Teachers College Press, Columbia University, New York, 1973.

Reports a survey of 2,677 children aged seven to fifteen, examining how and when children acquire attitudes toward war (specifically the Vietnam war) and what the primary sources of children's information are.

Torney, Judith V.: "The Implications of the I.E.A. Cross-National Civic Education Data for Understanding the International Socialization of American Adolescents," paper presented at 1974 annual meeting of the American Political Science Association, Chicago.

Reports findings on the sources of individual differences in international orientations and the comparative dimension of international socialization. Reinforces the conclusion that the years before age fourteen seem to be critical in the acquisition of knowledge and attitudes about international organizations and processes. American students know more about and are more interested in national than international matters.

————: "Research in the Development of International Orientations during Childhood and Adolescence," paper presented at the 65th annual meeting of the American Political Science Association, New York, September 1969.

Examines the nature of children's images of international relations, nationality preferences, and the variables contributing most to the child's orientation to world affairs.

Torney, Judith V., A. N. Oppenheim, and Russell F. Farnen: *Civic Education in Ten Countries: An Empirical Study,* Wiley, New York, 1975.

A report of the IEA study designed to show how and to what extent the educational objectives of producing well-informed, democratically active young citizens are attained. Looks at other influences besides the school, such as the family, mass media, peers, and political structures. In no country did students score above average on all four outcome measures: knowledge of civics, support for democratic values, support for the national government, and civic interest/participation.

Virginia State Department of Education: *A National Survey on International Education/Global Issues in the Curriculum, Kindergarten–Grade Twelve,* Jerri Sutton, Coordinator, Virginia Department of Education, Richmond, 1977.

Found that state departments of education, state boards of education, and legislative bodies of states do not have policies and/or regulations on international education/global issues in the curriculum. Indicates need for conceptualization and guidelines for implementation of programs in schools.

Yebio, B.: "Measuring 'World Citizen Responsibility': A Preliminary Test Battery," *Educational and Psychological Interactions,* no. 34, School of Education, Malmö, Sweden, 1970.

Contains instruments administered to 538 students from grades 4–9 in the Swedish comprehensive school. Describes instruments for measuring (1) attitudes to foreign nations and ethnic groups; (2) attitudes to international relations and cooperation; (3) knowledge of other peoples and nations; (4) broader personality characteristics (e.g., rigidity-flexibility, authoritarian-democratic tendencies, dogmatism, anxiety, etc.).

————: "World Citizen Responsibility: Some Characteristics of the Attitude Development," *Educational and Psychological Interactions,* no. 168, School of Education, Department of Educational and Psychological Research, Malmö, Sweden, 1972.

Index